IMAGES
of America

DURHAM

A CENTURY IN PHOTOGRAPHS

IMAGES
of America

DURHAM
A CENTURY IN PHOTOGRAPHS

William E. Ross and Thomas M. House

ARCADIA
PUBLISHING

ISBN 978-0-7385-8959-6

Published by Arcadia Publishing
Charleston, South Carolina

Printed in the United States of America

For all general information contact Arcadia Publishing at:
Telephone 843-853-2070
Fax 843-853-0044
E-mail sales@arcadiapublishing.com
For customer service and orders:
Toll-Free 1-888-313-2665

Visit us on the Internet at www.arcadiapublishing.com

Contents

Acknowledgments

History is dependent on those who come before us. They bequeath to us with both subject matter and an accumulation of historical resources for our interpretation. For that reason, we wish to acknowledge the contributions of those individuals, most especially the photographers, archivists, librarians, historians, and donors, whose actions, effort, and generosity made this book possible. Their gifts enrich our work; any errors are ours.

The authors wish to thank the many people who contributed time, assistance, and insight to the development of this book. These include Maryanna Hatch and William Hawkes of the Durham Historic Association Museum. Their familiarity with the collections, knowledge of Durham history, and most importantly, great patience, added much to this work. Thanks also go to Gary Samson, Ron Bergeron, Michelle Bergeron, and Lisa Nugent of the UNH Photographic Services. Their fine work in producing copy negatives and prints, and particularly, their expertise in making excellent prints from original glass-plate negatives, enhance this collection greatly. Many thanks to our colleagues in Special Collections and University Archives, namely Becky Ernest, Roland Goodbody, Erik Tuveson, Mylinda Woodward, Justina Lane, and Dave Doughan, who helped with the research, took up the slack, and put up with our clutter while we worked on this book.

And finally, special thanks and love go to Pat and Jo Nell.

Introduction

Europeans first came to the area that is now called Durham in the 1630s. Most left the settlement of Dover Neck for the fertile land and undisturbed forests along Great Bay and the tidal rivers that fed into it. As they cleared forests for timber, crops, and grazing, many moved their residences along the river called Shankhassick by those native to the region. By 1640, the richest waterfront parcels had been claimed and much of that land was being cleared.

Residents named the river for the extensive oyster beds located near its mouth. For a while, Exeter claimed the land south of the Oyster River; however, the Dover settlement maintained legal authority over settlements on both sides of the river.

Although both Exeter and Dover laid claim to the rich land, the residents along the Oyster River strove for independence as they built their homes and garrisons. By 1650, the area became known as Oyster River Plantation, a district within Dover. In 1716, colonial authorities established the Oyster River Parish. The creation of an independent parish calmed ill feeling for a while but, by 1729, border disputes redeveloped between Dover and the Oyster River Parish. A petition by Oyster River residents put the controversy before the General Assembly which, in 1732, voted to make the Oyster River settlement an independent town. Reverend Hugh Adams suggested that the new town call itself Durham and the townspeople agreed.

The town not only survived Indian attacks, land disputes, and shifting colonial administrations, it flourished. By the mid-1700s, the population had grown to over 1,000, making it almost as large as Dover. The men of Durham saw limited action during the French and Indian Wars, but a few years later, a significant number took up arms against Great Britain. Durham patriots, a number of whom had taken part in the 1774 raid on Fort William and Mary, included General John Sullivan, General Alexander Scammell, and Lieutenant-Colonel Winborn Adams.

Residents returned to their homes following the war and resumed their lives as farmers, fishermen, and shipbuilders. The rhythms of rural life continued into the following century. Farmers added onto colonial homes and converted garrisons into farmhouses, not out of any preservation impulse but because it was the thrifty and expedient thing to do. As a result, many examples of colonial architecture continued to exist well into the nineteenth century and beyond.

Durham shipyards built two privateers used in the War of 1812, yet the war attracted few Durham volunteers until the British threatened Portsmouth in 1814. Following the war, Durham-built gundalows and schooners hauled goods across Great Bay and around the world. Andrew Simpson built ships; his son, Andrew Lapish Simpson, captained them around Africa's Cape Horn.

According to the 1860 census, the population of Durham numbered 1,534. Farming continued to be the primary occupation, but shipbuilding and small industry remained important components of the local economy. The following year, the Confederate bombardment of Fort Sumter would once again awaken this rural hamlet. By the end of the Civil War in 1865, over 125 Durham residents had served on the Union side. Twenty-three of those served in the U.S. Navy, while the rest served as infantrymen and faced Confederate fire in such places as Fort Wagner, Gettysburg, and Cold Harbor.

Following the war, Durham suffered the population loss felt by many New Hampshire communities as residents migrated west. In 1870, Durham had a population of 1,260, but by the end of the century, it dropped below 1,000. Those farmers remaining in Durham increasingly employed scientific farming methods to improve yields. Alongside this agricultural economy, Hamilton Mathes manufactured bricks, Samuel Runlett ran a major lumber mill, and Thomas Wiswall made wallpaper in nearby Packer's Falls. Durham's most dramatic change, however, resulted from the bequest of one of its more prominent citizens.

Ben Thompson, a prominent farmer and landowner, died in 1890. He left his estate, which included his farm and assets totaling over $400,000, to the state of New Hampshire for the establishment of an agricultural college. In 1891, Governor Hiram Tuttle signed an act accepting the conditions of Thompson's will. This resulted in the relocation of the New Hampshire College of Agriculture and the Mechanic Arts from Hanover to Durham in 1893. That one event would change the town of Durham forever.

Within a few years, mills and manufacturing would give way to retail and service businesses. Visitors from across New England were drawn to the college and to the inns and camps lying outside Durham Village. In spite of the college and subtle changes to the economy, the town tried to hold steadfastly to its rural roots, and in some respects, it was successful.

Over time, the railroad drew the town's focus away from the landing on the Oyster River. The internal combustion engine gradually replaced draft horses and oxen. As the town entered the twentieth century, it would consolidate schools and provide services that occasionally seemed at odds with the town's rural roots.

The new century brought a war to end all wars and the college became a university. Durham remained tied to the past with a historical pageant in 1919 and with the celebration of its bicentennial in 1932. Nevertheless, by the eve of World War II, the University of New Hampshire had become Durham's primary "business." By 1940, it was clear that the centuries-old tension between farmer and wilderness had been replaced by the sometimes uneasy bond between the town and the university.

Photography came to Durham two full centuries after the first settlers put down roots. The earliest photograph in this collection is a daguerreotype of Mary E. Smith dating back to around 1850. Although there are few extant photographs of Durham people or events prior to that time, all is not lost. Many homes, buildings, and certain aspects of rural life changed little during much of the nineteenth century. As a result, even this limited photographic record provides us with glimpses of Durham prior to the advent of photography.

Clearly, photographs provide us with an important historical record. They capture structures, faces, places, events, and ways of life that seem all too distant today. This information reflects both a vision of what was, as well as what the particular photographer wanted viewers to see. The result provides us with a more tangible idea of what life in Durham was like during the one hundred years covered by this book.

The images reproduced were copied from original photographs in a variety of processes and formats. Included are images from daguerreotypes, tintypes, albumen prints, cyanotypes, glass-plate negatives, lantern slides, as well as more modern negatives and prints. Some have been published in other works, but many are presented in print for the first time.

This book contains only a fraction of the photographs surveyed. Most of the images in this book come from the over 40,000 images maintained by the University of New Hampshire Special Collections and Archives. Although individual collections are not identified within the captions, those represented in this book include: the University Archives Photographic Collection; the Thompson Family Papers; the Adams Family Papers; the Edwin Jay Roberts Negative Collection; the Henry Bailey Stevens and Agnes Ryan Papers; the Works Project Administration: Historic American Buildings Survey of New Hampshire Papers; and the Durham Town Records. The remainder of the photographs in this collection are from the collections of the Durham Historic Association Museum. Captions identify these items, as well as the names of known donors.

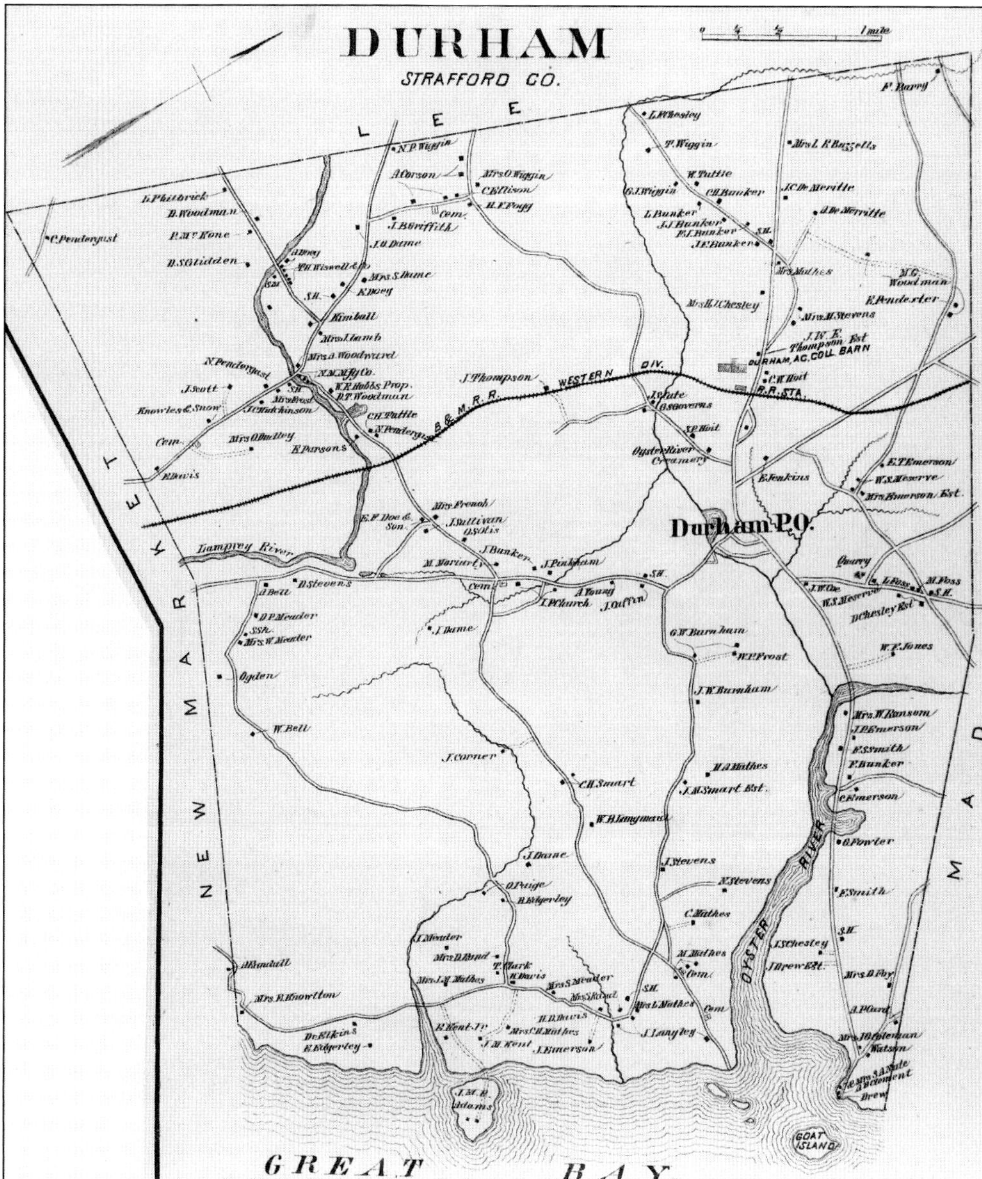

Map of Durham, 1892, from the *Town and City Atlas of the State of New Hampshire* (Boston: D.H. Hurd and Co., 1892).

One

Stream, Field, and Forest

In a 1652 deposition, John Ault reported "that in the yere 1635, that the land about Lamprile River was bought of the Indians & made use by the men of Dover & myselfe both for planting & fishing & feling of Timber." (*New Hampshire Provincial Papers*, Vol. I, p. 204). Other settlers, many from Dover Neck, soon joined Ault in settling the area that would become known as Oyster River Plantation, and a century later, Durham.

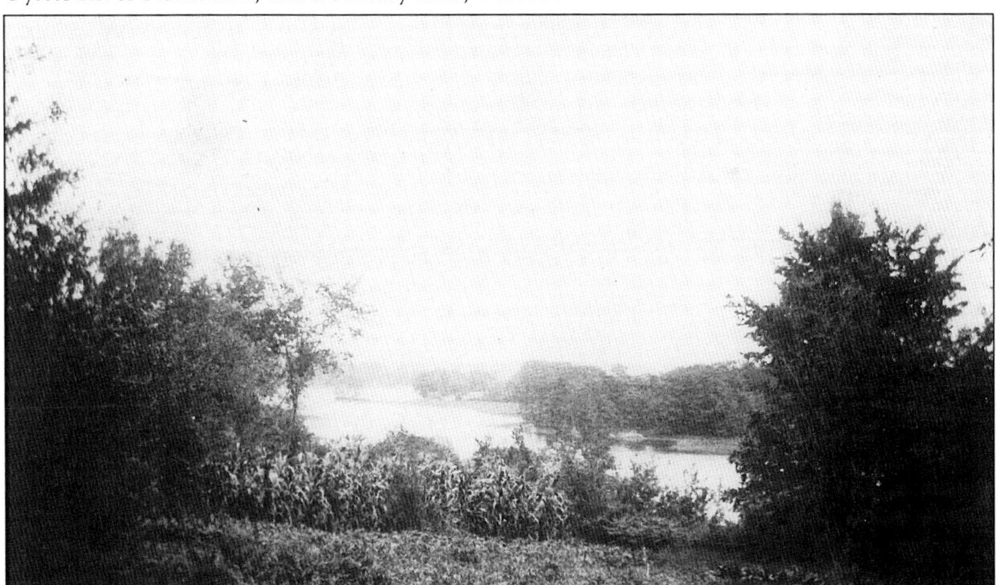

The Shankhassick or Oyster River, the focal point of what became Oyster River Plantation, c. 1910. The English name came from the large oyster beds found near the mouth of what is now Bunker Creek.

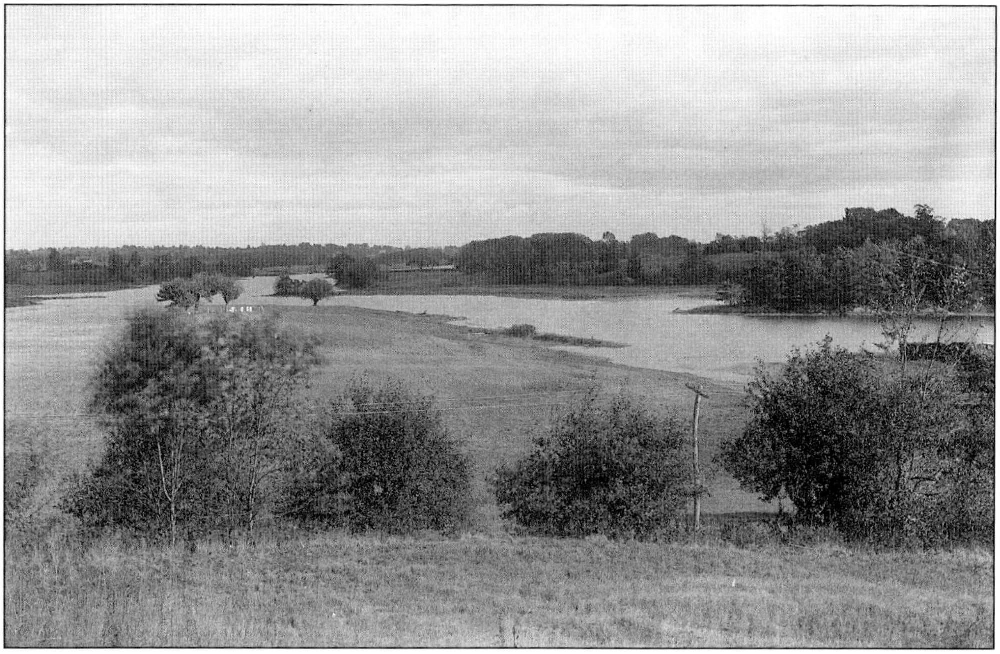

A view of the Oyster River at high tide, 1895. The Young family graveyard appears center left.

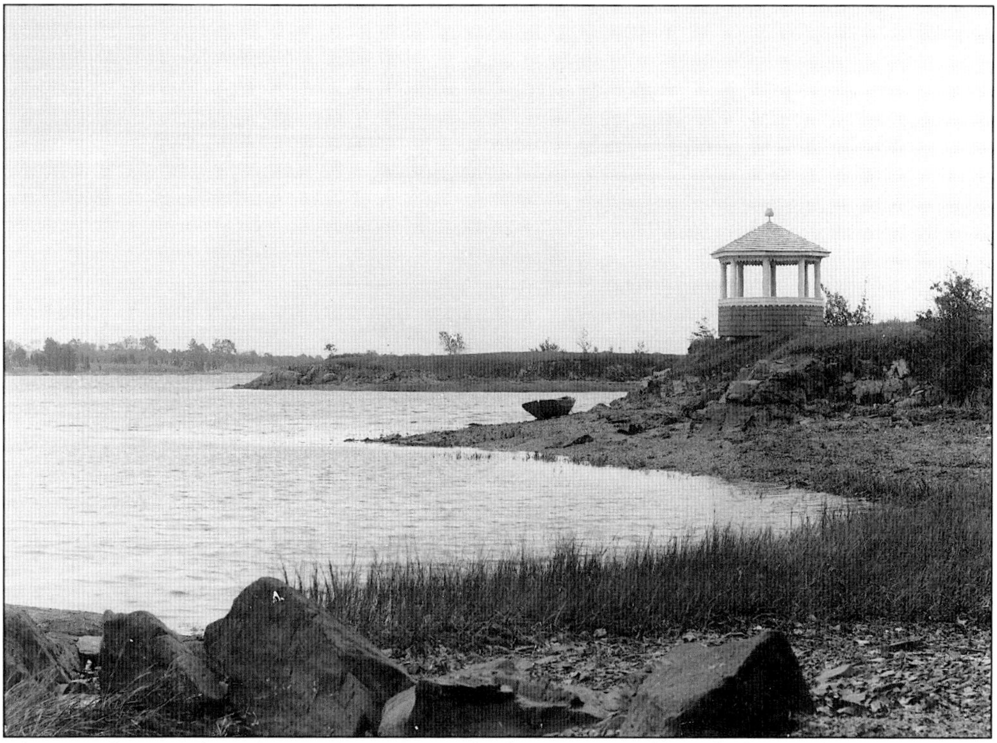

The pagoda on Adams Point, Great Bay, which was originally called "Matthews or Mathes Neck," c. 1910. The columns on the pagoda came from the Second Meeting House, which stood on the site of the Sullivan Monument. John "Reformation John" Adams, a prominent Methodist minister, bought and tore down the church in 1848.

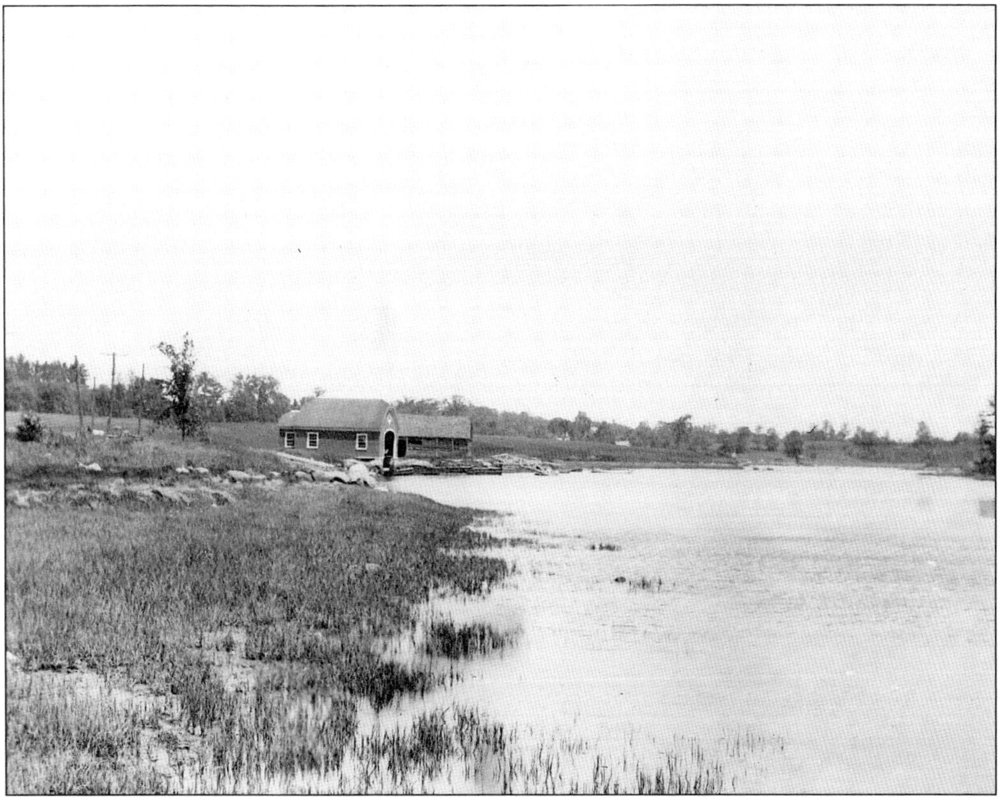

The north bank of the Oyster River, *c.* 1900. This area was the site of Durham's shipyards and warehouses during the eighteenth and nineteenth centuries.

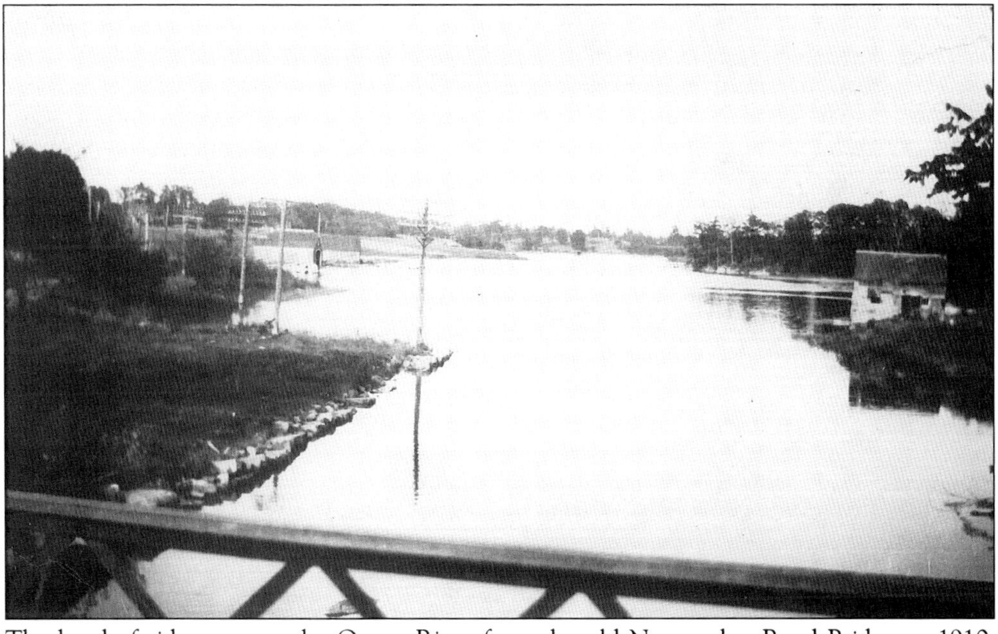

The head of tidewater on the Oyster River from the old Newmarket Road Bridge, *c.* 1910. General John Sullivan's dock appears on the right, the old town landing on the left.

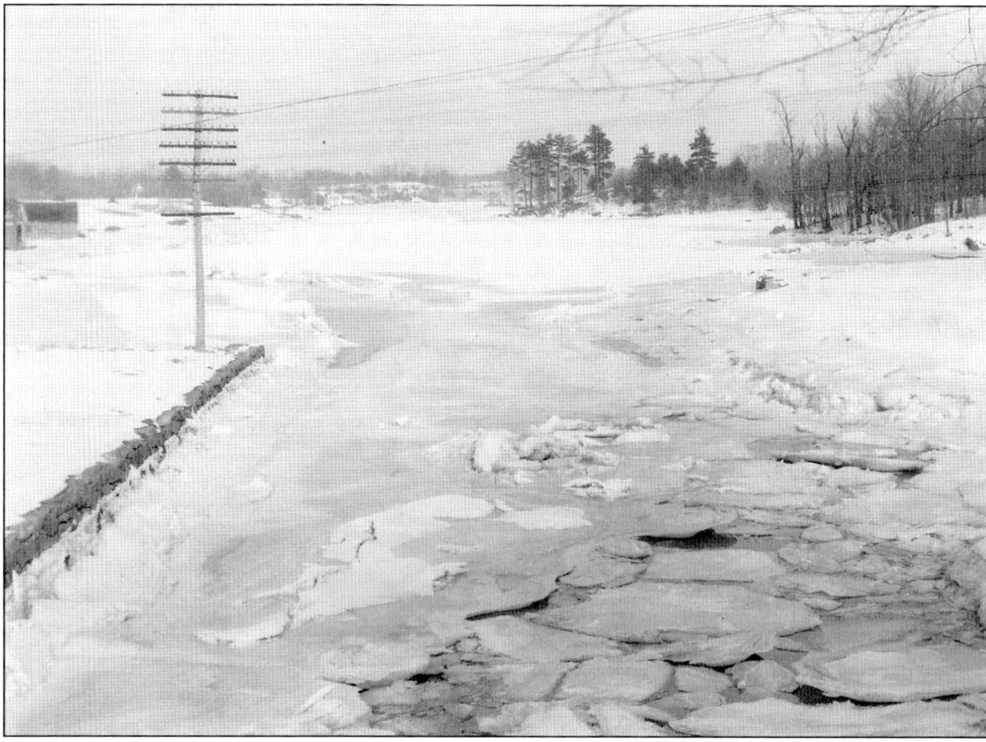
The same view from the bridge in February 1934.

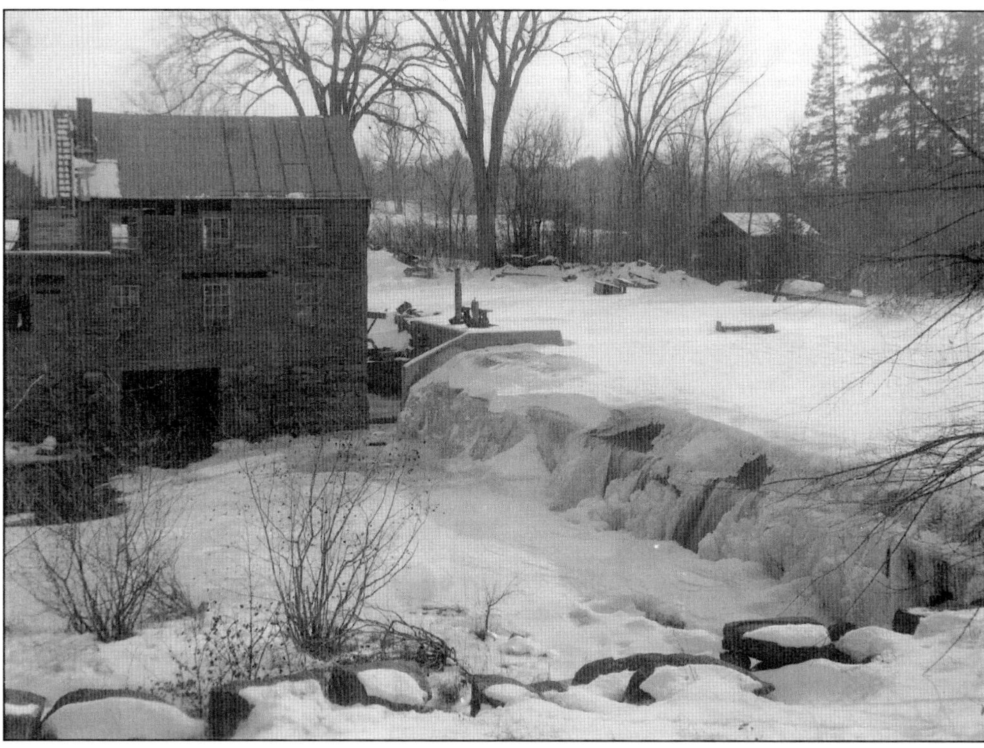
Ice formations on the Falls, upstream from the bridge, February 12, 1934.

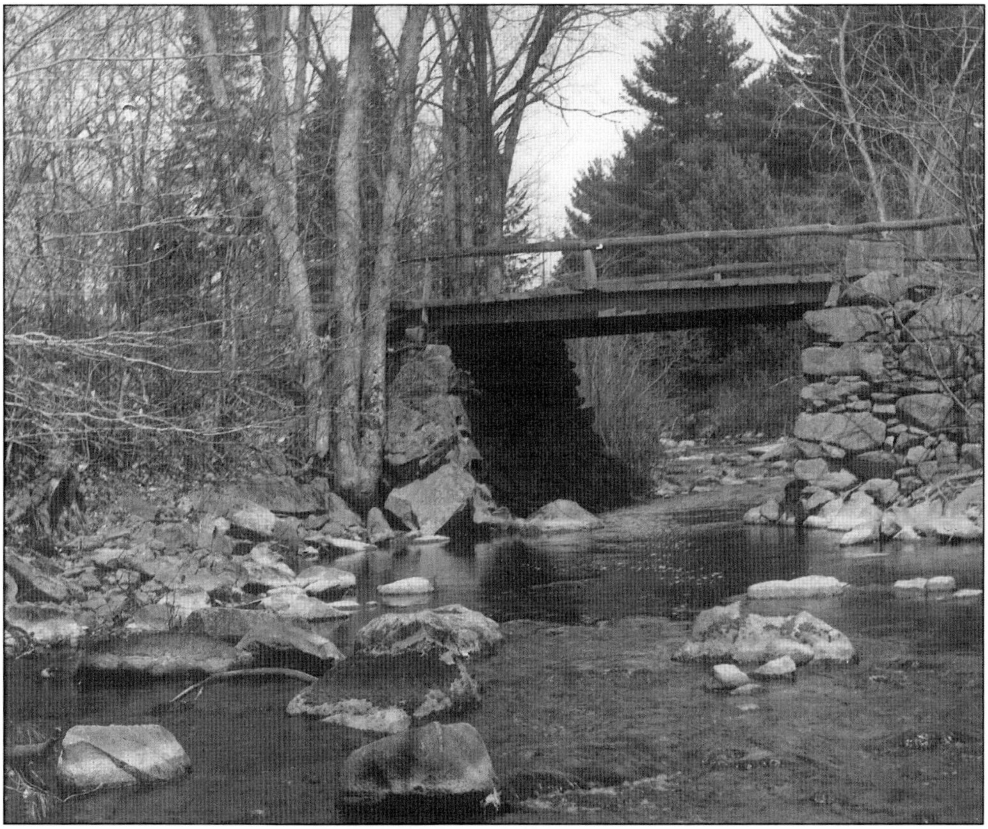

The Mill Road Bridge over the Oyster River, *c.* 1890.

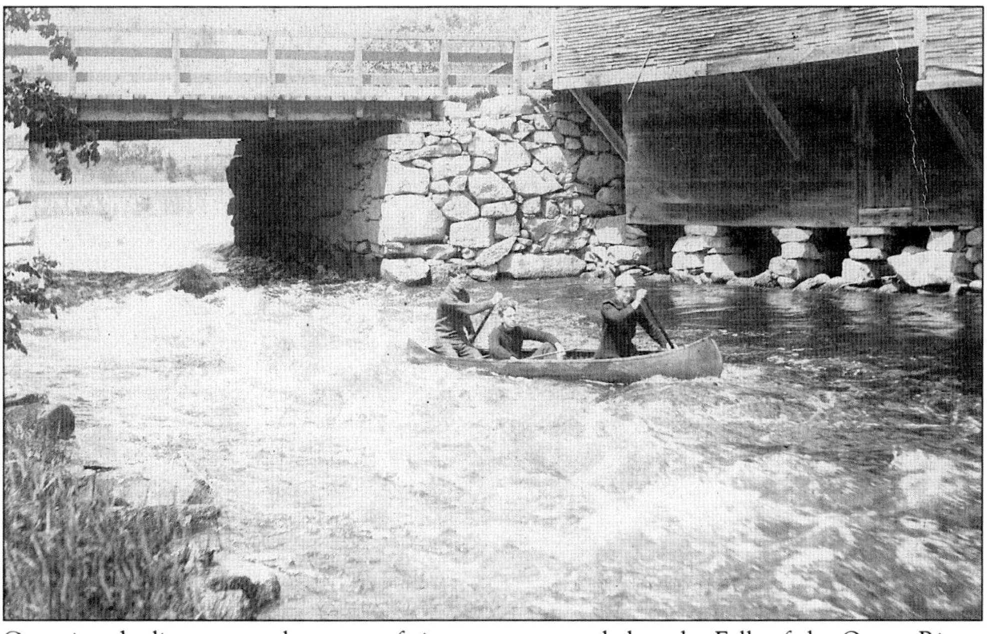

Canoeists duplicate an early means of river conveyance below the Falls of the Oyster River, June 1897. (Durham Historic Association, gift of Alvena Pettee Nelson.)

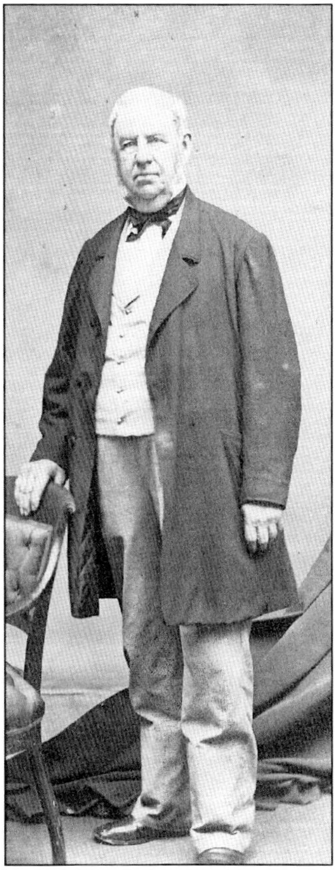

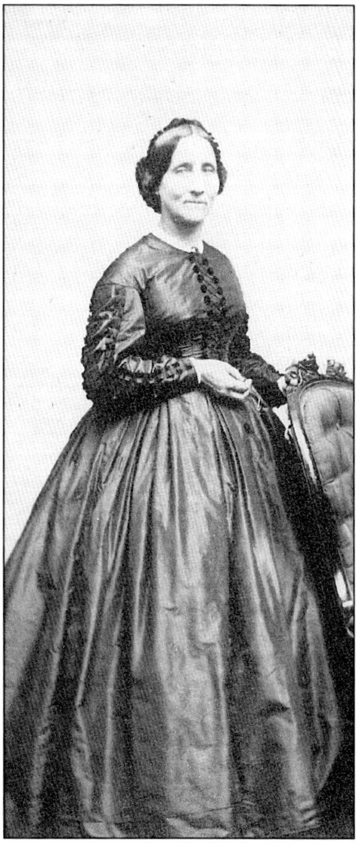

LEFT: Captain Andrew Lapish Simpson, c. 1860. Over the centuries many Durham residents have made their living from the sea. Chief among them was Captain Simpson, a noted sea captain who, during his career, rounded the Cape Horn of Africa twenty-six times.

RIGHT: Mrs. Lydia Kelley Simpson, c. 1860. Mrs. Simpson was a longtime supporter of the Durham Congregational Church and the Durham Library Association. At her death in 1895, she bequeathed her home to both the church and library. The church purchased its share from the library and used the home as its parsonage.

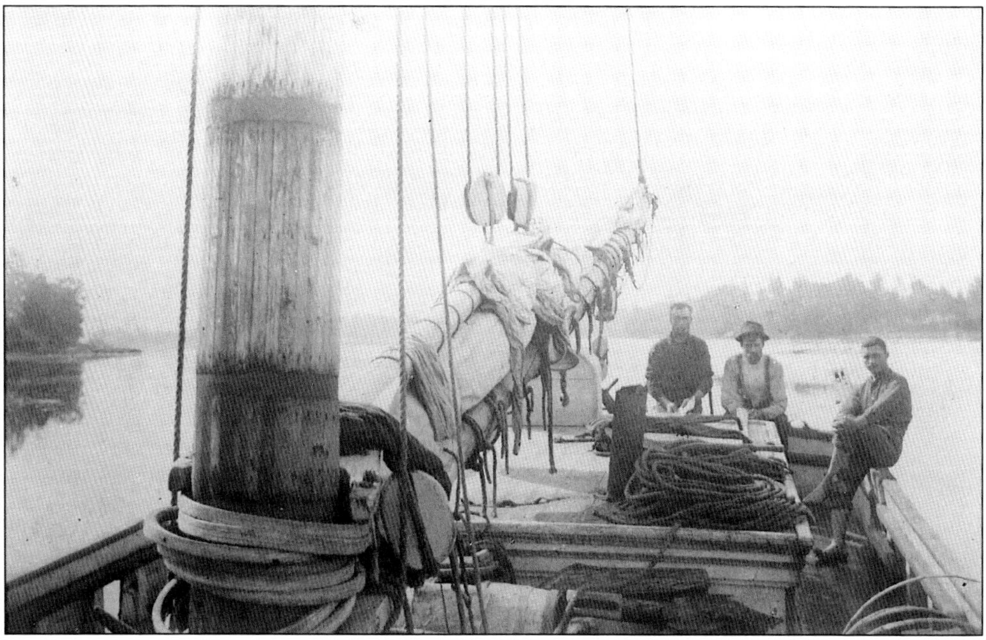

An unidentified crew hauling bricks on the Oyster River near the mouth of Bunker Creek, c. 1890.

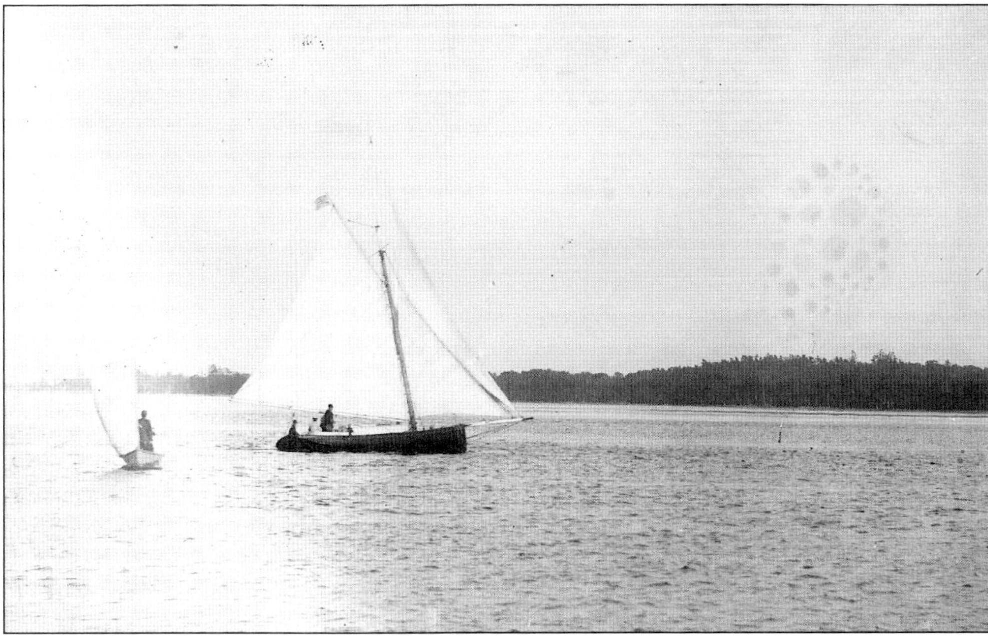

Sailboats on Great Bay, c. 1900.

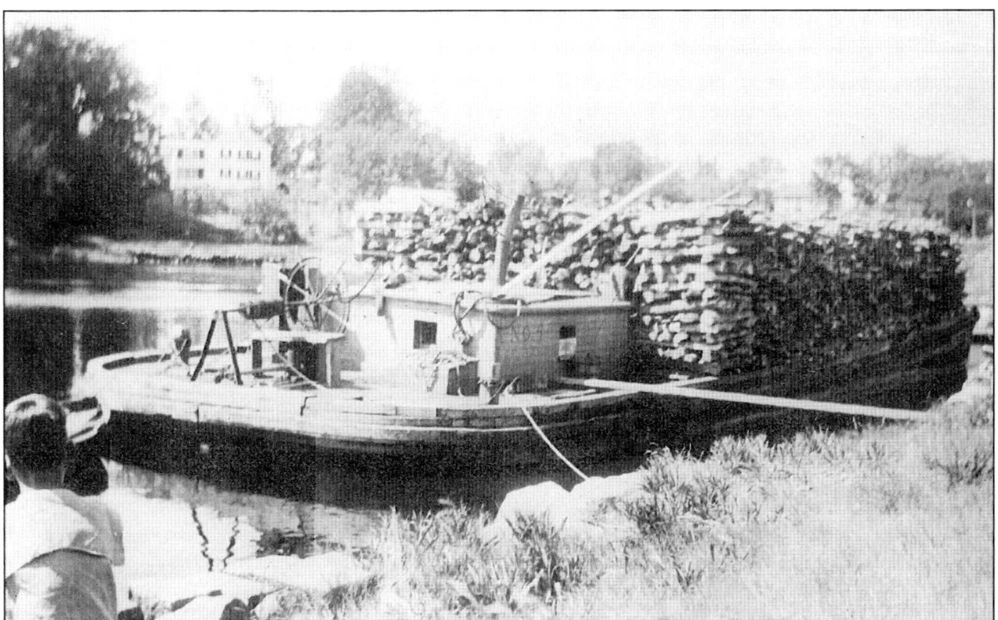

A gundalow, loaded with 40 cords of wood, 1913. Gundalows, shallow-drafted boats used primarily for shipping cargo, were peculiar to the Piscataqua region. They carried timber, bricks, and farm products over local waters from colonial days until the early twentieth century. (Durham Historic Association.)

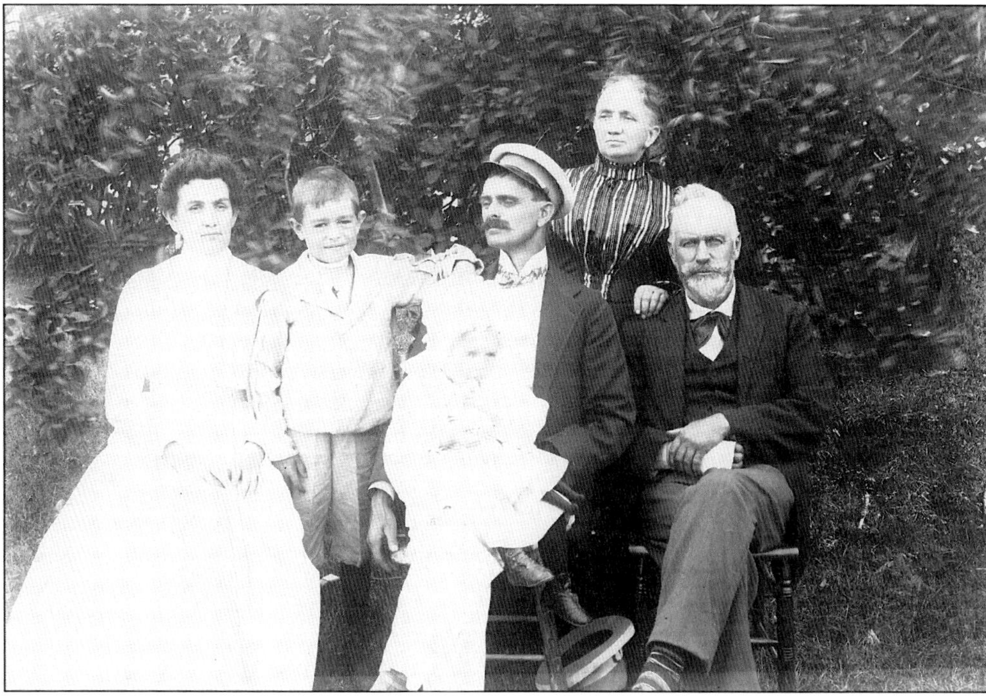

Captain Edward Hamlin Adams (1860–1951) with his wife, Frances Harvey Adams; his parents, Joseph Martin Reuter and Olive Esther Libbey Adams; and his children, Edward Cass and Avis Susanne Adams, *c.* 1900. Captain Adams, grandson of "Reformation John" Adams, owned and captained the *Fanny* M., one of the last working gundalows on Great Bay.

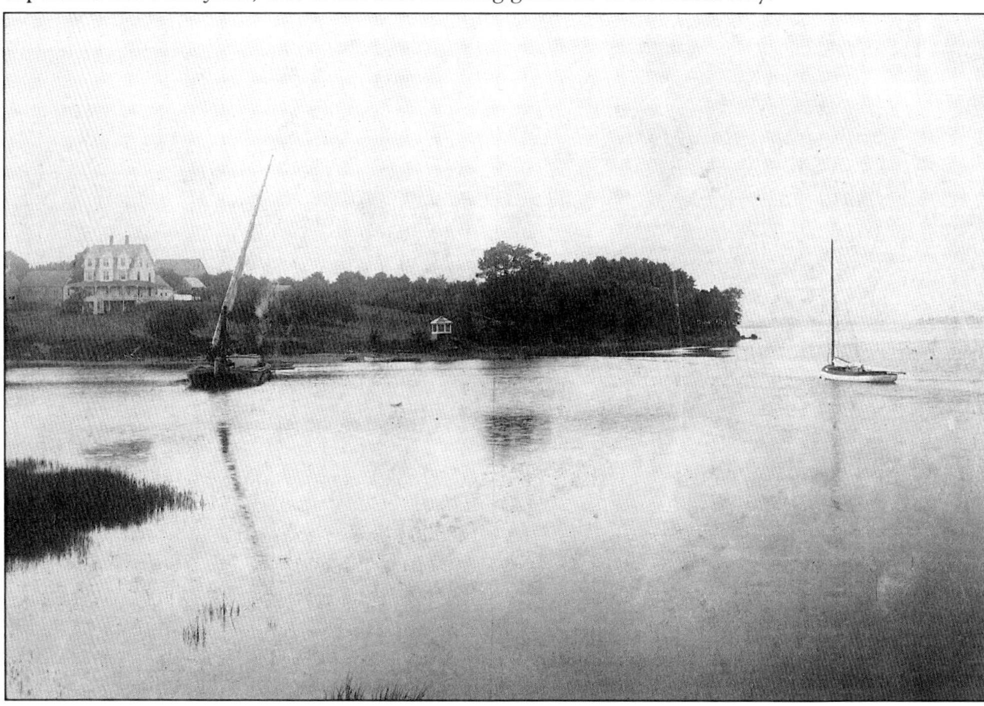

The *Fanny* M., shown at its mooring at Adams Point, around 1898.

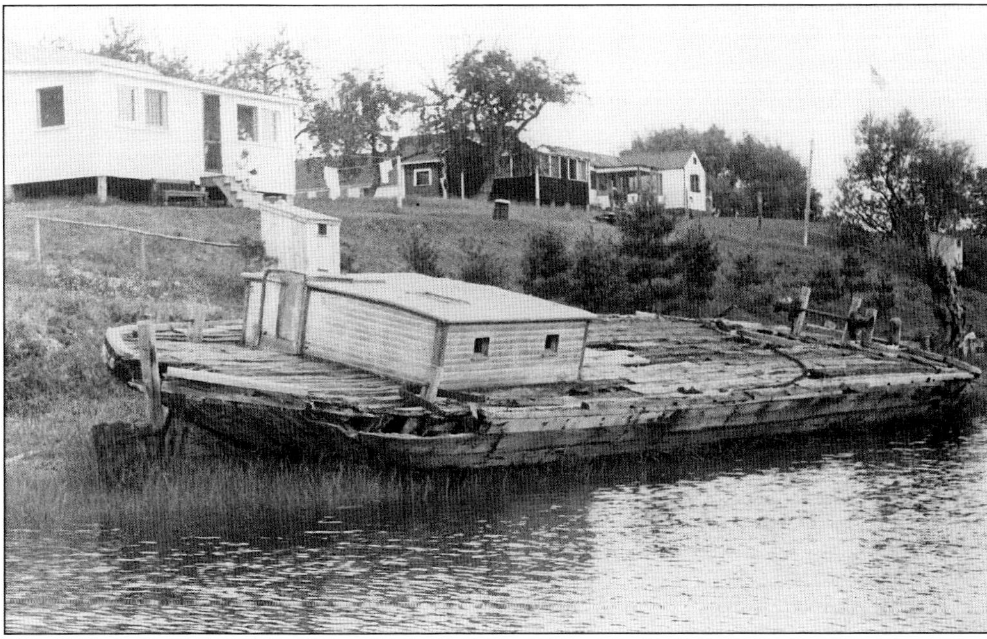

The *Fanny M.* aground on Dover Point, after it broke up in a heavy ice pack during the winter, 1925. It had already been stripped of its rigging and other hardware.

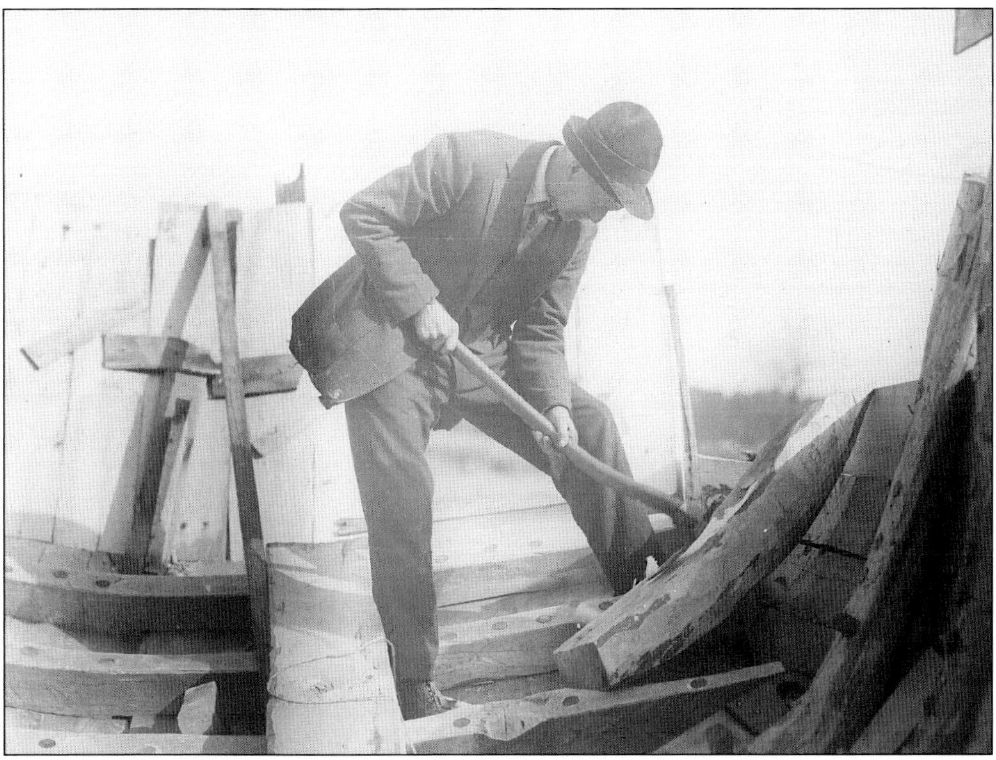

Captain Adams using an adze to shape the *Driftwood*'s frame in the mid-1930s. In 1931, Captain Adams and his son Cass began constructing a new gundalow, the *Driftwood*. The pair finally launched the ship in 1950, shortly before Captain Adams' death.

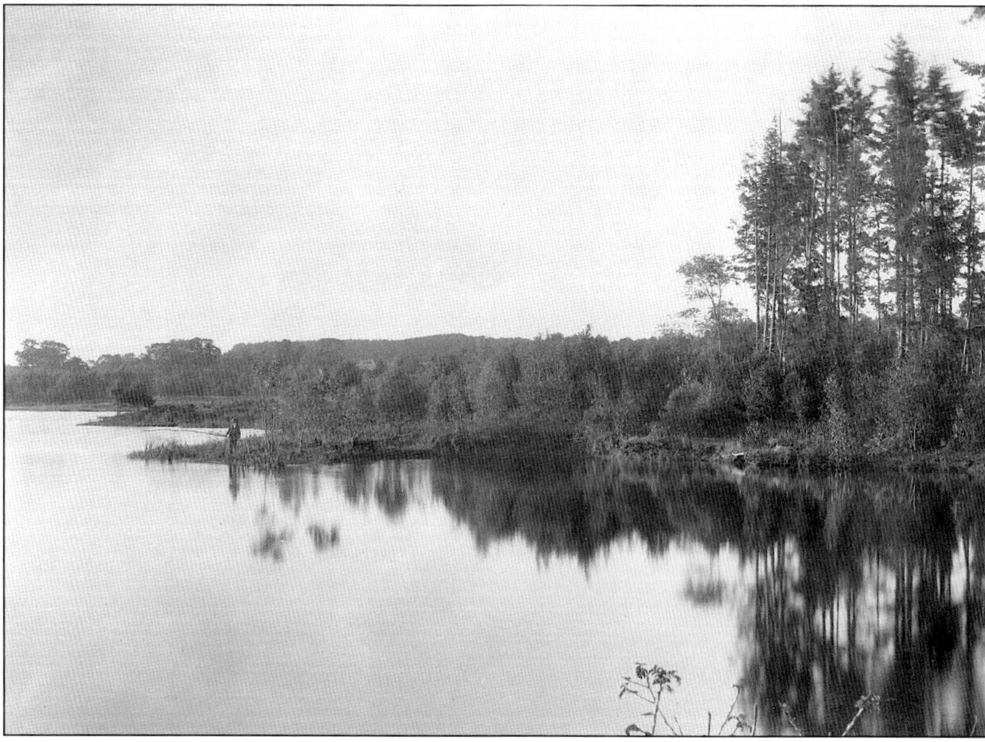

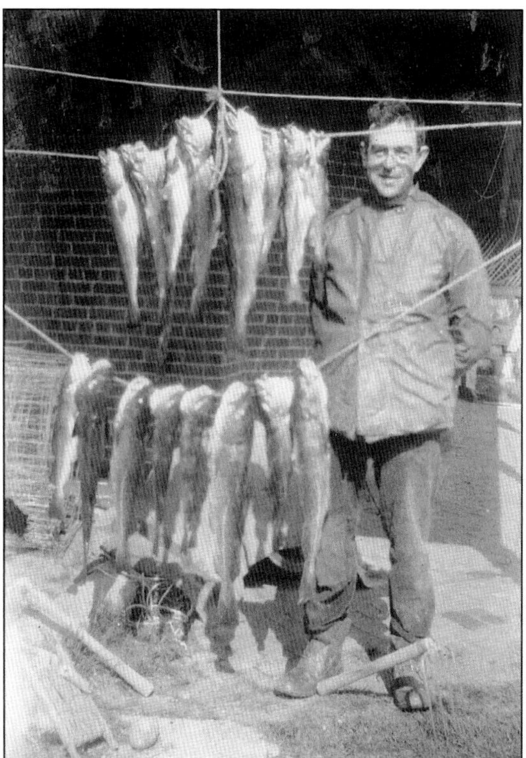

An unidentified angler, possibly near the mouth of the Oyster River, c. 1890s. From the beginning, the waters surrounding Durham have provided residents and visitors alike with food and sport.

Cass Adams showing off his catch in a snapshot from the early 1930s.

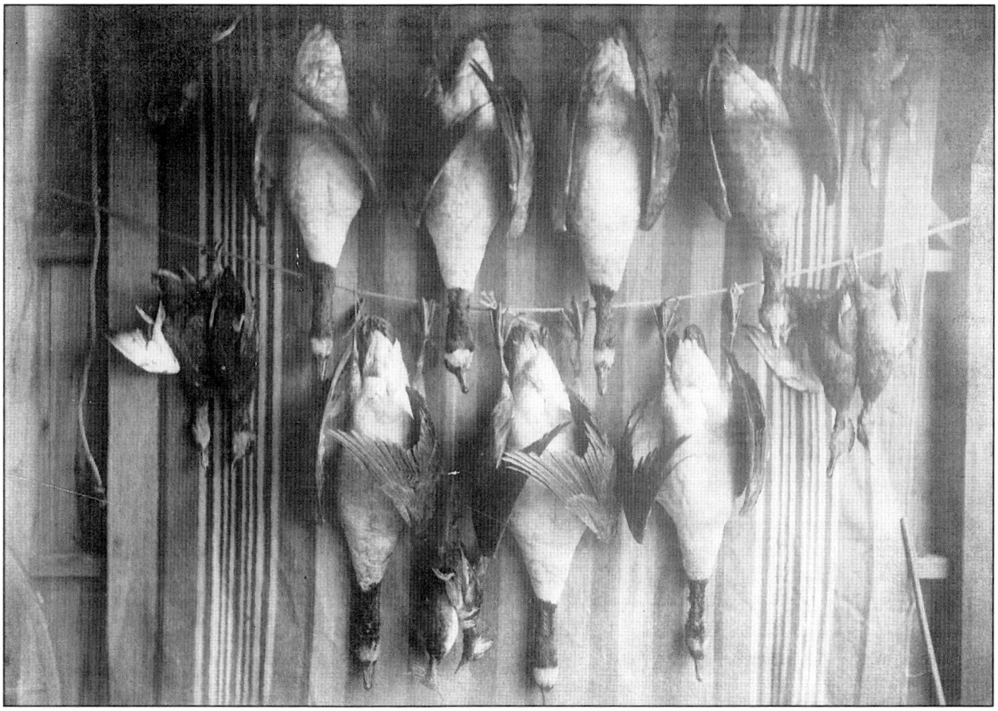

Ducks and geese shot on Great Bay, March 28, 1912. On the verso, it was noted that the largest goose weighed 12 pounds, the total take, 68 pounds.

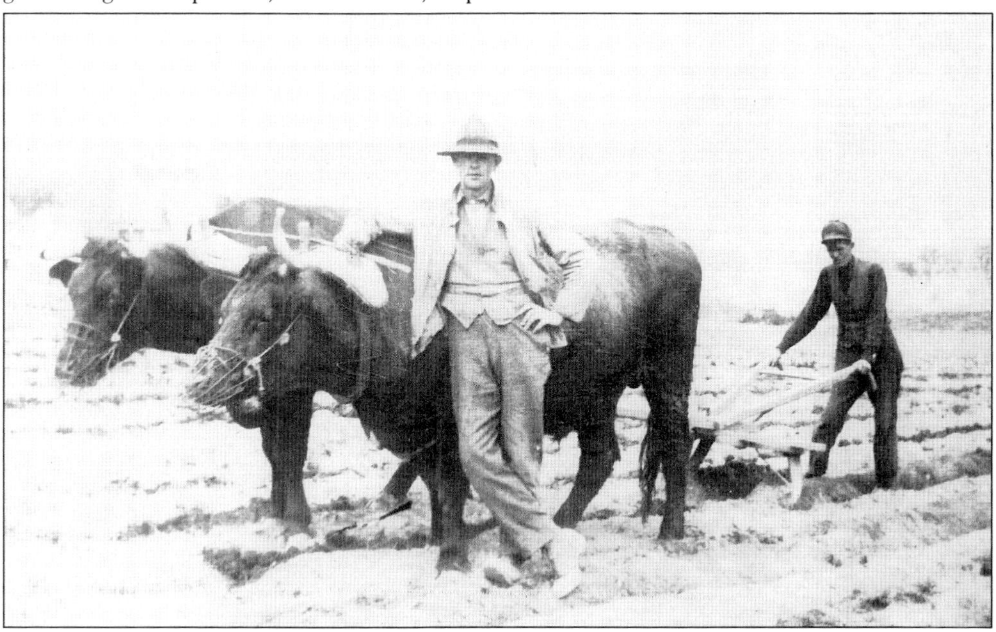

Captain Adams and Cass Adams (behind plow) turning land with an ox-drawn plow, *c.* 1910. Methods of farming changed little from the first settlement through the nineteenth century. While many early residents engaged in trade, fishing, fur trapping, and lumbering, settlers increasingly began to claim the fertile land along the Oyster River. Within a generation, these improved lands were central to the economy of Oyster River Plantation.

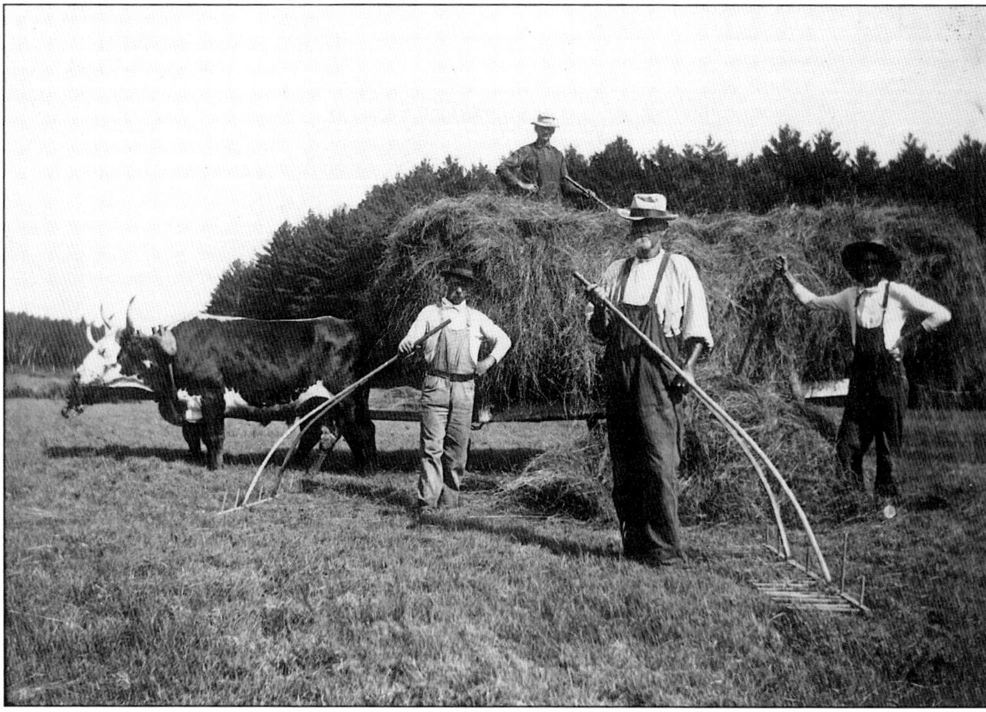

Unidentified farmers raking hay with wooden hay rakes, *c.* 1890. (Durham Historic Association.)

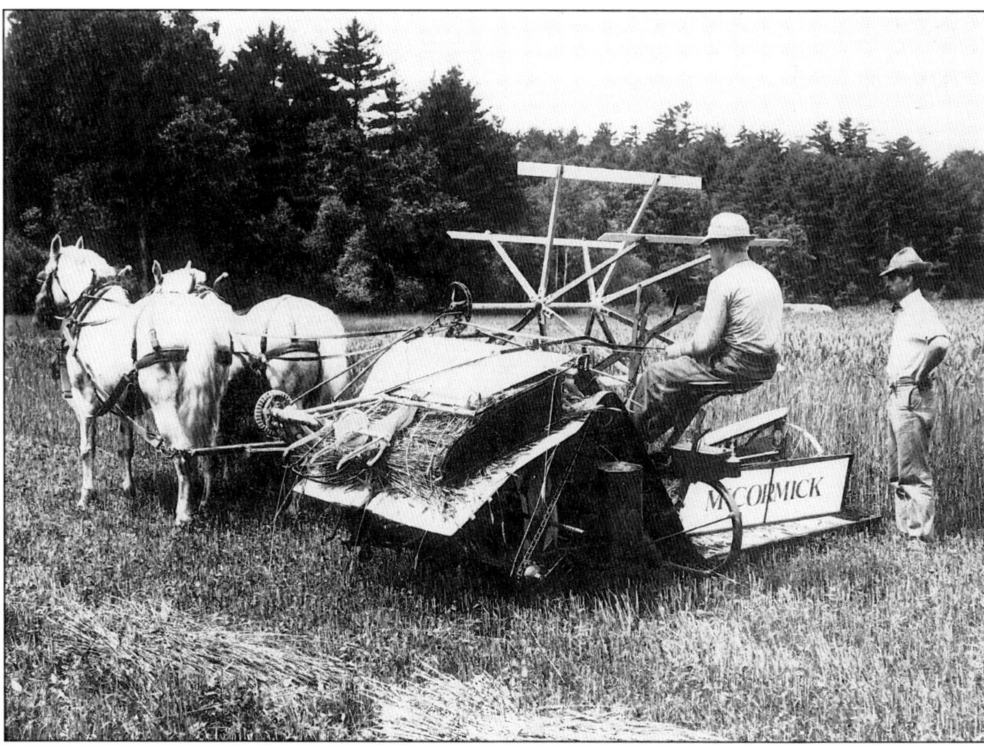

Cutting wheat with a horse-drawn McCormick reaper, 1907.

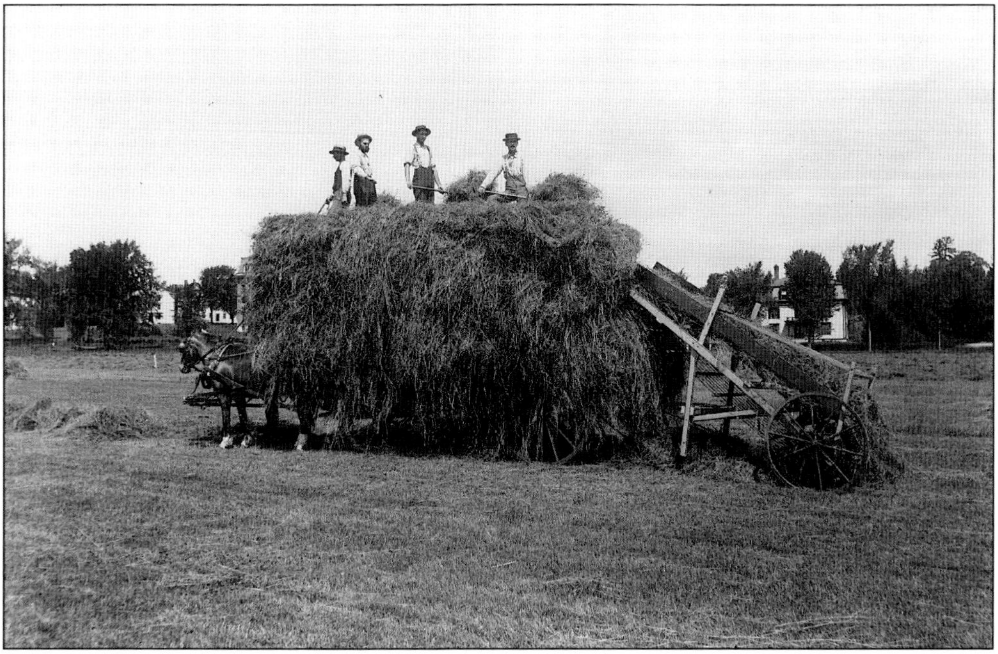

A horse-drawn hay loader, c. 1904.

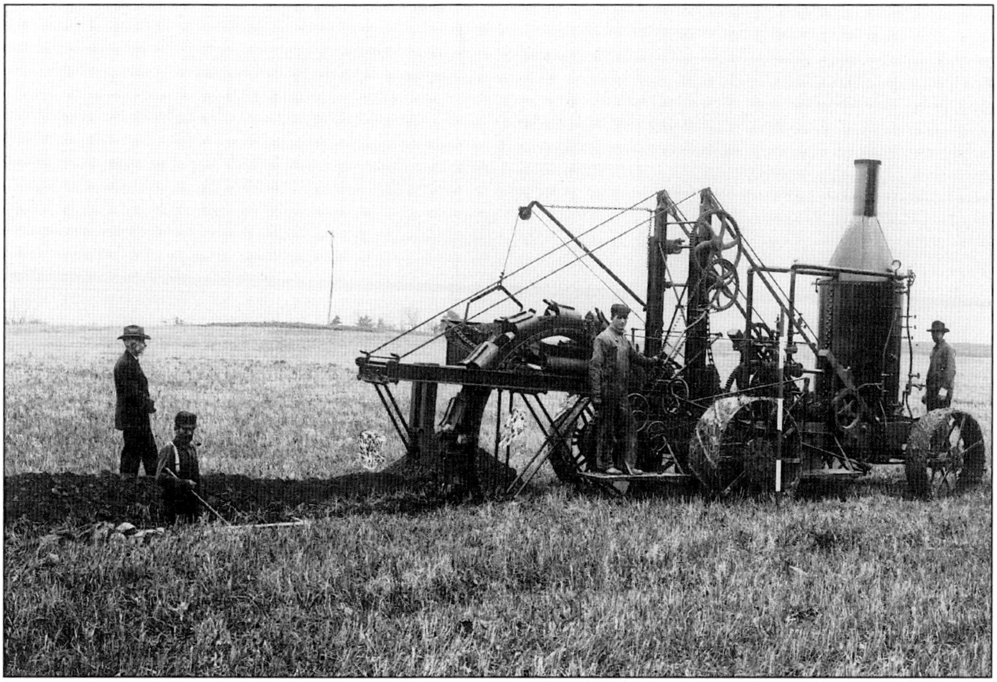

A steam-powered ditching machine, used to lay drain tiles, 1904. The development of steam and later gasoline-powered farm equipment changed the face of farming in Durham.

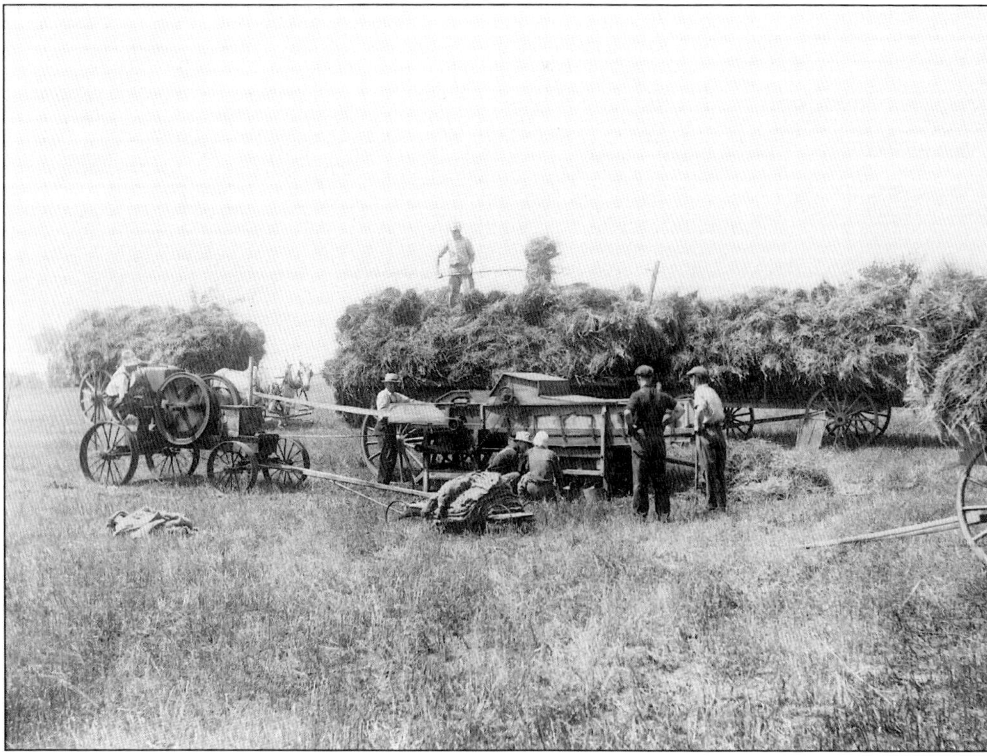

A gasoline-powered engine used to separate grain from the stalk, Adams Point, *c.* 1910. Note men bagging the grain.

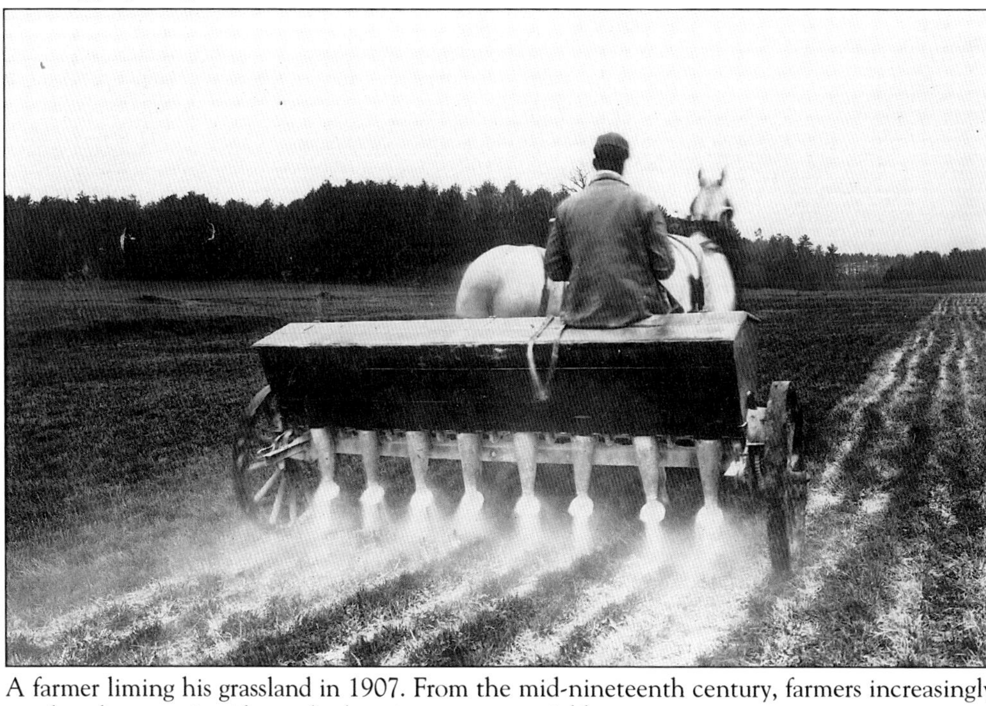

A farmer liming his grassland in 1907. From the mid-nineteenth century, farmers increasingly employed more scientific methods to increase crop yields.

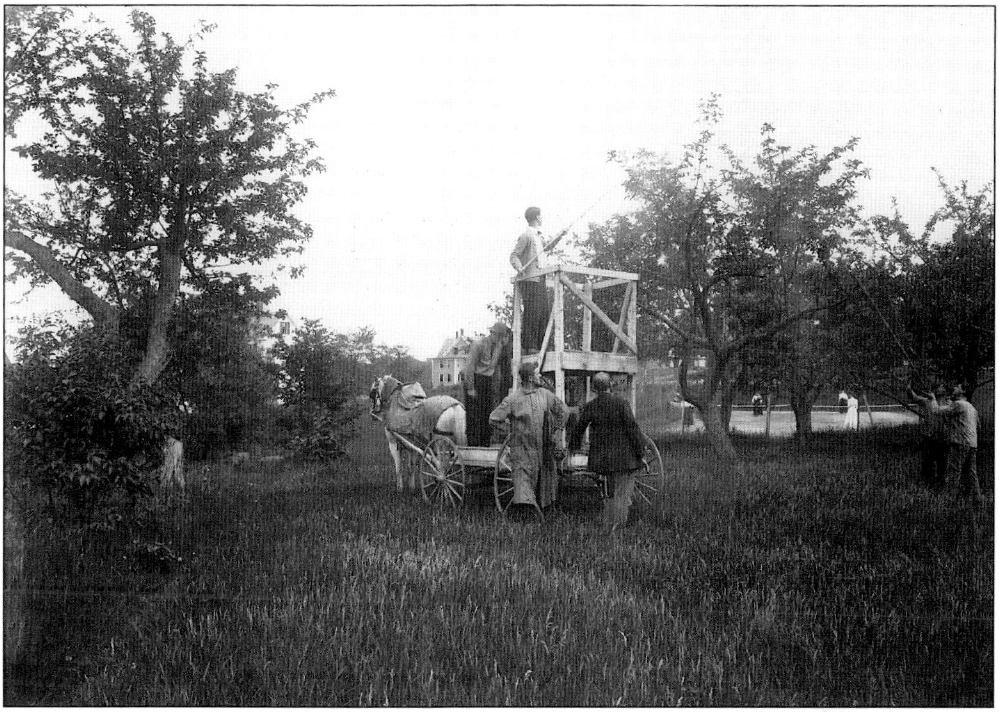

Spraying apples near the campus tennis courts, 1920.

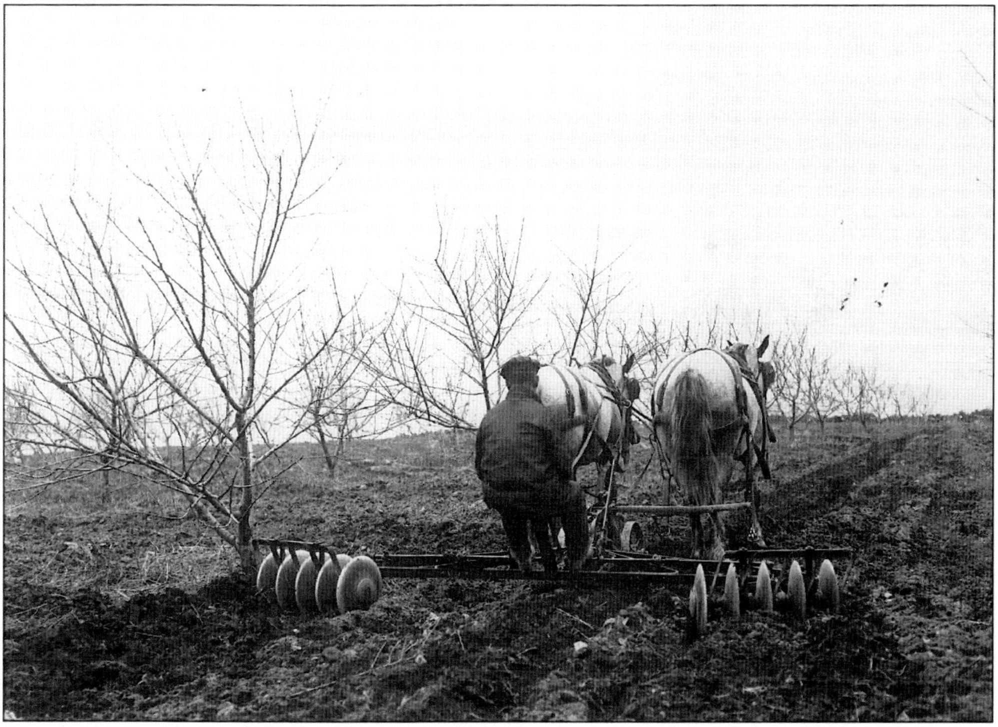

Experimental plowing in the Reno Orchard, 1890s.

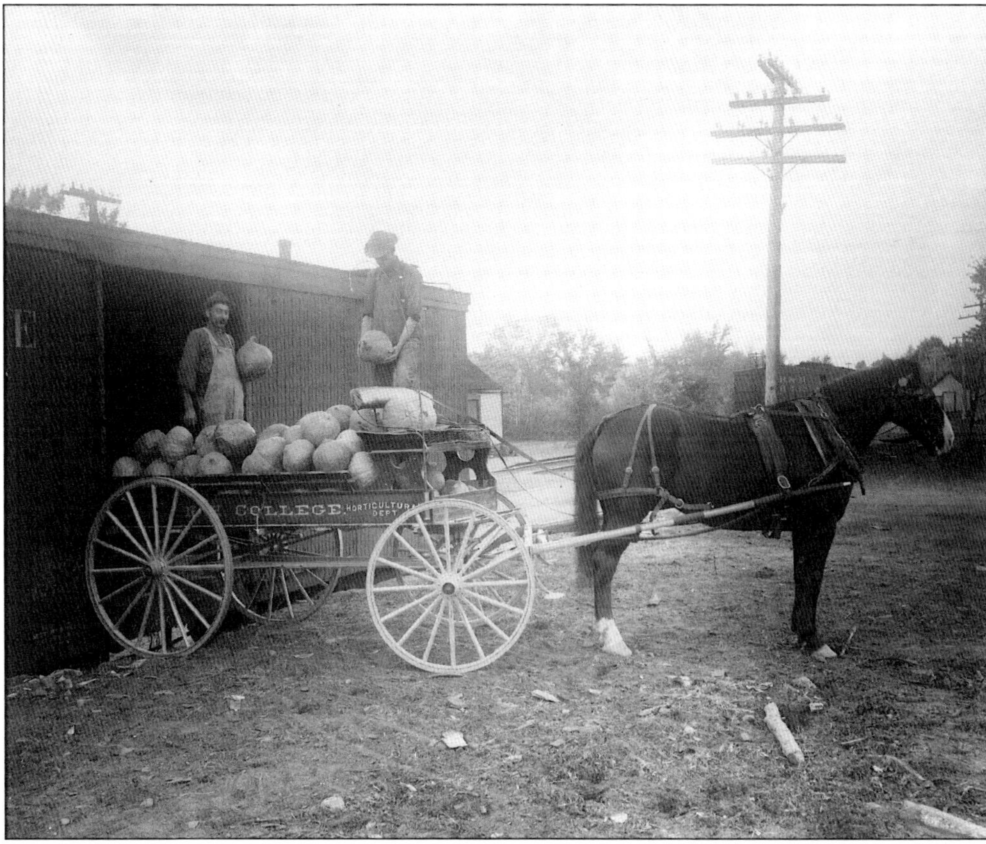

Loading Hubbard squash from the New Hampshire College farms, 1904.

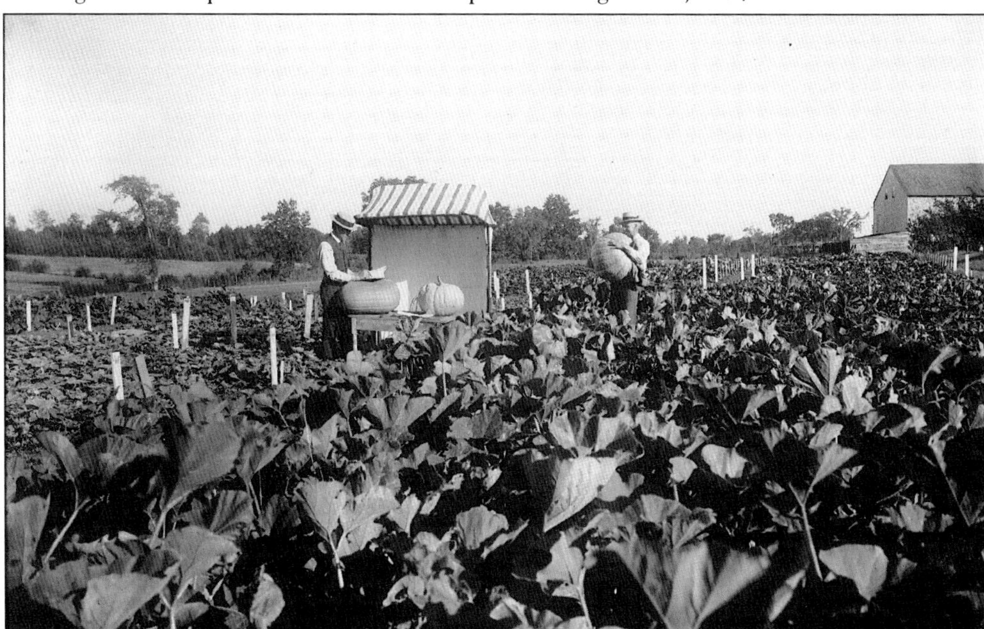

Harvesting pumpkins, *c*. 1918.

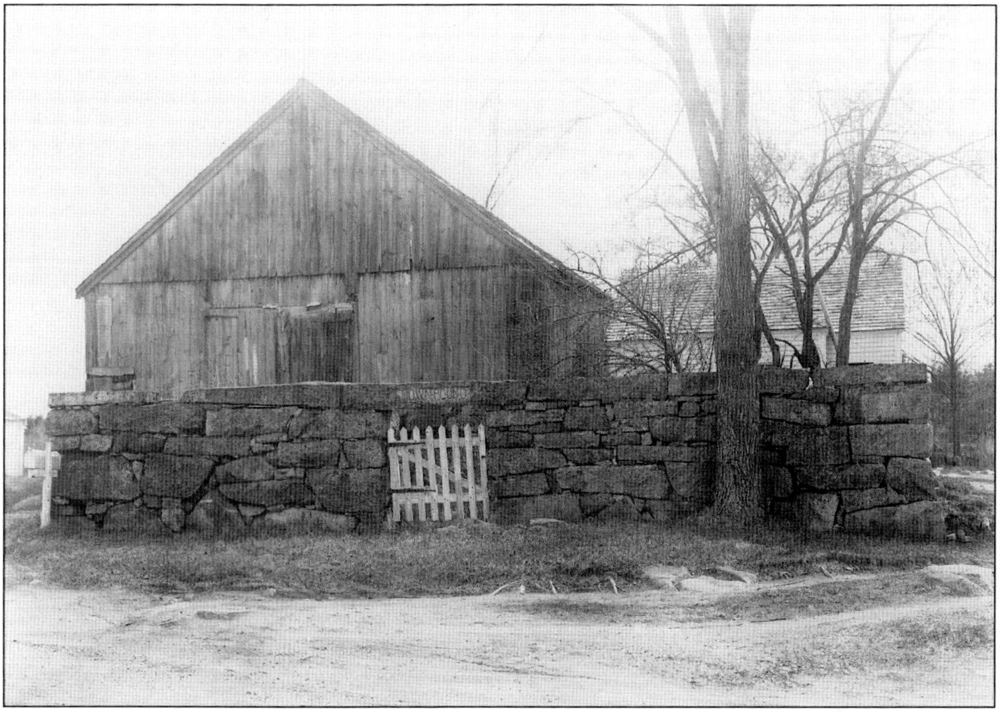

The town pound, *c*. 1920. During the colonial period, most towns constructed pounds, roofless corrals usually constructed of stone blocks, to confine animals found straying into neighboring farms or gardens. Owners would later reclaim their animals and pay a fine. The residents of Oyster River Plantation constructed a pound in 1708. It was rebuilt in 1808 and restored in 1909.

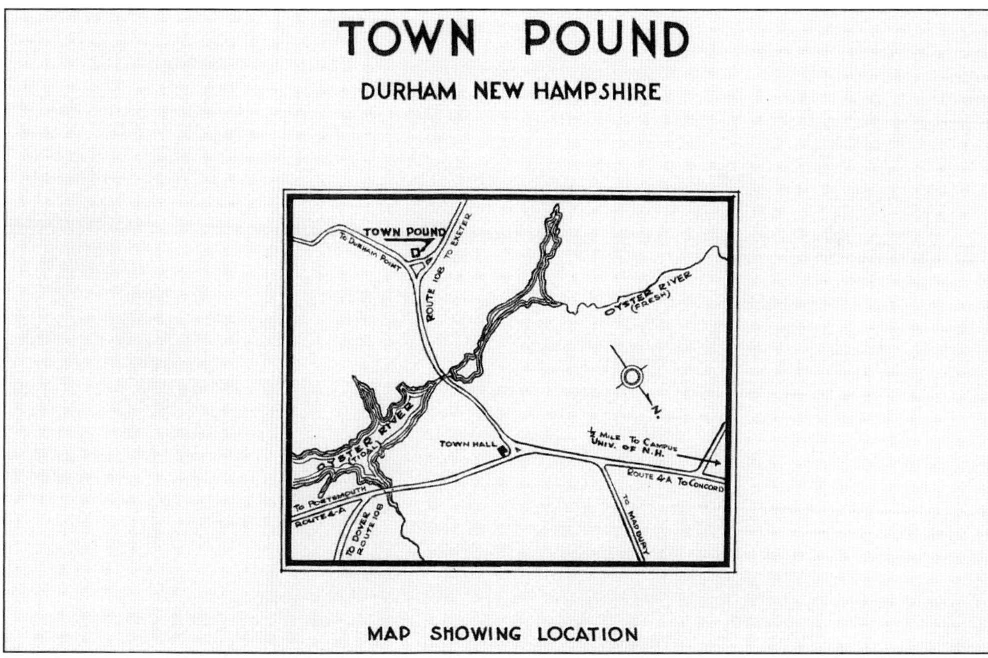

An Historic American Buildings Survey map showing the location of the town pound, 1935.

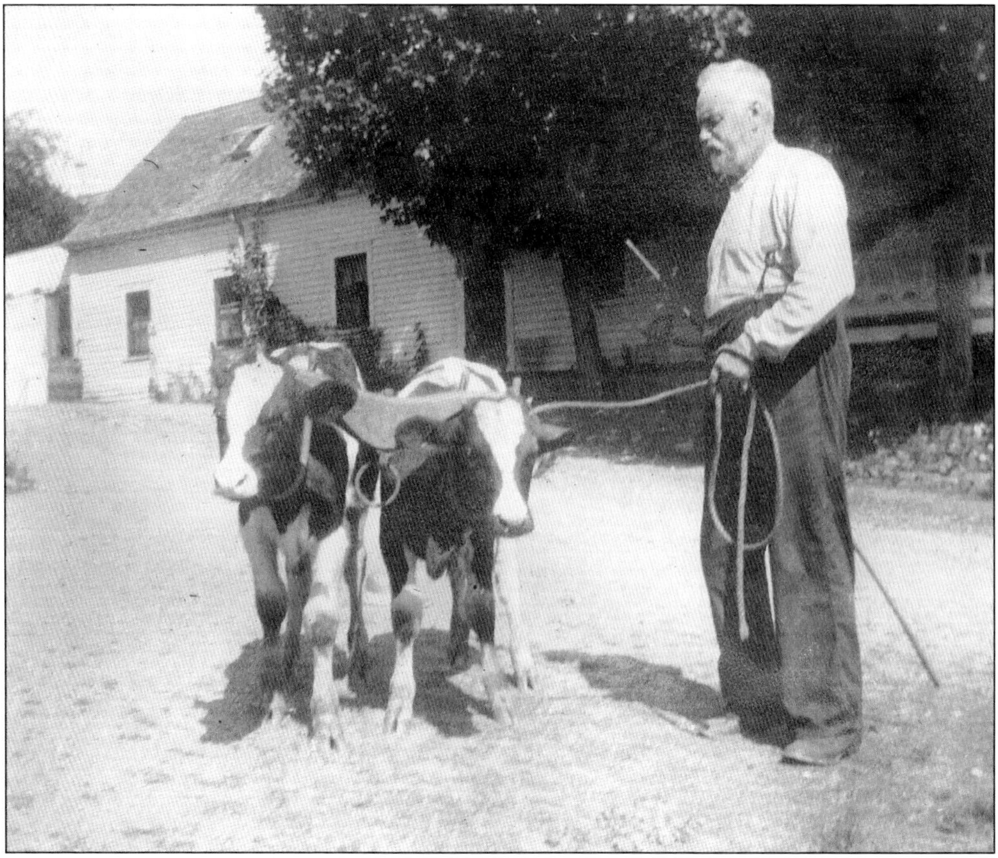

Joseph Martin Adams with a yoked pair of young oxen, Adams Point, *c*. 1905.

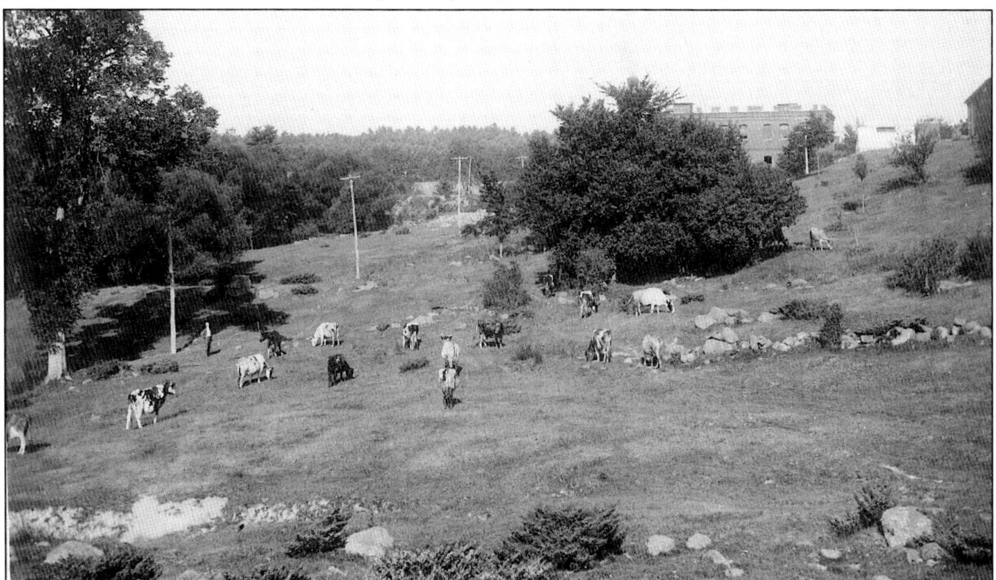

Cattle grazing on land formerly belonging to Benjamin Thompson. Note newly constructed Conant Hall in the background, *c*. 1900.

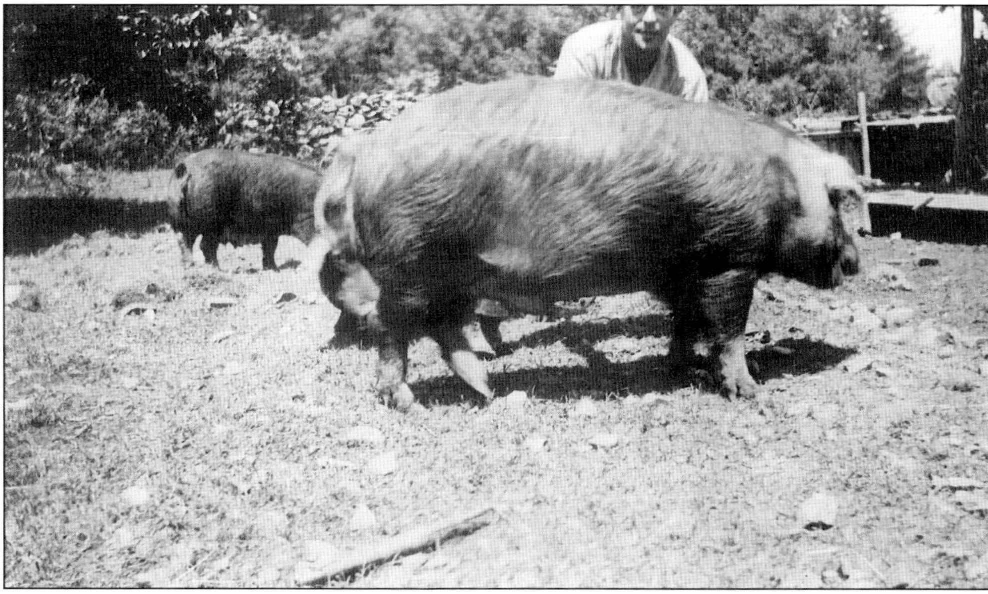

Cass Adams with a Duroc boar, c. 1917.

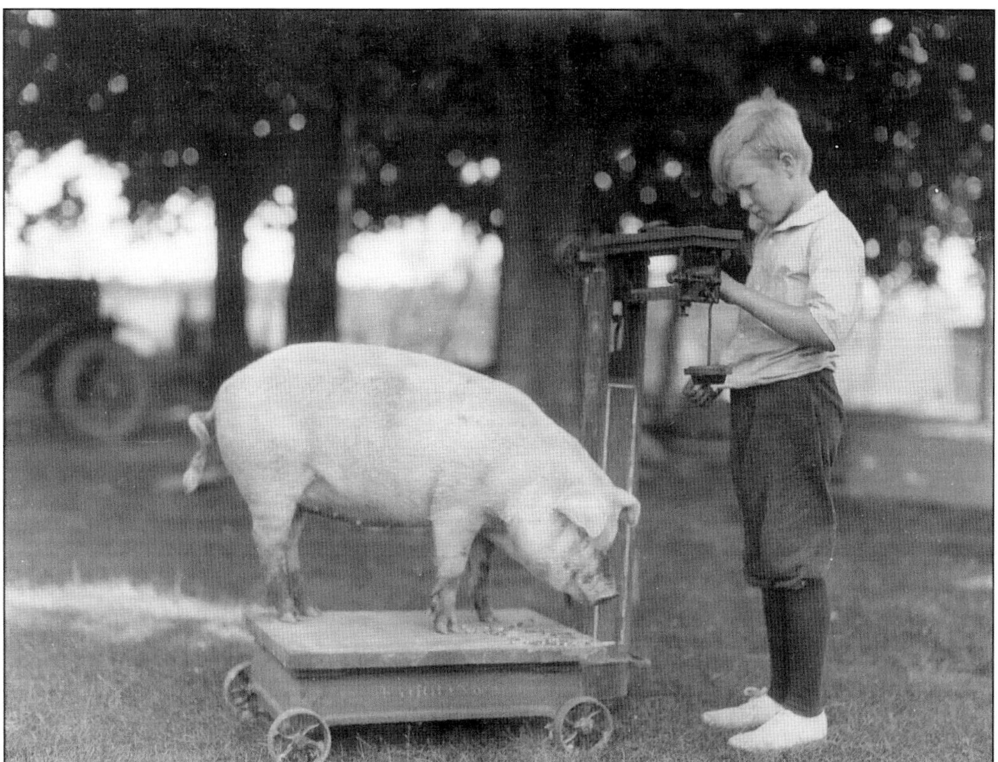

Mr. Meeker weighing his pig, part of a program operated through UNH Cooperative Extension, 1925.

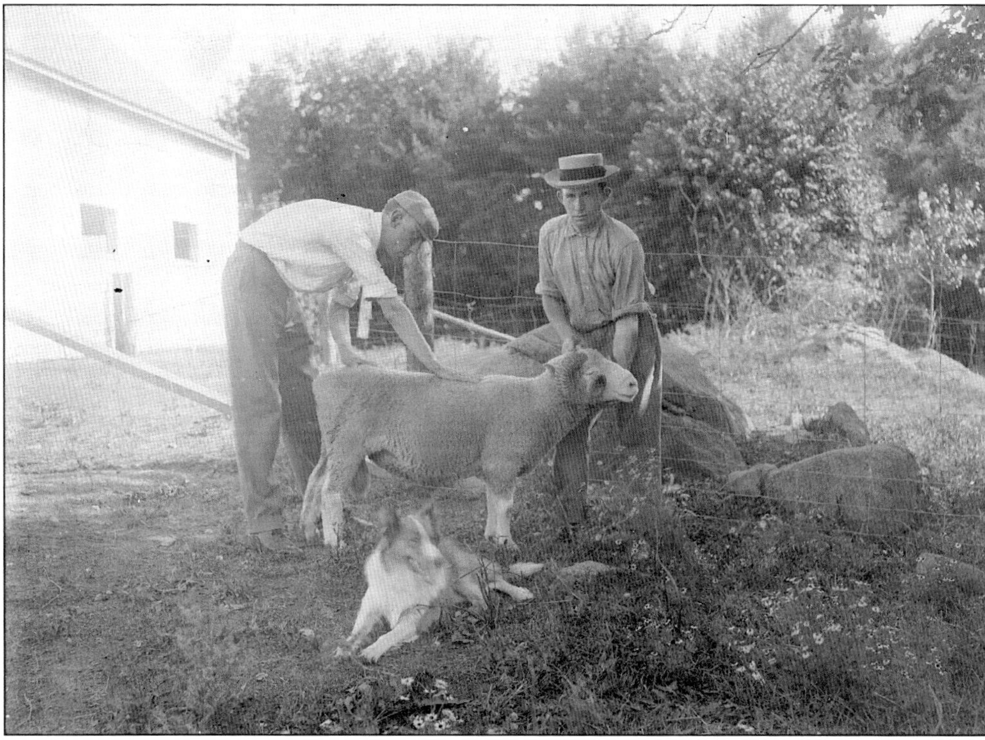

Albert D. Littlehale (right) and extension agent T.R. Arkell examine a sheep, 1910. In later years, it was not uncommon for Littlehale to herd his flock down Main Street.

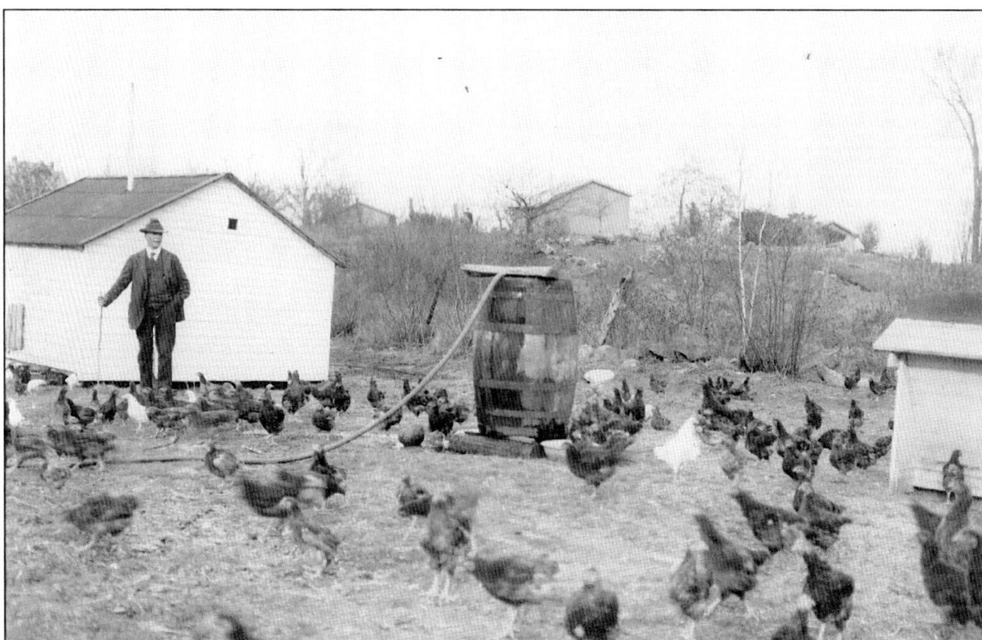

Oren V. "Dad" Henderson with his chickens, c. 1925. (Durham Historic Association.)

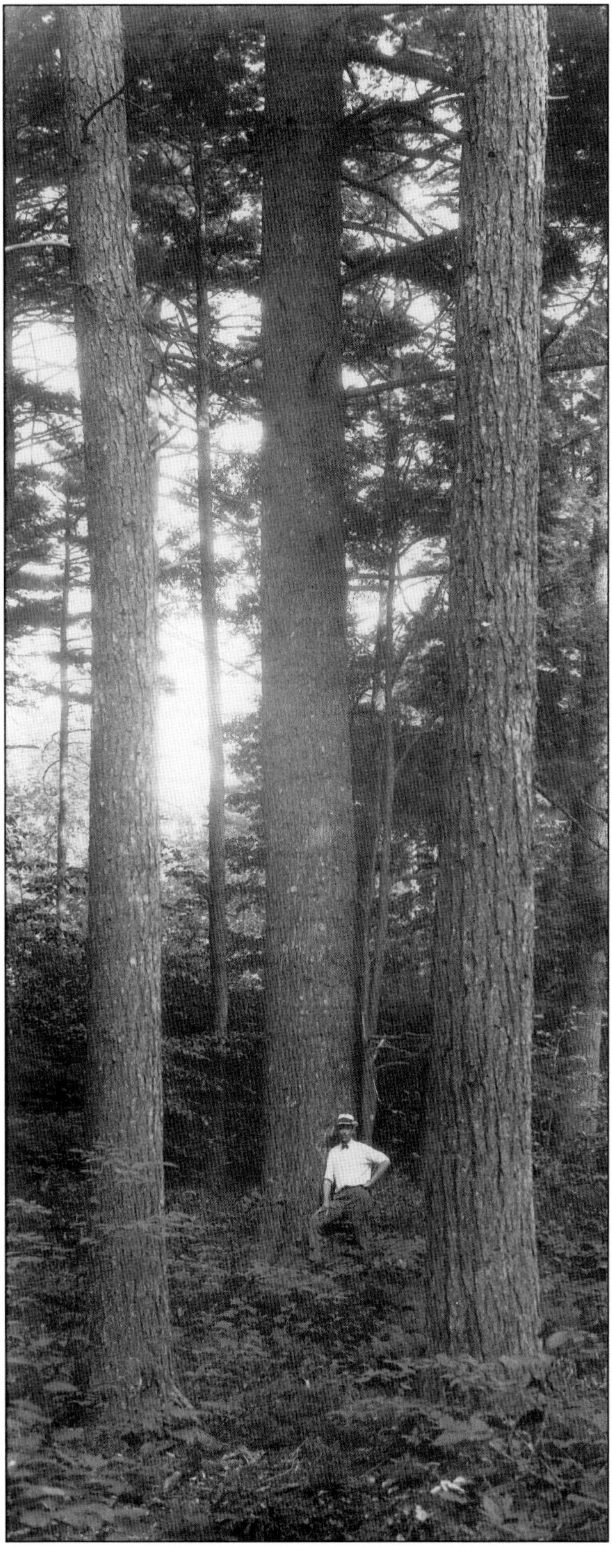

The "Paul Bunyan Tree," a 250-year-old white pine in College Woods, formerly Ben Thompson's woodlot, 1925. Early settlers quickly realized the value of the region's timber resources. By the 1630s, the residents of Dover Neck were hand-sawing boards for shipment back to England. In 1652, Ambrose Gibbons received permission to establish a sawmill on Johnson's Creek in what would later become Durham.

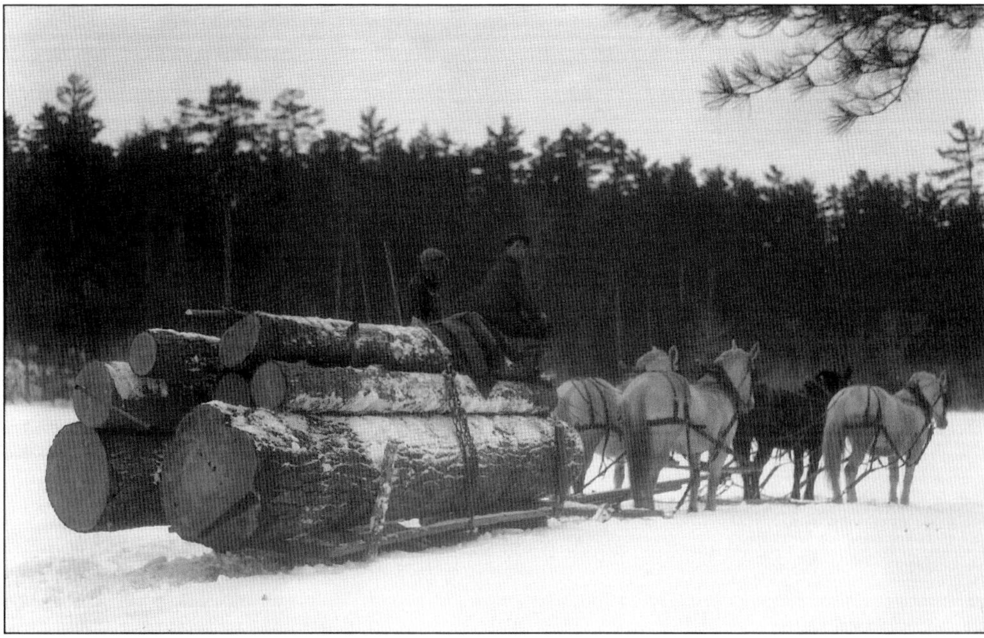

Logs loaded on a horse-drawn sled, 1926.

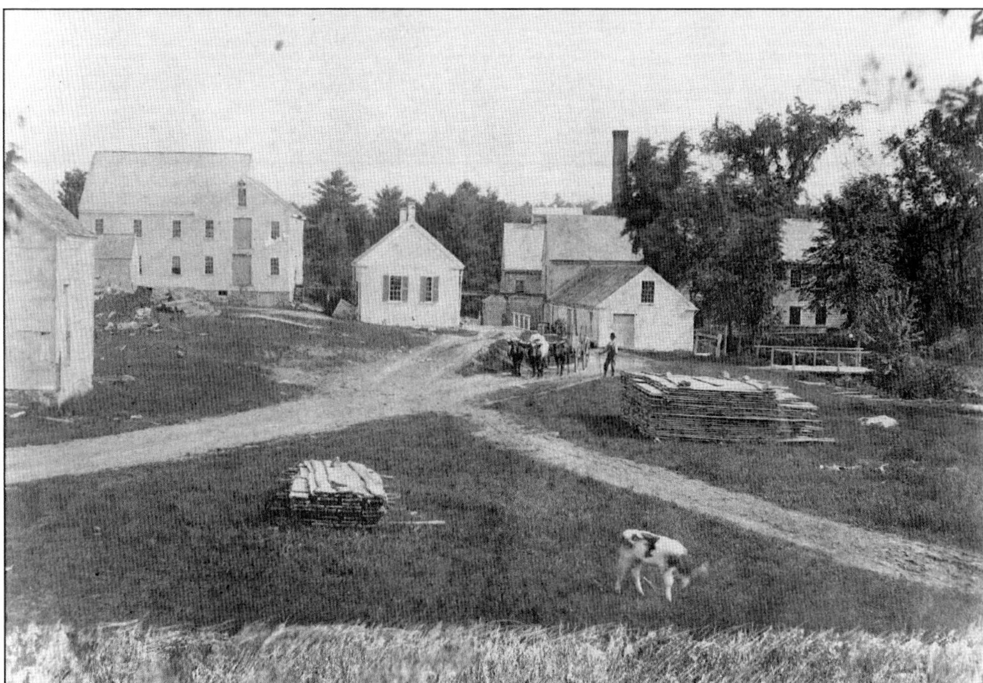

Wiswall's Mill near Packer's Falls in Durham, *c.* 1880. In 1853, Thomas H. Wiswall, son of an Exeter papermaker, purchased a sawmill along the Lamprey River. He added a grist and flour mill along with other small manufacturing facilities. Wiswall later added a paper mill, making the area the manufacturing center of Durham. A fire destroyed the paper mill and surrounding buildings in 1883, leaving only the lumber mill and dam. (Durham Historic Association, gift of Alice Kova.)

Two

Durham Homes, Inns and Camps

By 1640, much of the fertile land along the Oyster River had been claimed by residents of Dover Neck. As they cleared land for farming and their growing herds, many moved their residences to Oyster River Plantation. According to a 1648 tax assessment, twenty-three of Dover's fifty-three households were located in Oyster River.

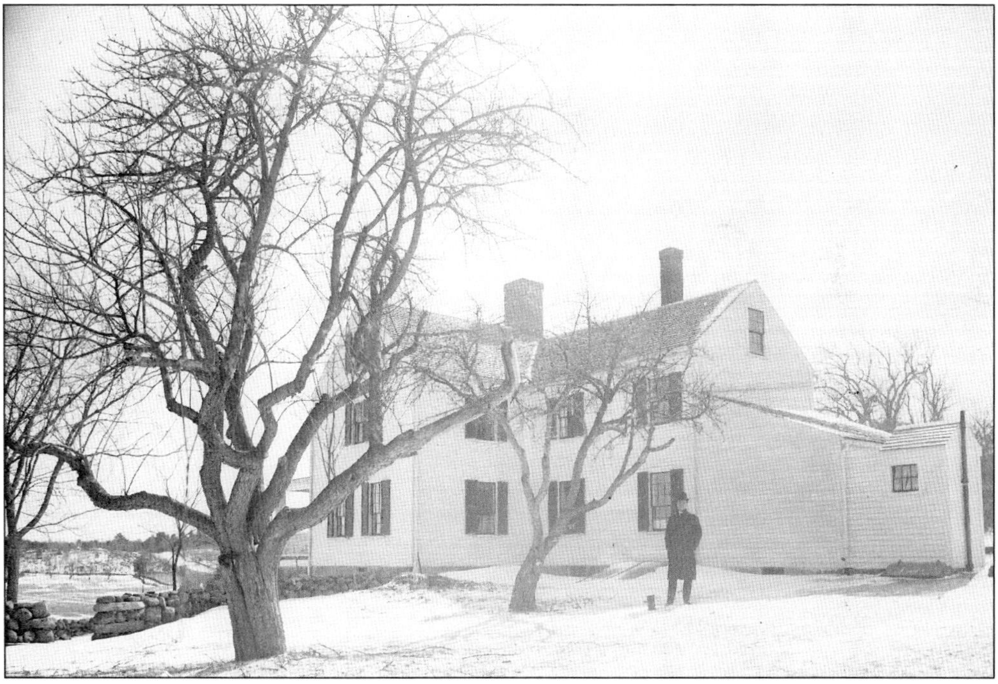

Author Ralph D. Paine at "Shankhassick Farm," c. 1920. A portion of the homestead, which was located off of Durham Point Road, was built by Robert Burnham in 1641.

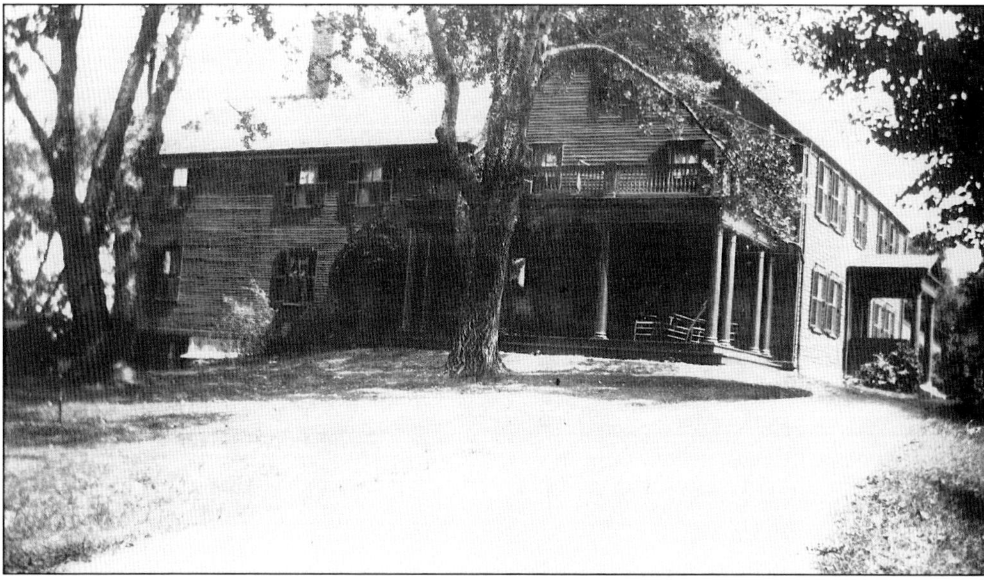

The Valentine Hill Home, *c.* 1910. According to early records, Valentine Hill built a home near his mill in 1649. Tradition has it that the oldest part of the Ffrost House is Valentine Hill's original home. Its location, uphill from the Oyster River dam and the site of the mill, seems to support this notion.

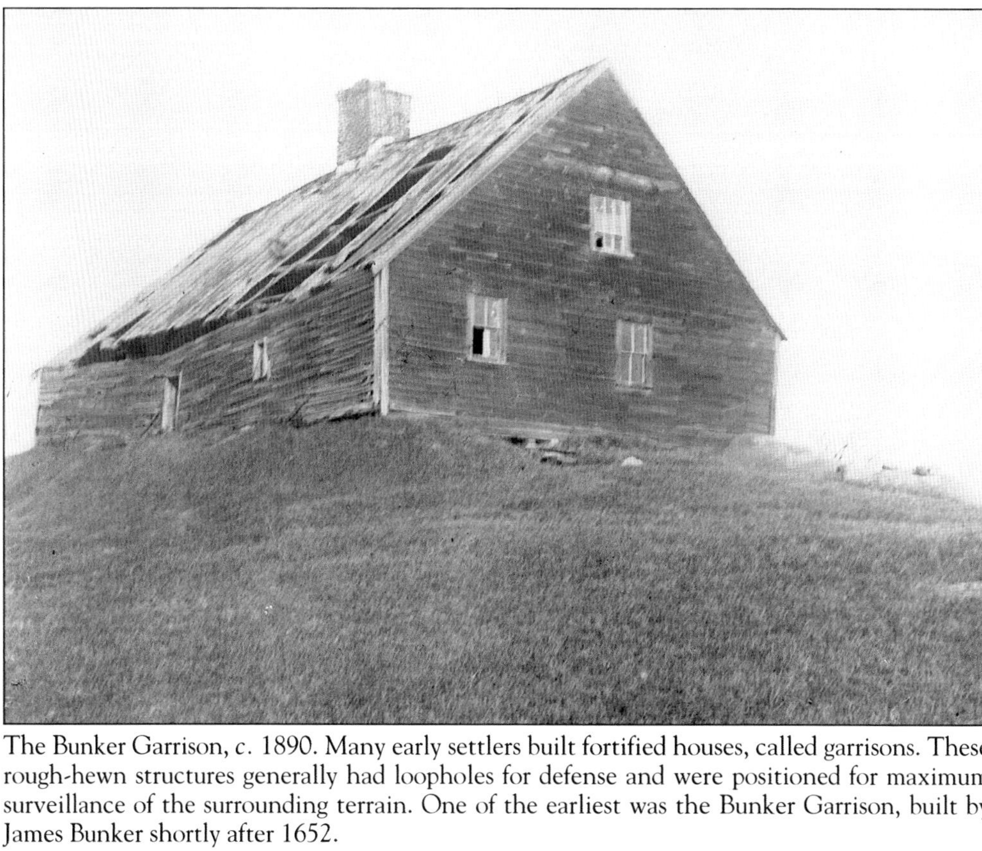

The Bunker Garrison, *c.* 1890. Many early settlers built fortified houses, called garrisons. These rough-hewn structures generally had loopholes for defense and were positioned for maximum surveillance of the surrounding terrain. One of the earliest was the Bunker Garrison, built by James Bunker shortly after 1652.

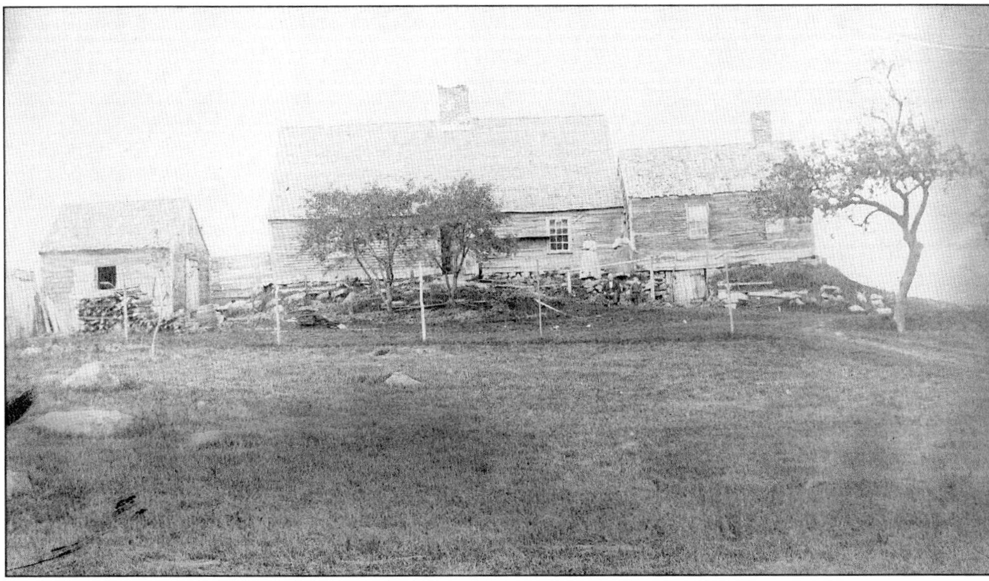

Additions to the original structure of the Bunker Garrison, from a c. 1875 albumen print. (Durham Historic Association.)

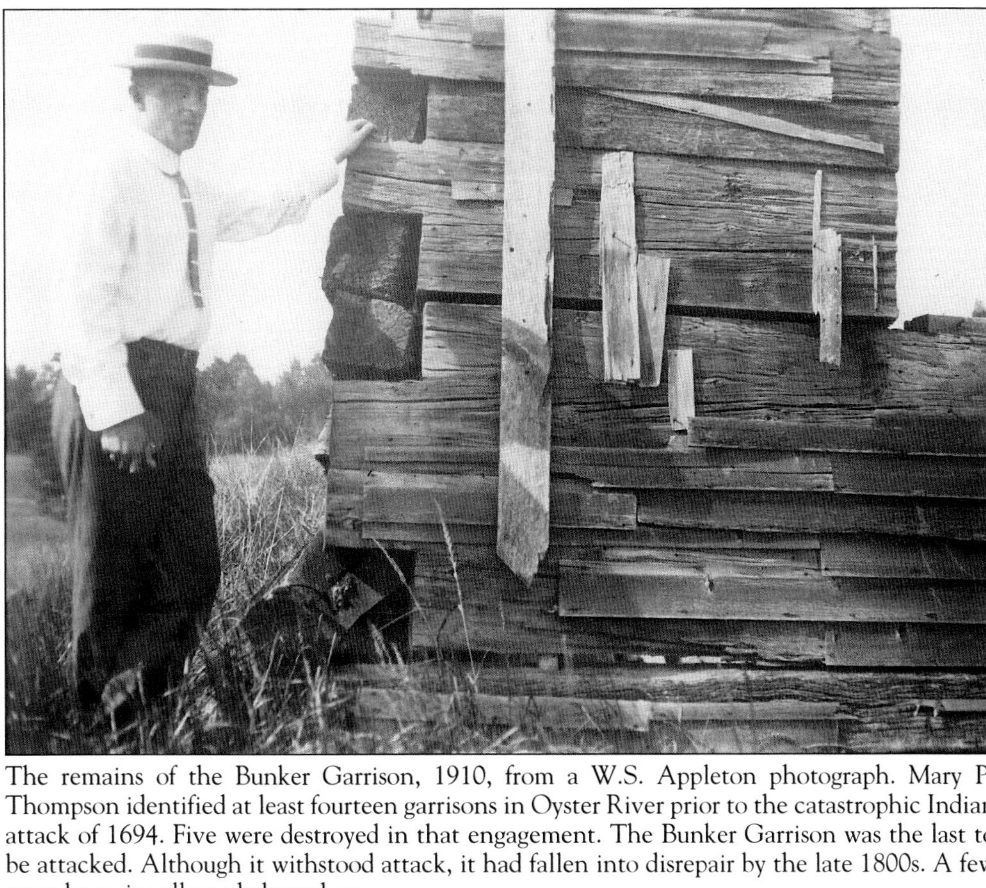

The remains of the Bunker Garrison, 1910, from a W.S. Appleton photograph. Mary P. Thompson identified at least fourteen garrisons in Oyster River prior to the catastrophic Indian attack of 1694. Five were destroyed in that engagement. The Bunker Garrison was the last to be attacked. Although it withstood attack, it had fallen into disrepair by the late 1800s. A few years later, it collapsed altogether.

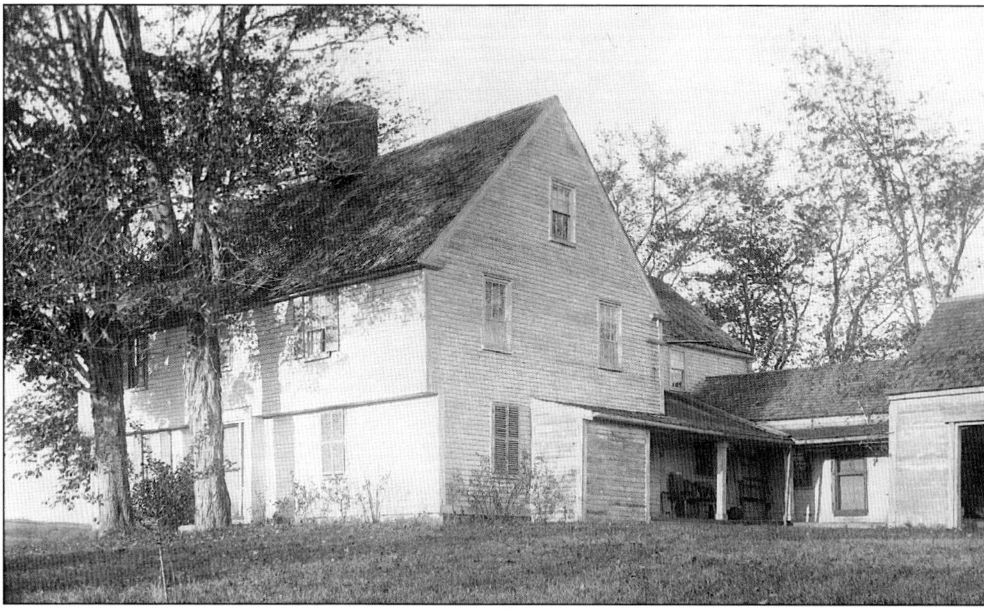

The Woodman Garrison, 1890s. Captain John Woodman built the garrison that bore his name soon after he moved to Oyster River in 1656. It was one of the largest and best fortified of the Oyster River garrisons.

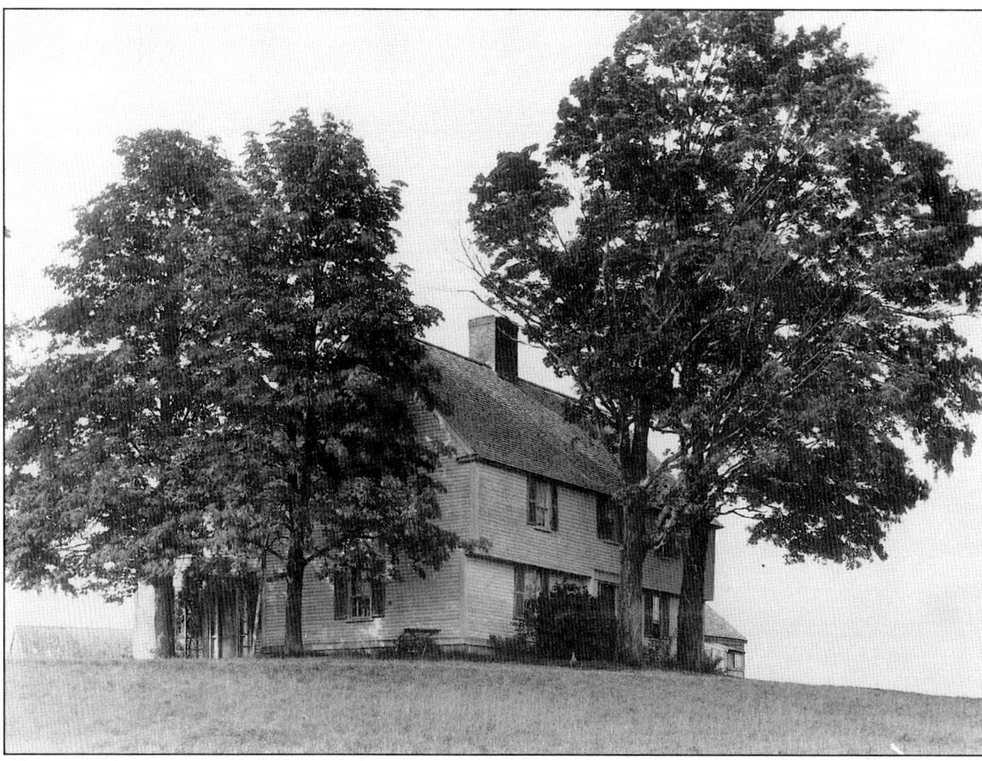

The Woodman Garrison. Located at the head of Beard's Creek off of what is now Madbury Road, the garrison afforded open views on three sides. The loopholes had been enlarged into windows long before this 1890s photograph was taken.

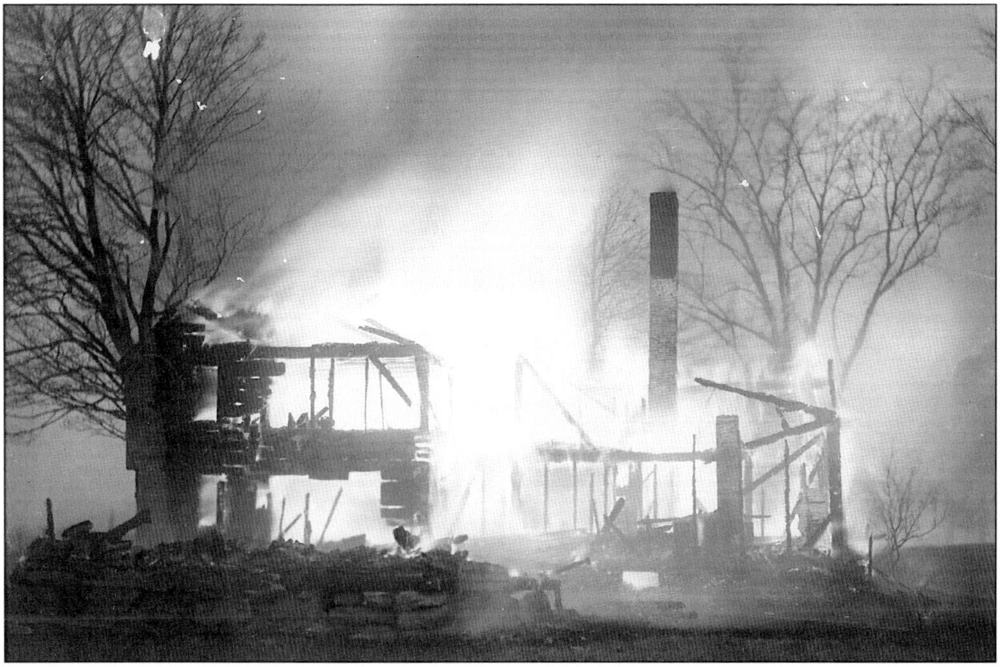

The Woodman Garrison fire. On the night of November 8, 1896, fire destroyed the Woodman Garrison, one of Durham's most treasured historical landmarks.

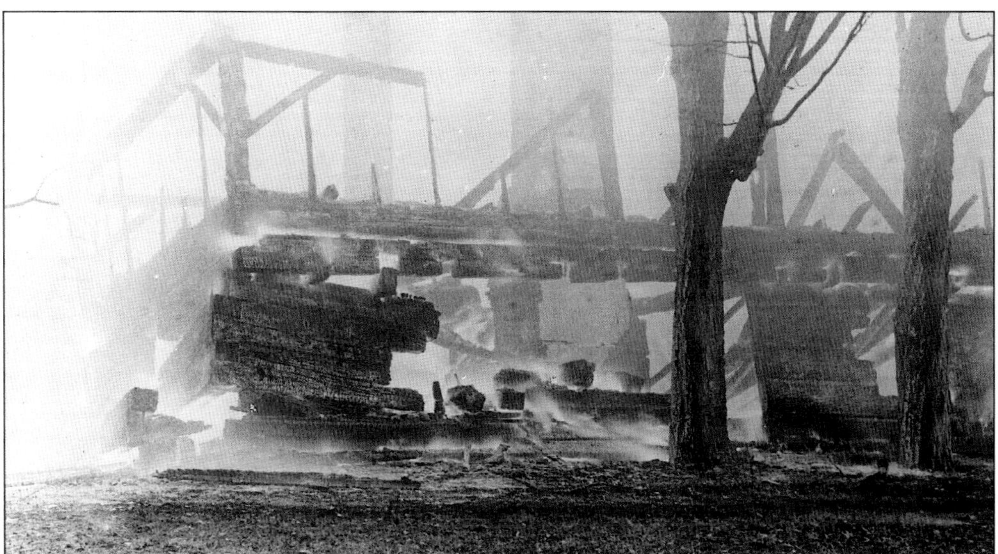

The ruins of the Woodman Garrison the morning after the fire, 1896.

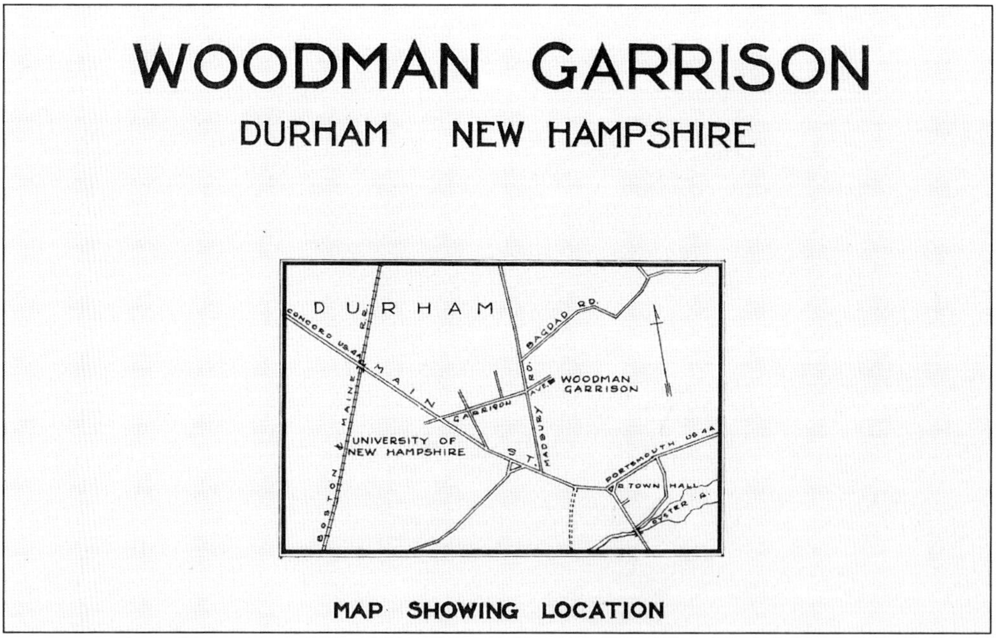

A map showing location of the Woodman Garrison. Professor E.F. Huddleston created this map in 1936 for the Historic American Buildings Survey, a Works Project Administration initiative.

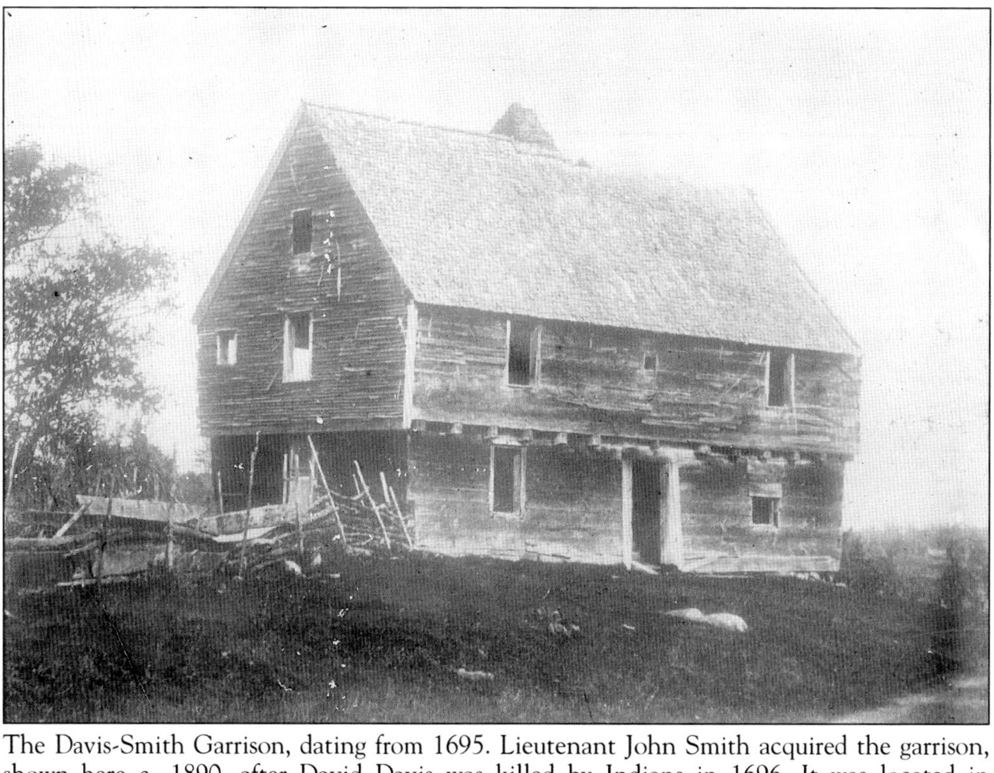

The Davis-Smith Garrison, dating from 1695. Lieutenant John Smith acquired the garrison, shown here *c.* 1890, after David Davis was killed by Indians in 1696. It was located in "Lubberland" along the border between Durham and Newmarket. Durham Point Road now runs through the site.

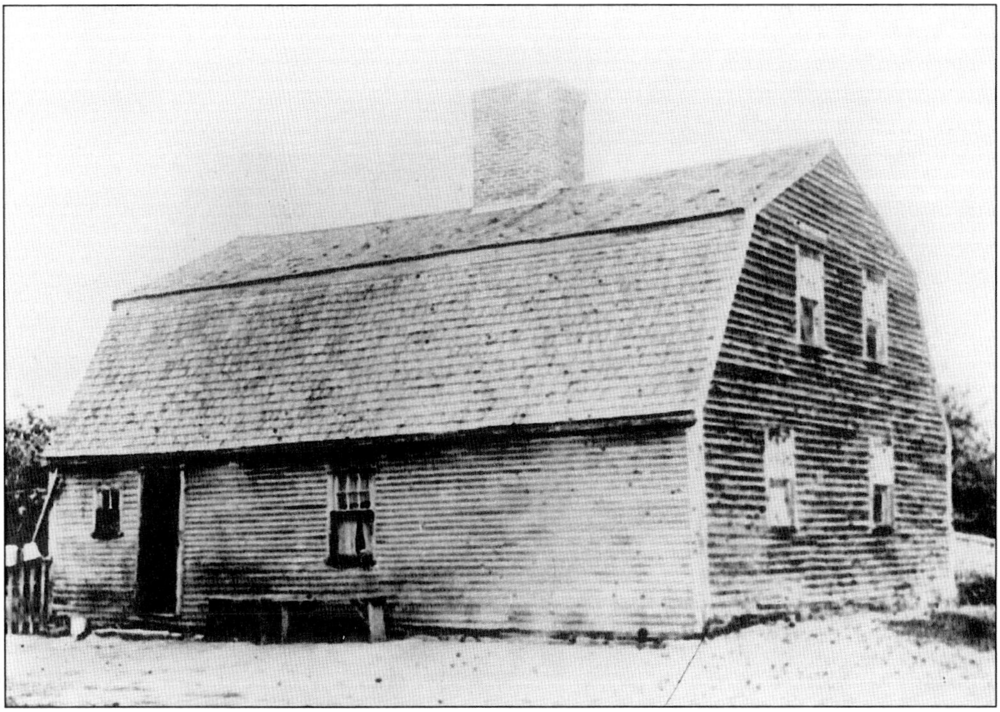

The western side of the Chesley Garrison, possibly 1920s. The Chesley Garrison, one of three garrisons to bear that name, was constructed in the early eighteenth century.

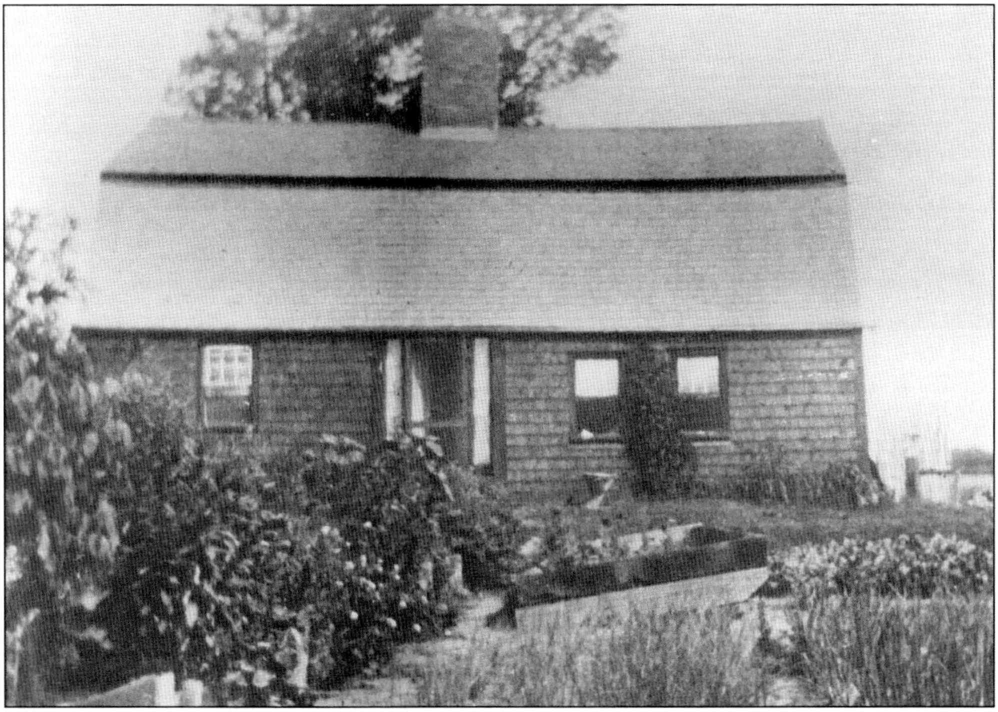

The eastern side of the Chesley Garrison, possibly 1920s. This structure still stands at the intersection of Bagdad and Old Bagdad Roads.

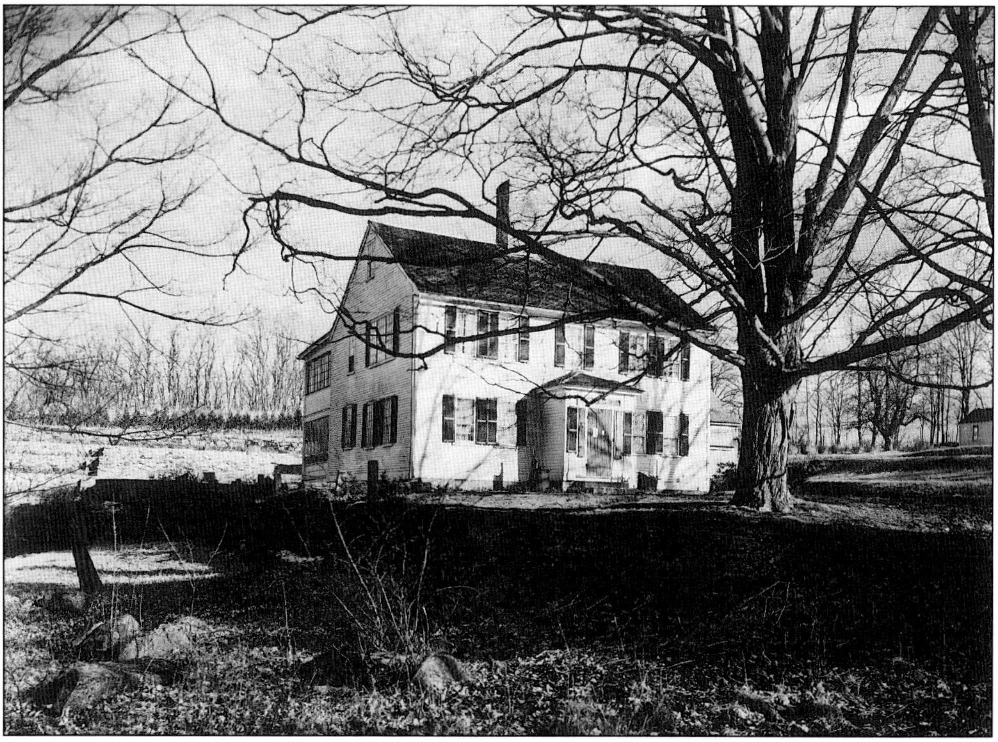

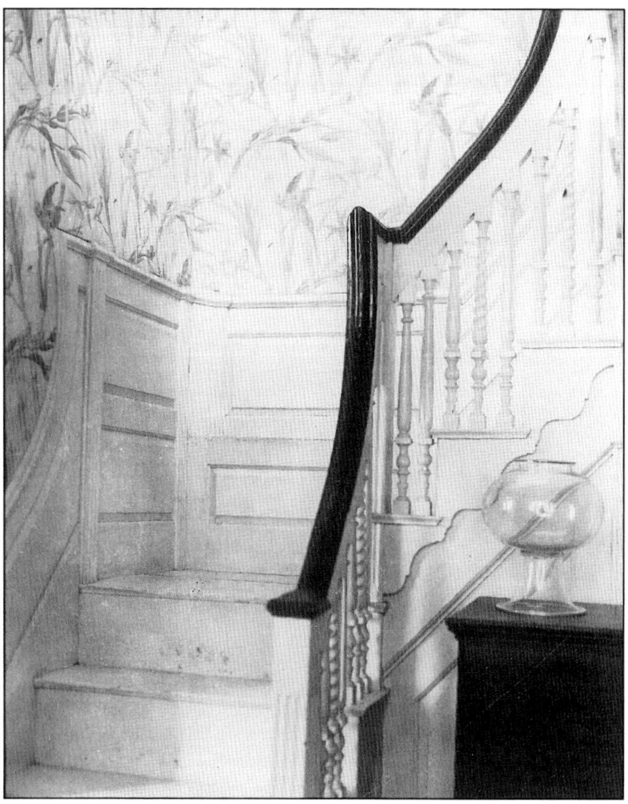

The Sullivan House, *c.* 1900. Built prior to 1750 by Reverend Samuel Adams, this house bears the name of a later owner, Revolutionary War hero General John Sullivan.

An interior shot of the main stairway of the Sullivan House, *c.* 1910.

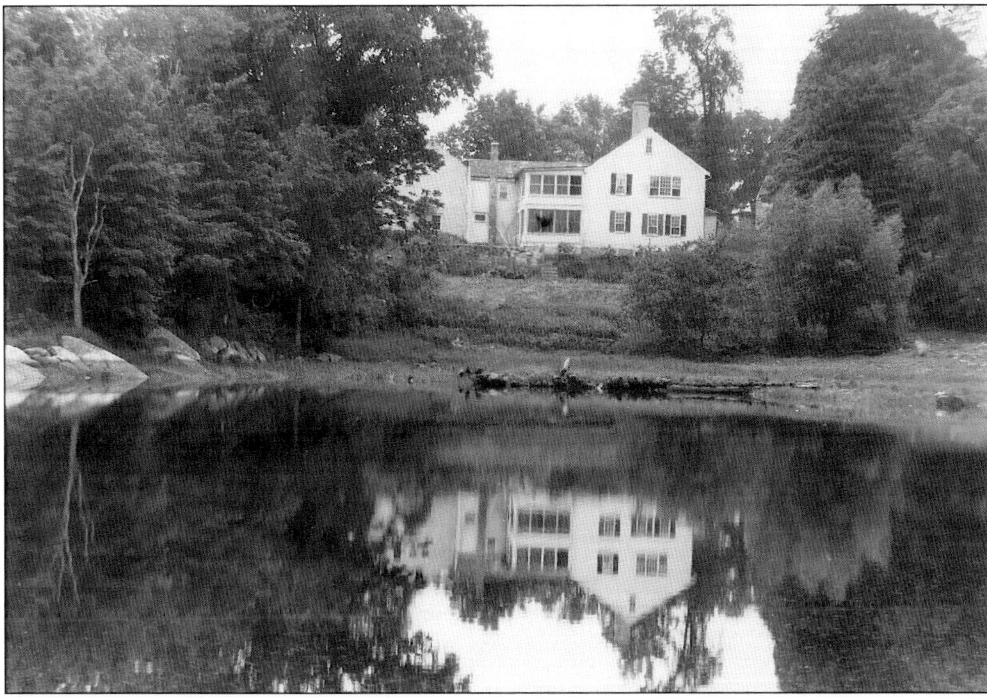

The Sullivan House, seen across the Oyster River from Durham Landing, *c*. 1910.

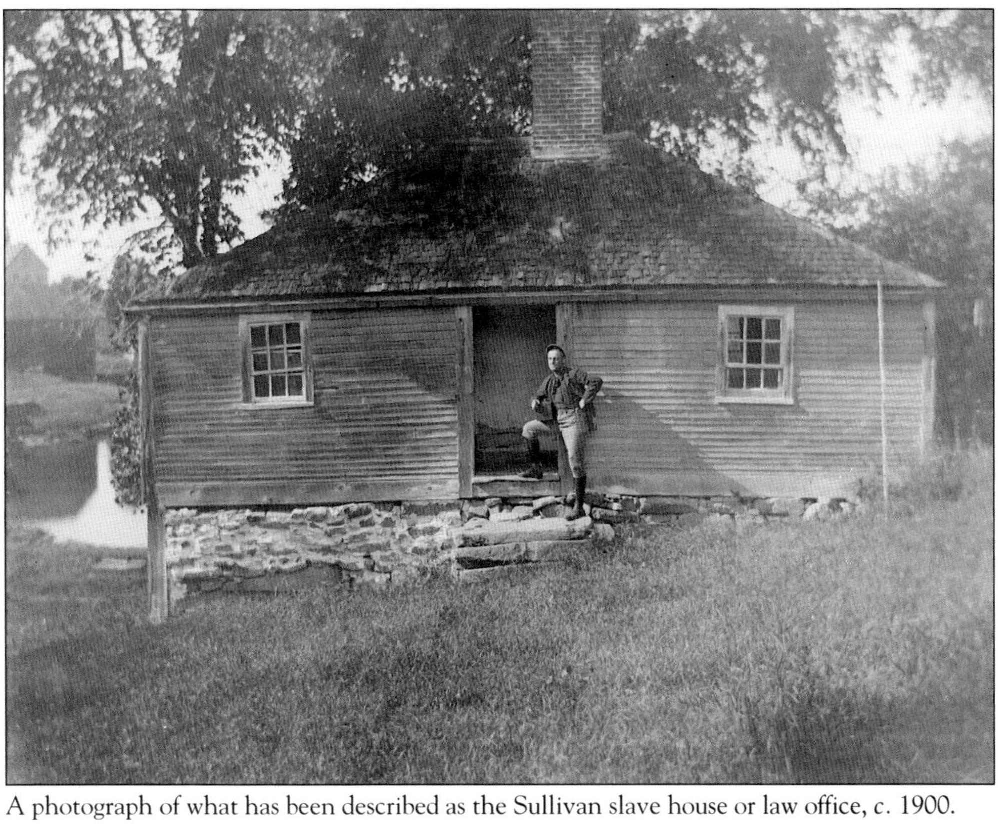

A photograph of what has been described as the Sullivan slave house or law office, *c*. 1900.

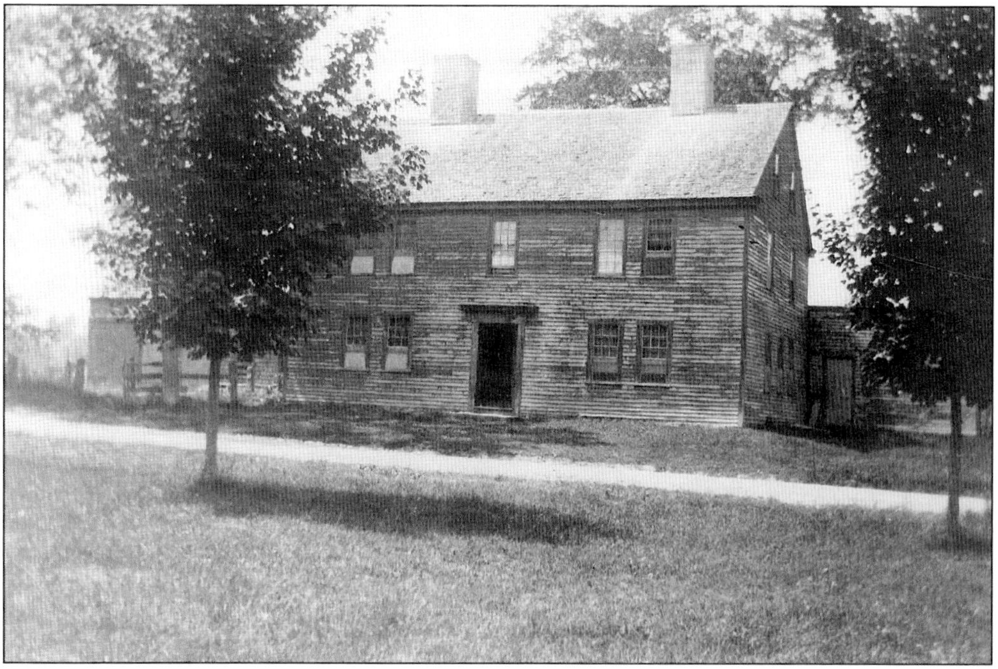

The Inn of John Smith, *c.* 1900. The inn was built soon after 1700 in the area known as Broth Hill. As early as 1686, James Smith was licensed to keep a "public house"; his grandson John, who died in 1739, was called "innkeeper."

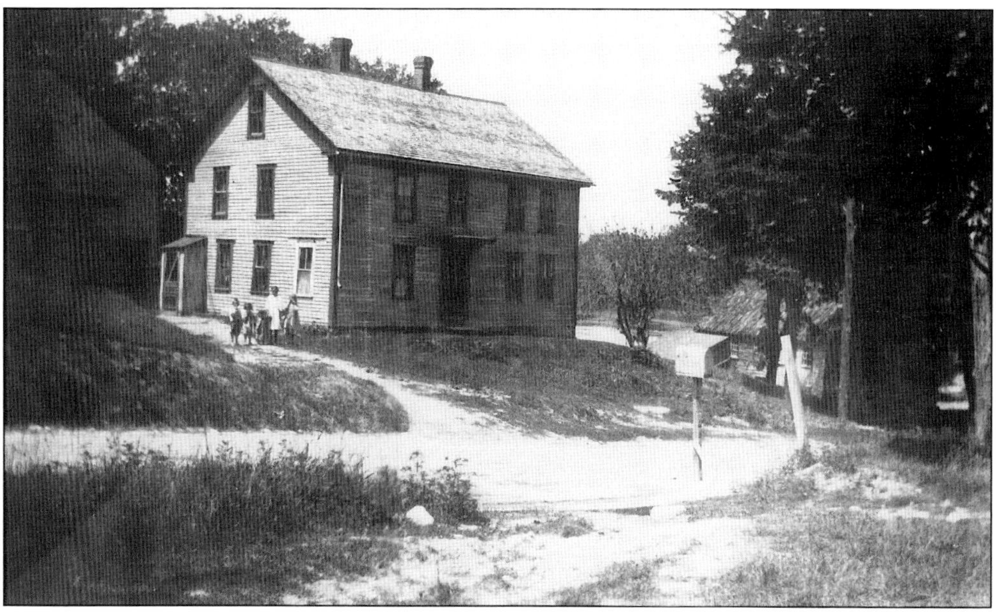

The Lieutenant Colonel Winborn Adams Inn, built around 1750 and shown here *c.* 1910, located on the south side of Newmarket Road opposite the Sullivan Monument. In addition to his military service, Adams worked as a surveyor and innkeeper. Lieutenant Colonel Adams was killed during the Battle of Bemis Heights, in 1777. His wife, Sarah Bartlett, kept the inn for a time after her husband's death.

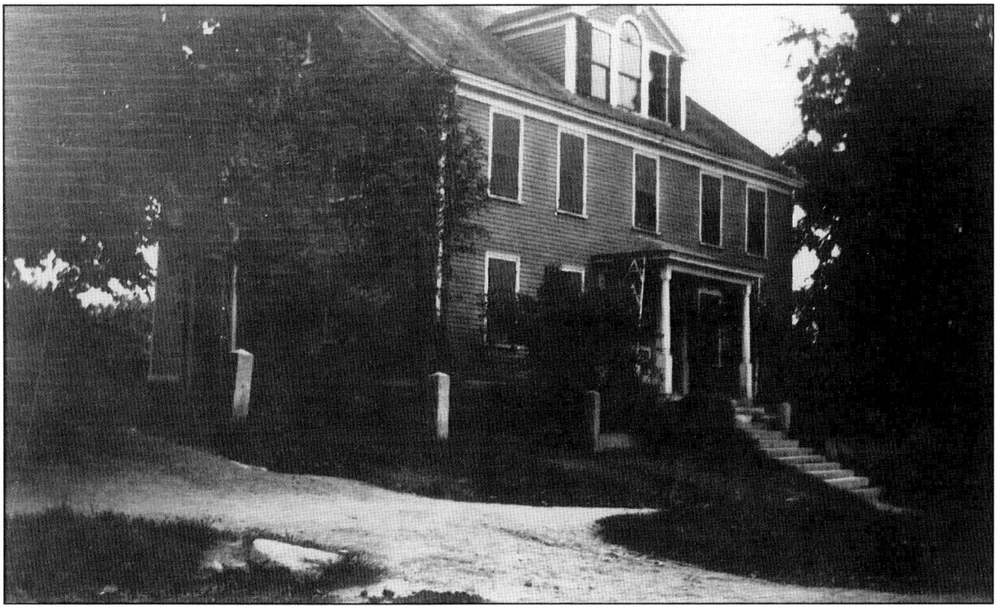

The Captain Joseph Richardson Inn, built between 1780 and 1800 and shown here *c*. 1910. This building was a meeting place for town officials prior to 1840. In the early 1900s it was the residence of George and Mary Mendell. In the 1930s the house was purchased by Harold Loveren and divided into apartments.

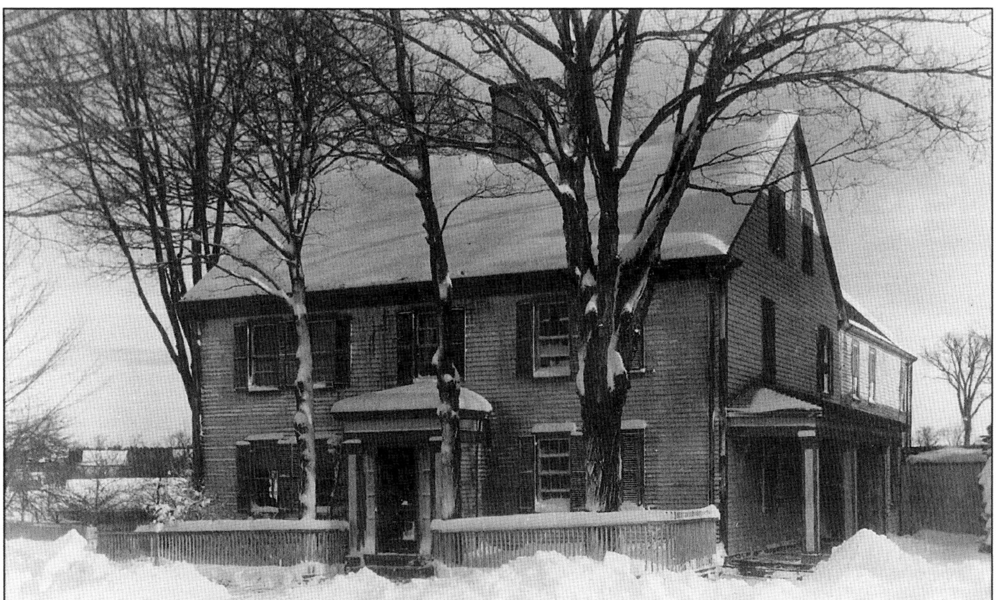

A *c*. 1890 photograph of a house that originally belonged to Ben Thompson. Thompson, a prominent farmer, bequeathed the bulk of his estate to establish an agricultural college in Durham. From 1893 to 1895 the building was the residence of Charles S. Murkland, president of the New Hampshire College of Agriculture and Mechanic Arts. It then served as a women's dormitory before it burned in December 1897.

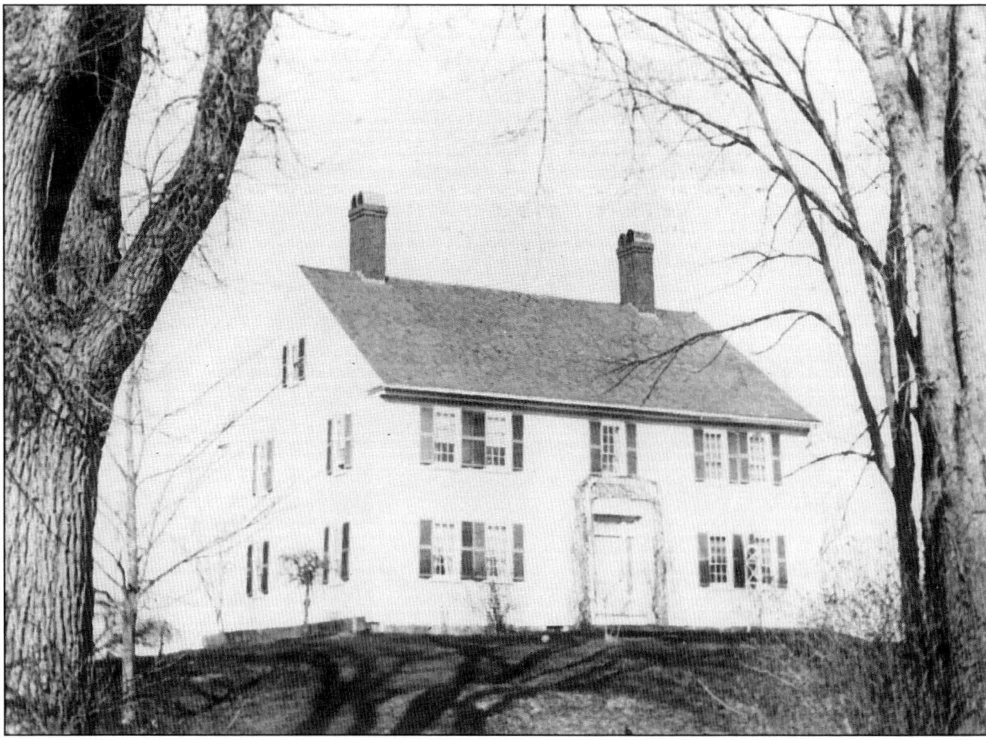

A front view of the Chesley or Mathes House from Main Street, *c.* 1890. Originally built by Philip Chesley in 1764, it was later owned by Charles Mathes.

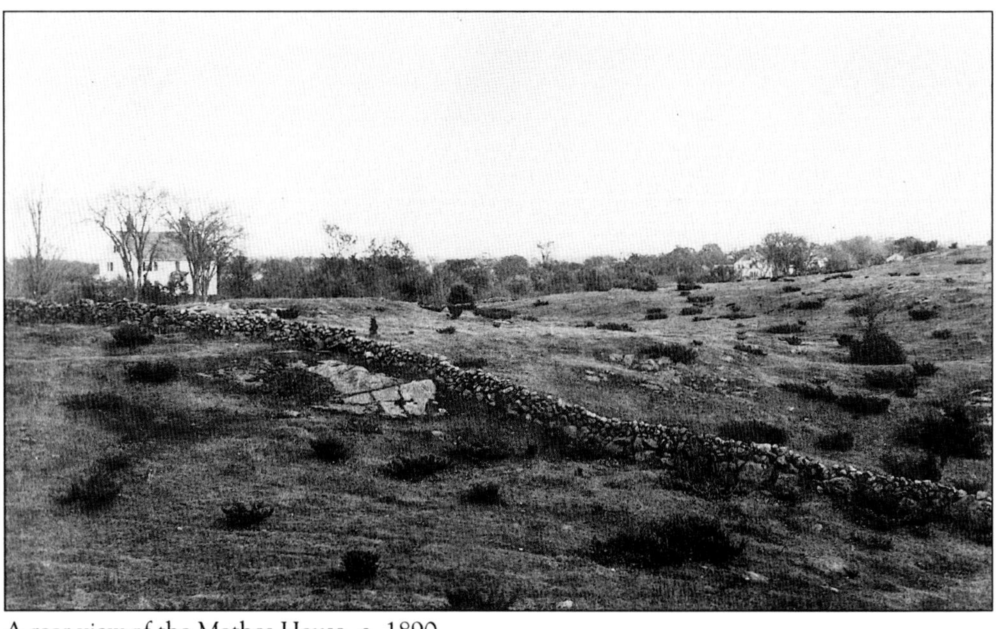

A rear view of the Mathes House, *c.* 1890.

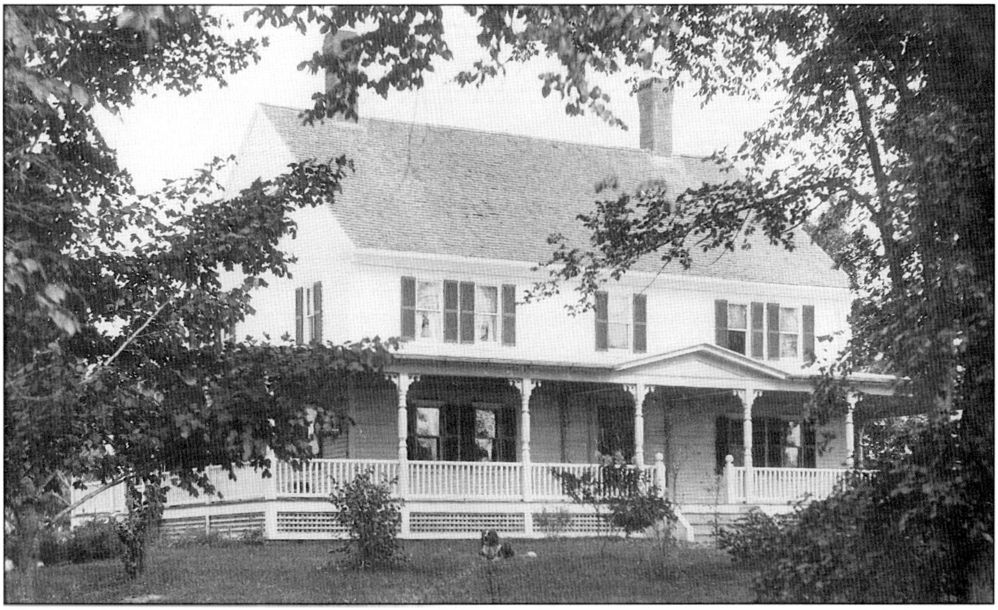

The Mathes House, *c.* 1900, after it was renovated to serve as the home of the president of the New Hampshire College of Agricultural and Mechanical Arts. The house burned to the ground in 1903, days after the the new president, William D. Gibbs, had moved in his family's belongings.

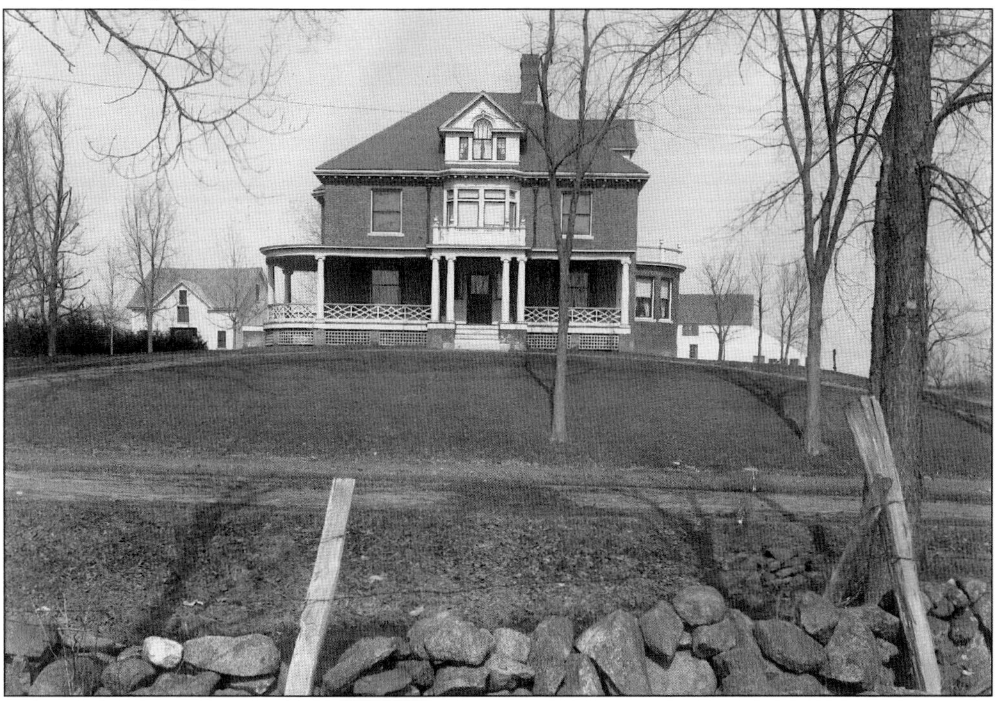

The home of the president of the University of New Hampshire. In 1905 New Hampshire College replaced the Mathes House with a $5,500 home built by Walter M. Parker of Manchester. Shown here shortly after it was completed, it continues to serve on the same site as the home of the university president.

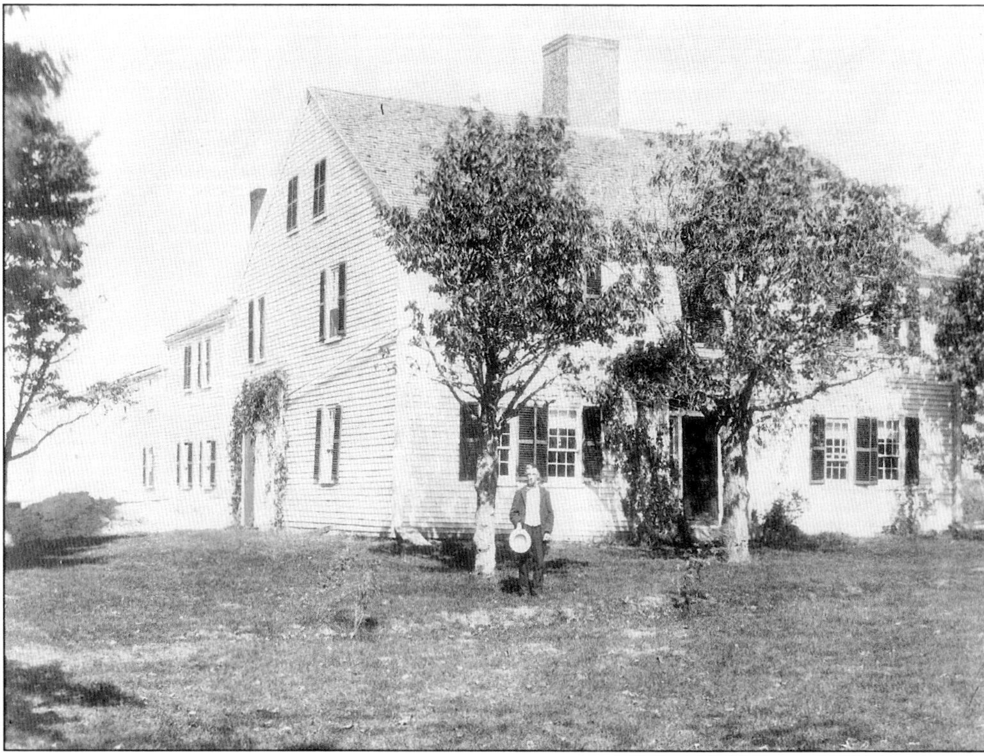

The Thompson House, *c.* 1910. Judge Ebenezar Thompson built this house soon after the American Revolution. This photograph shows both Lucien Thompson, who later owned the home, and a two-story addition that contained the library of Mary P. Thompson, Lucien's aunt.

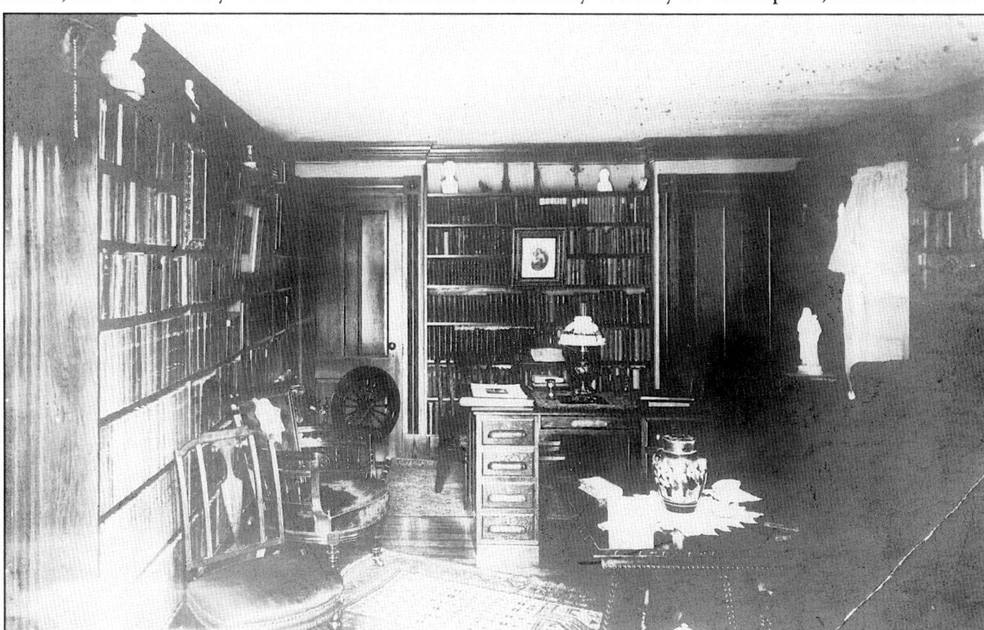

An interior photograph of the Thompson House, showing the library of Mary P. Thompson, c. 1910.

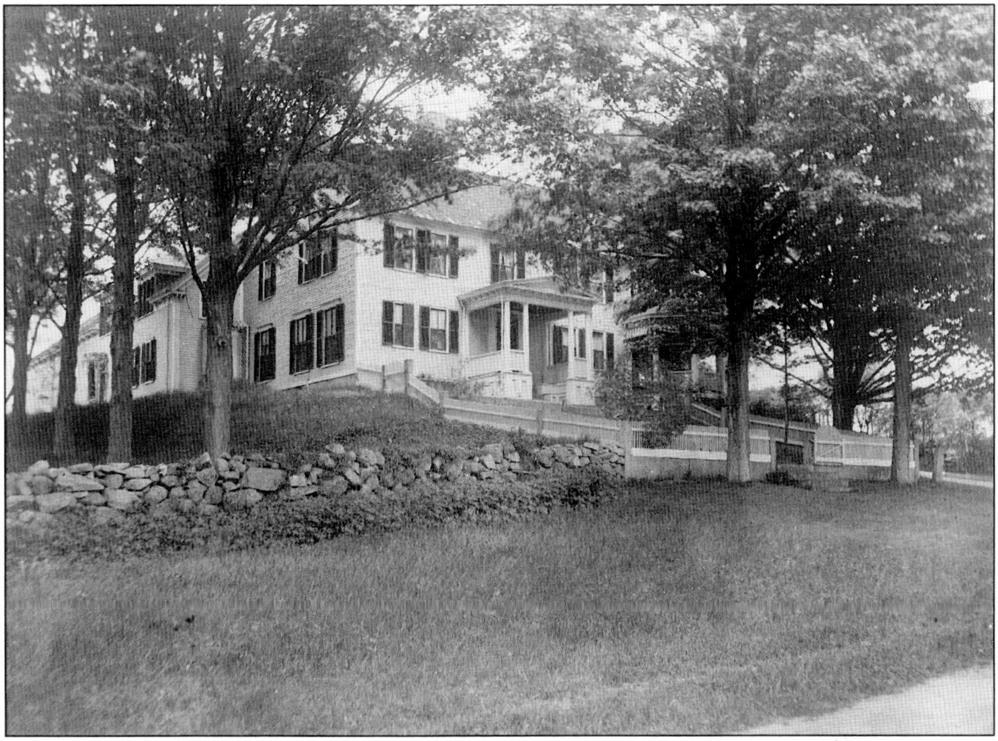

The Smith House, *c.* 1910. This residence, which commanded views of both the Oyster River and Little Bay, was built in 1803 by Major Daniel Smith and his son, Major Winthrop Smith. Forrest S. Smith later remodeled the home, adding heat, running water, and a bathroom.

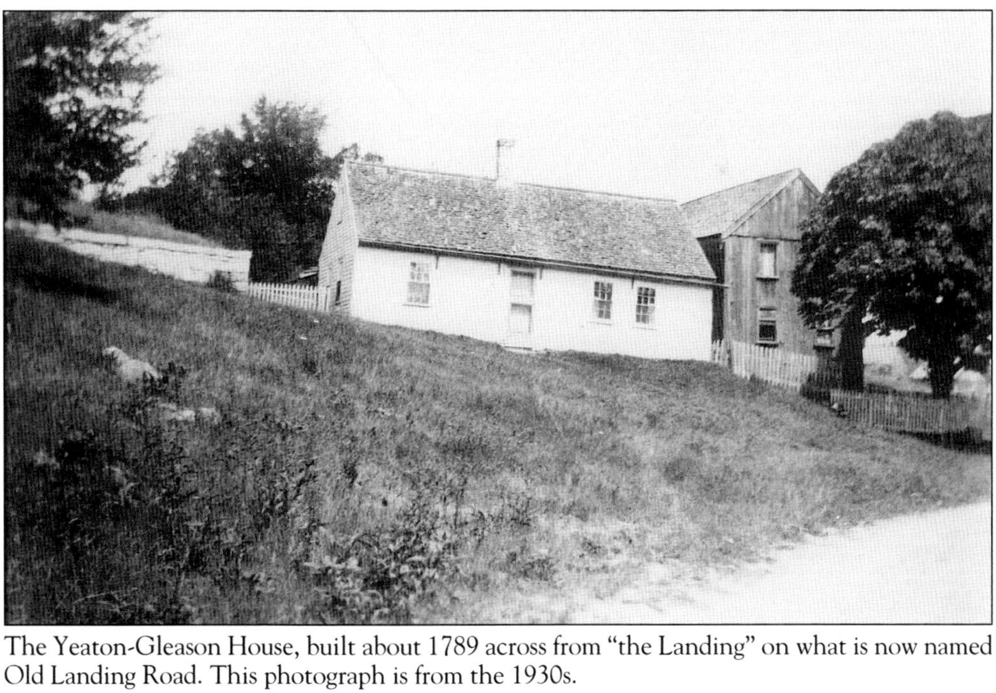

The Yeaton-Gleason House, built about 1789 across from "the Landing" on what is now named Old Landing Road. This photograph is from the 1930s.

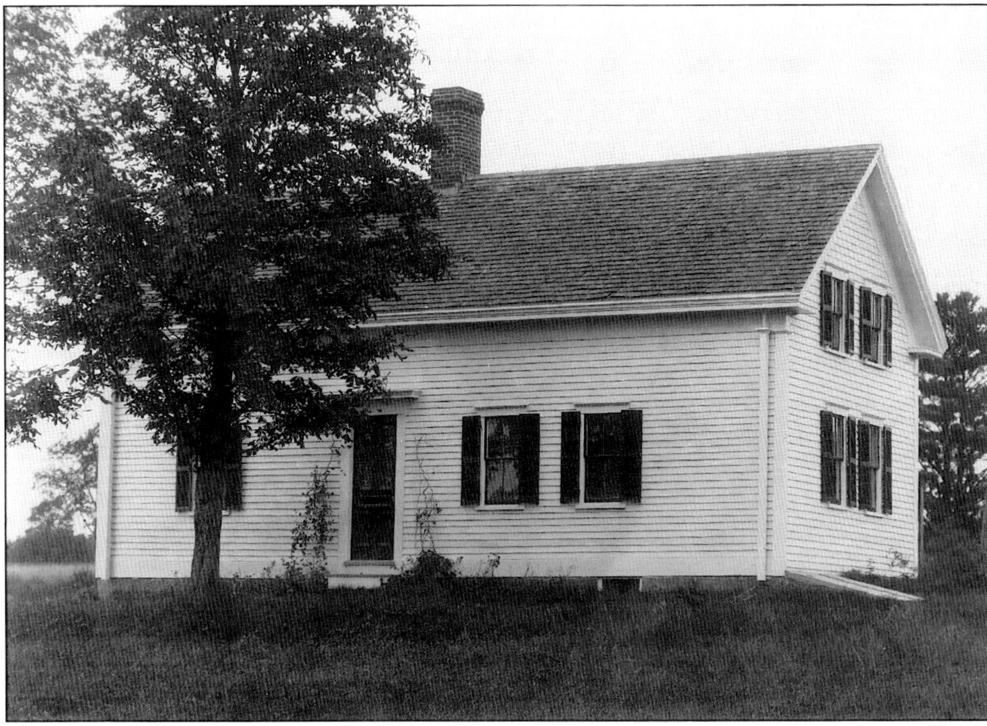

The home of John Woodman, c. 1890. Woodman, born in 1760, built this home near the intersection of Mast Road and the Concord-Portsmouth Turnpike. The property housed both the old Durham tollbooth, and after 1921, the New Hampshire College detention hospital.

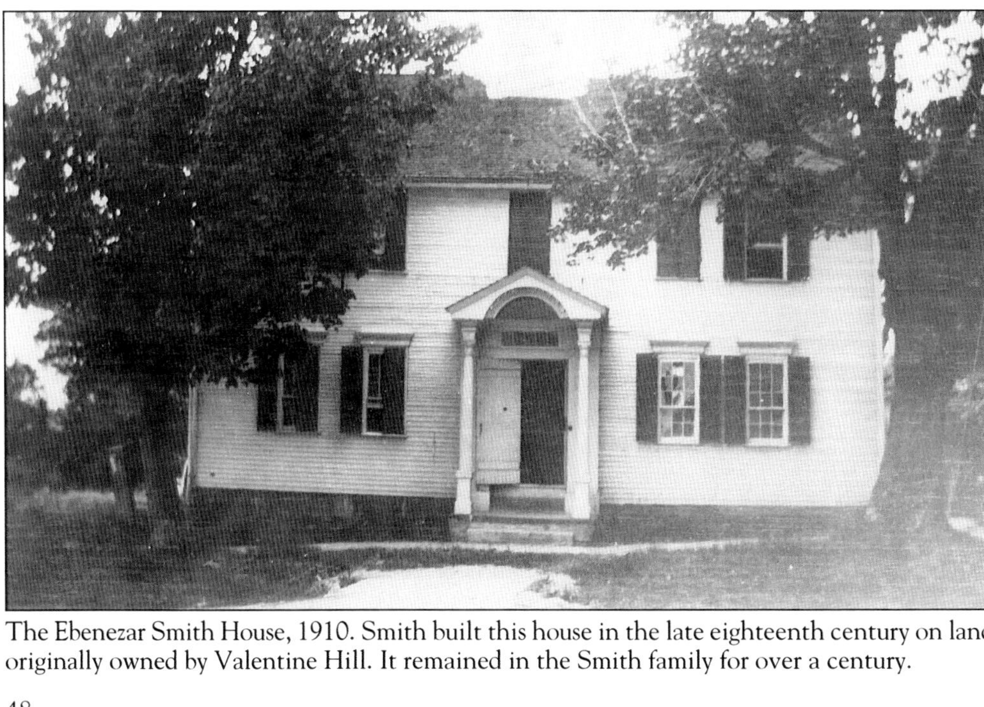

The Ebenezar Smith House, 1910. Smith built this house in the late eighteenth century on land originally owned by Valentine Hill. It remained in the Smith family for over a century.

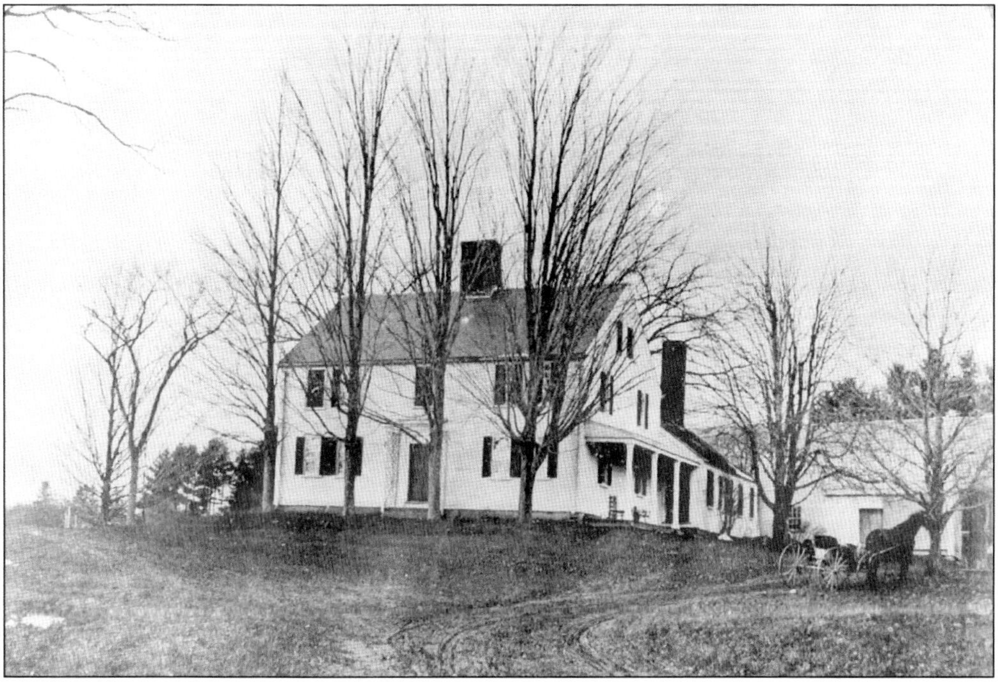

The Albert Demeritt farm, *c.* 1910, built in 1808 on land granted to Eli Demeritt in 1699. Albert Demeritt was a chief supporter of moving New Hampshire College from Hanover to Durham.

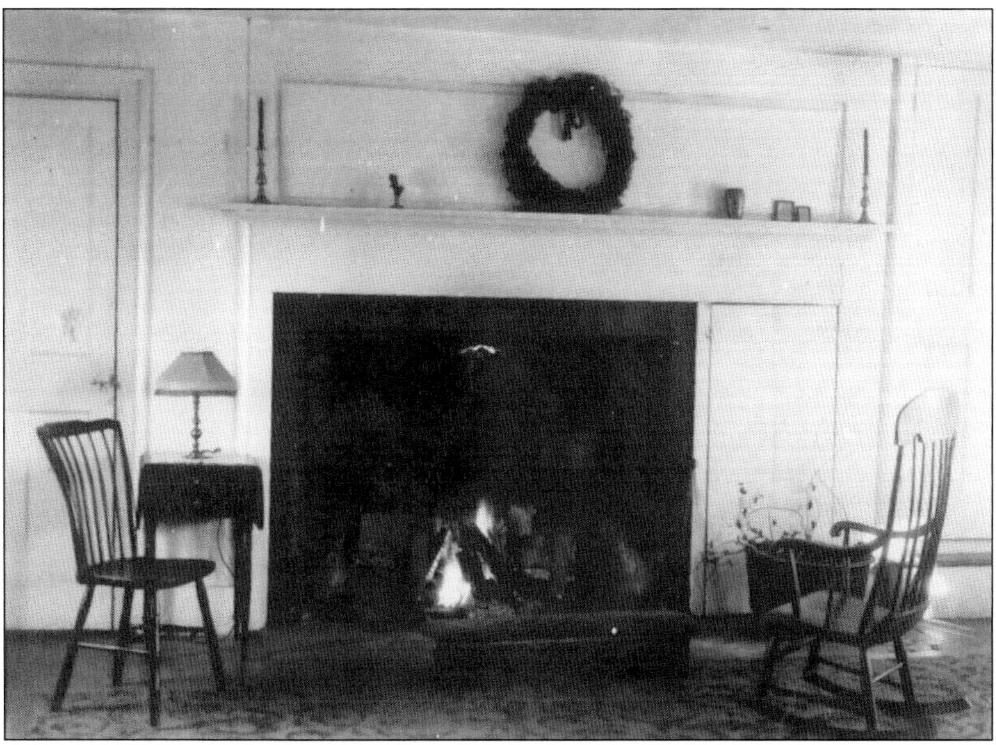

A fireplace in the Albert Demeritt House, *c.* 1910.

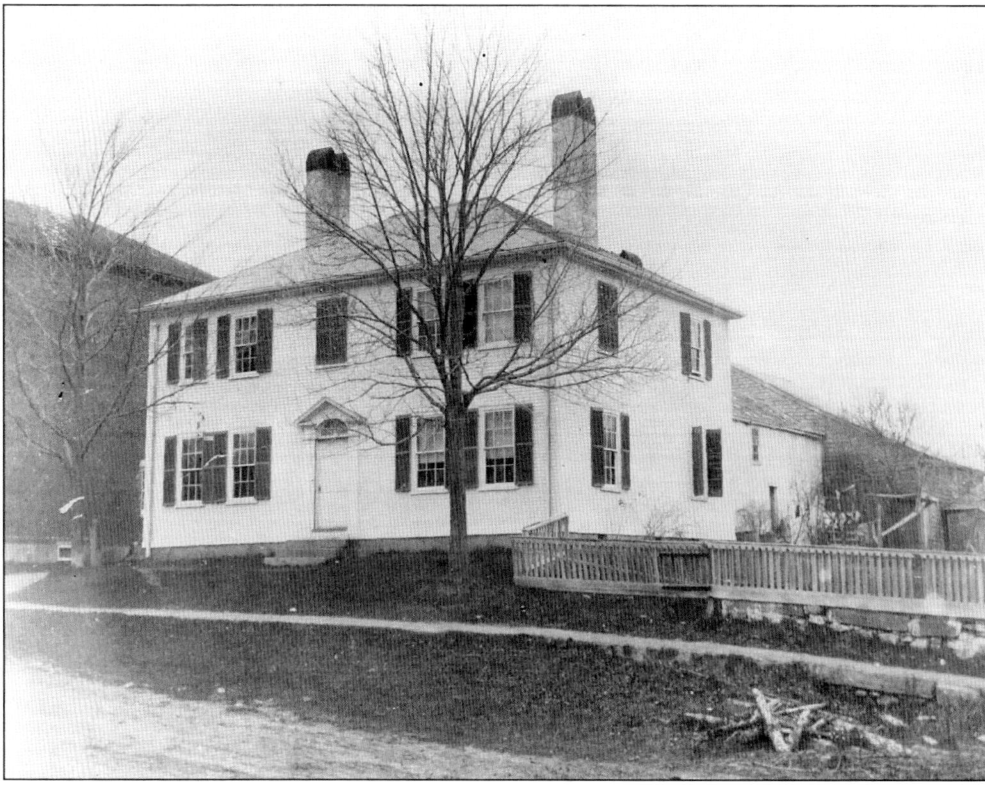

The Coe-Buzzell House, 1910s. Built by James Joy about 1825, this home stood behind the old town hall, now the Durham Historic Association Museum. Owned by William Coe and John E. Buzzell, it later belonged to the Delta Pi Epsilon fraternity.

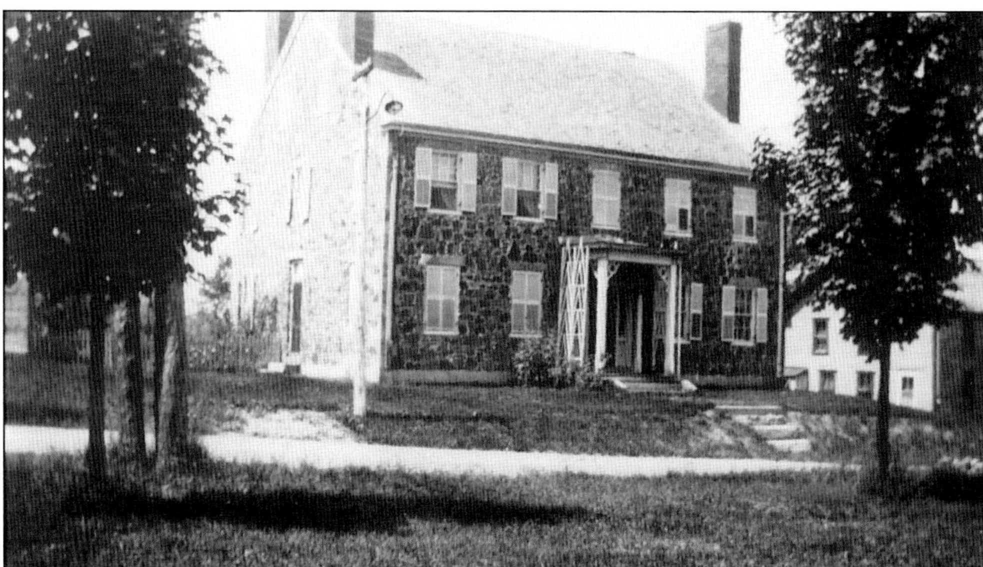

The stone house, c. 1900, built by Howard and James Paul. While taking down the scaffolding, James Paul fell, broke his neck, and died.

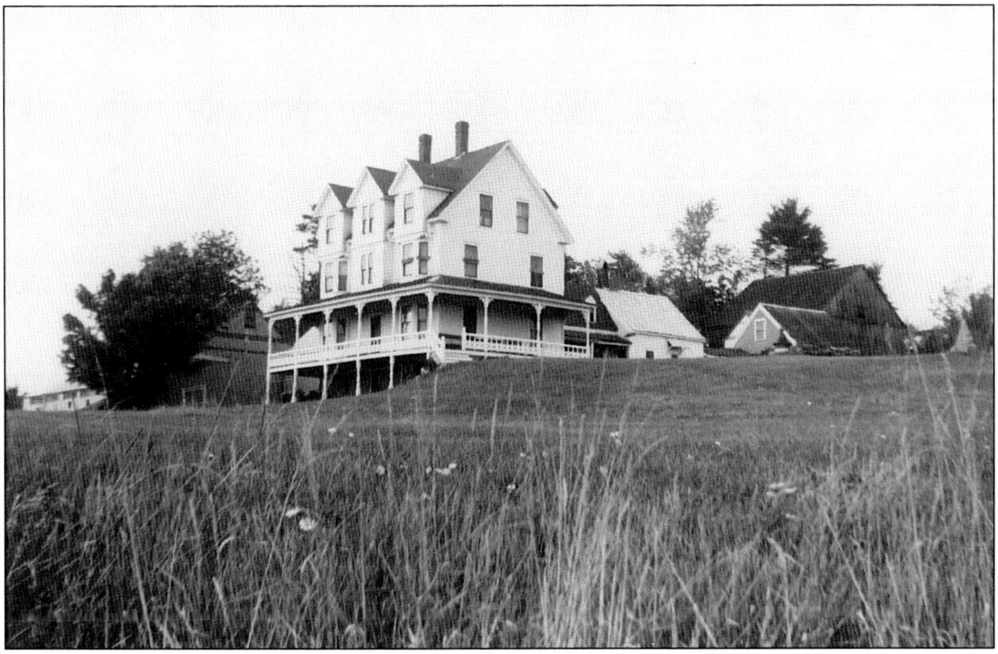

The Adams family home on Adams Point, *c.* 1900. Originally constructed by "Reformation John" Adams in 1835, it remained in possession of the Adams family until 1960.

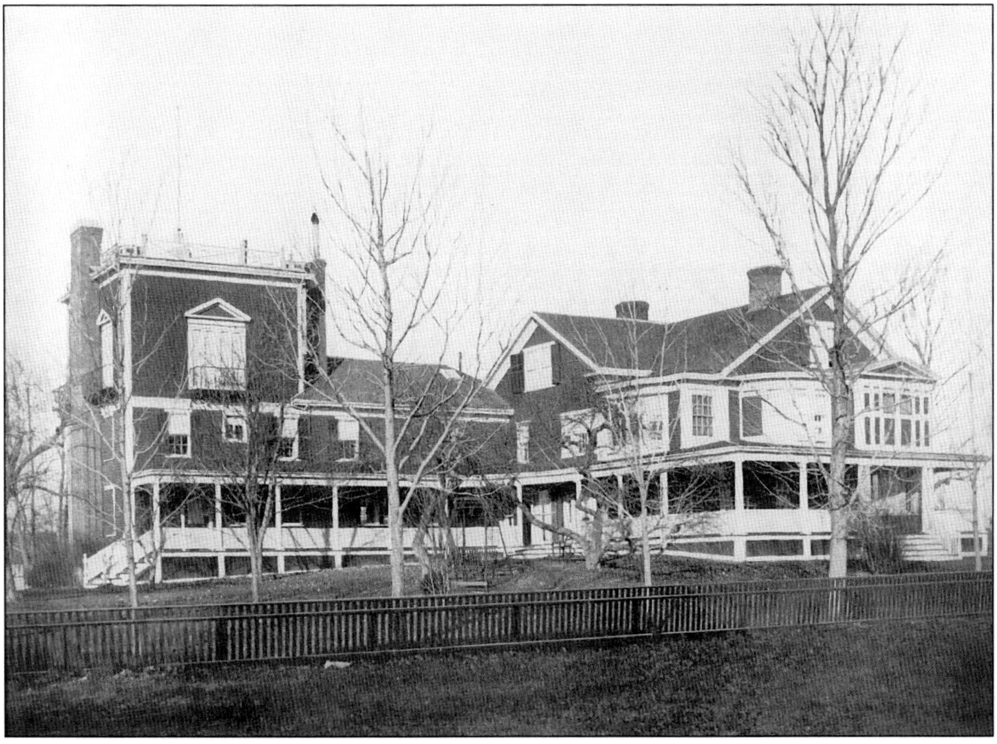

The Hamilton Smith House, known as Red Tower, originally built in the early nineteenth century by Reverend John Blydenburgh. Smith bought the home and several surrounding tracts in 1895. The photograph shows a view from the eastern side of Red Tower in 1907.

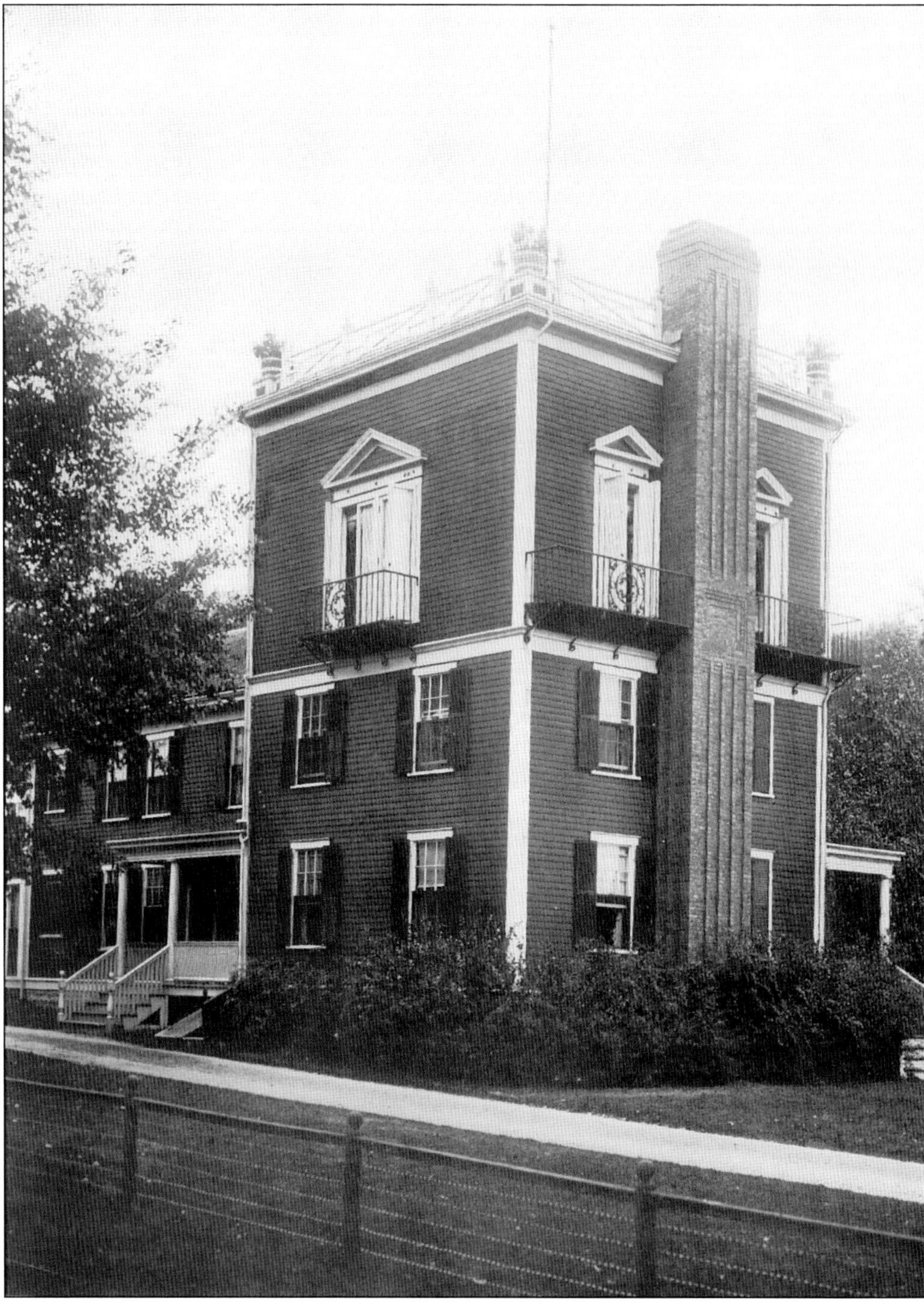

A view from the western side of Red Tower, 1907. Hamilton Smith, Durham's first *bona fide* millionaire, purchased land from Main Street to the Oyster River. When his renovation was complete, Red Tower reflected an opulence that set it apart from other Durham homes.

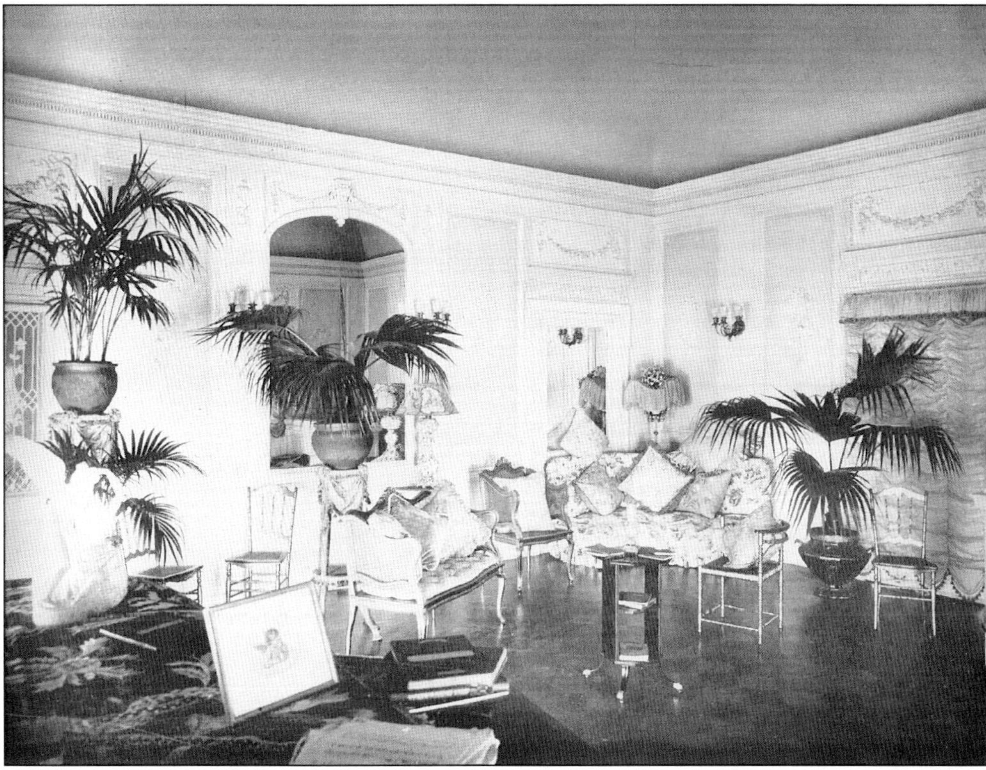

The Music Room in Red Tower, 1907. Although Red Tower was atypical of most Durham homes, its splendor resembled homes constructed in more opulent communities during the Gilded Age.

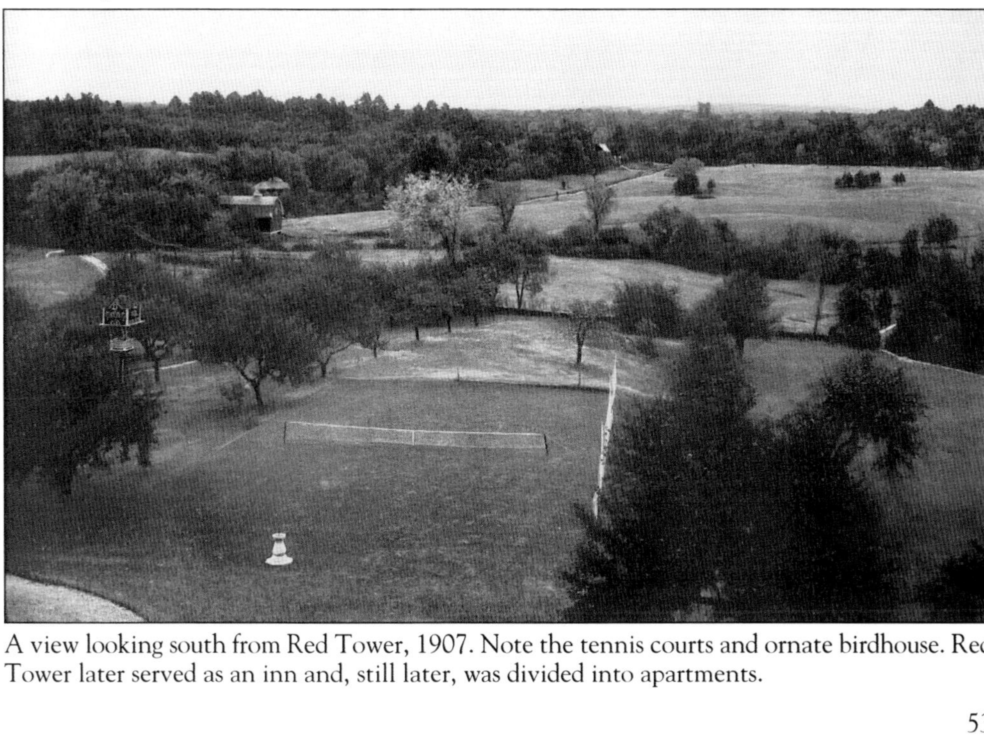

A view looking south from Red Tower, 1907. Note the tennis courts and ornate birdhouse. Red Tower later served as an inn and, still later, was divided into apartments.

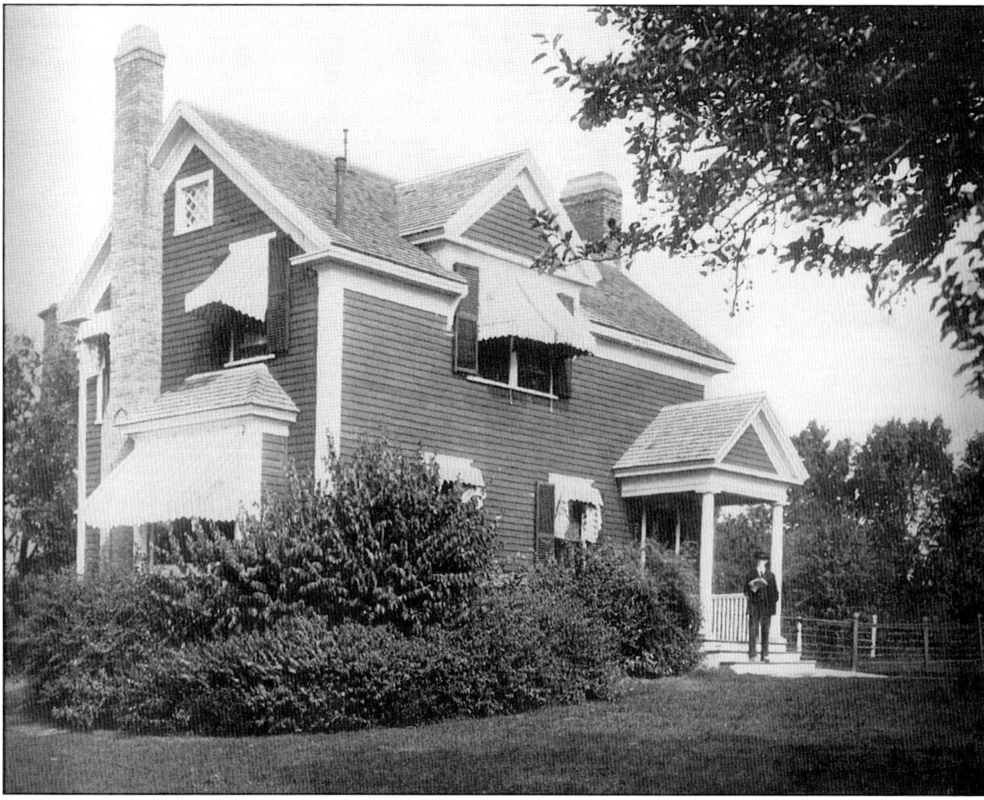

The Billiard House on the Red Tower estate, 1907.

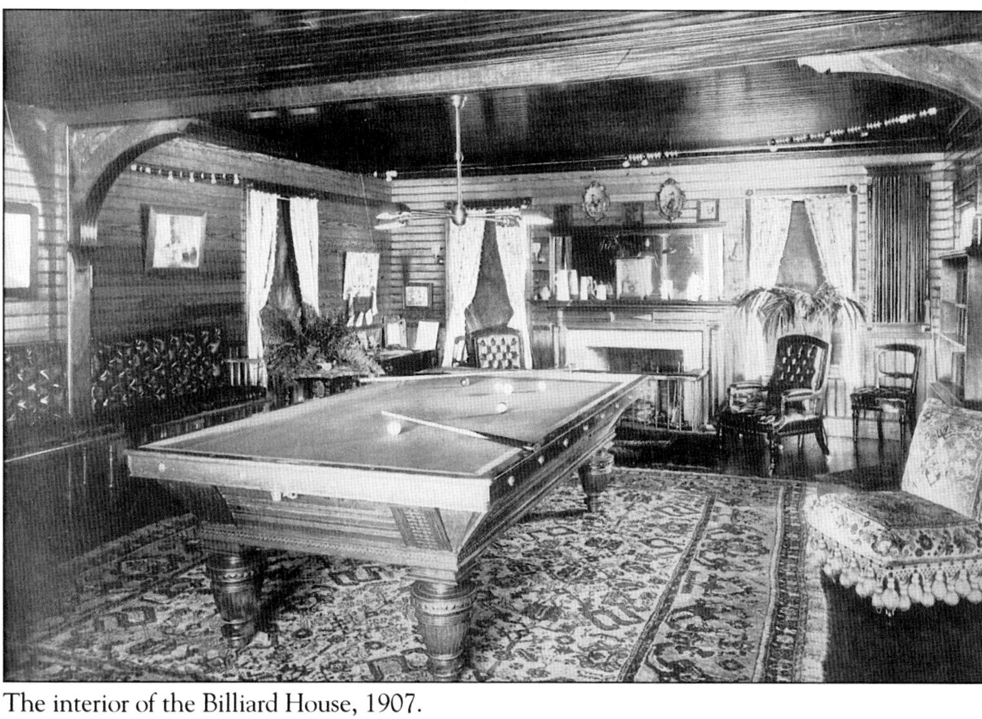

The interior of the Billiard House, 1907.

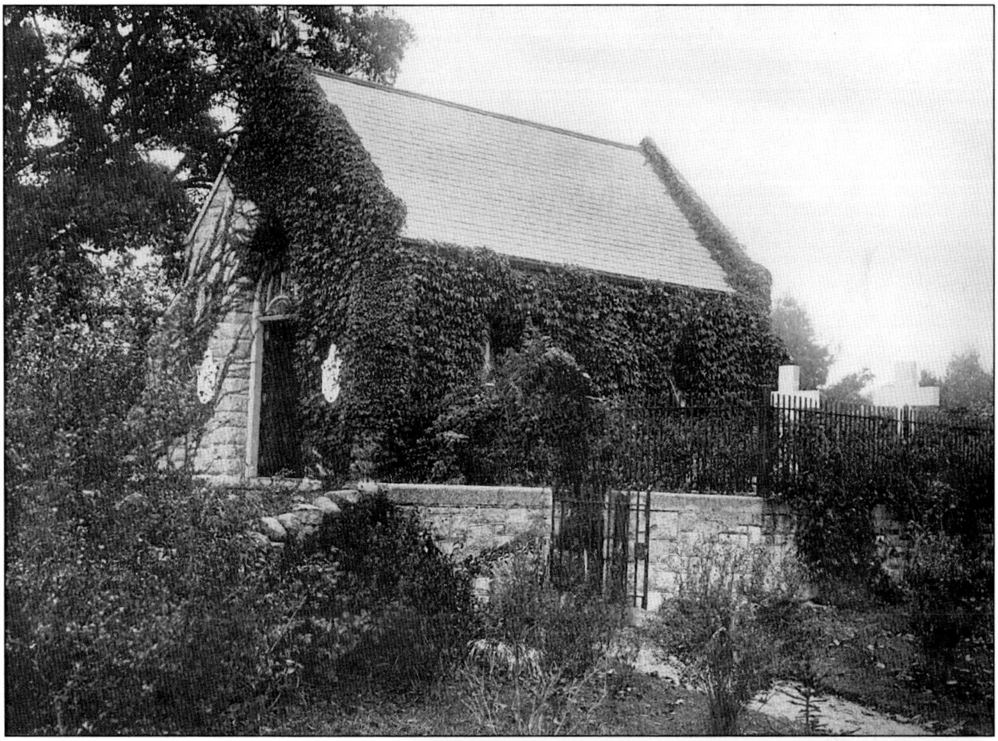

The Smith Park Chapel, between the Oyster River and what is now Mill Pond Road, 1907. The chapel was constructed as part of Hamilton Smith's Red Tower estate.

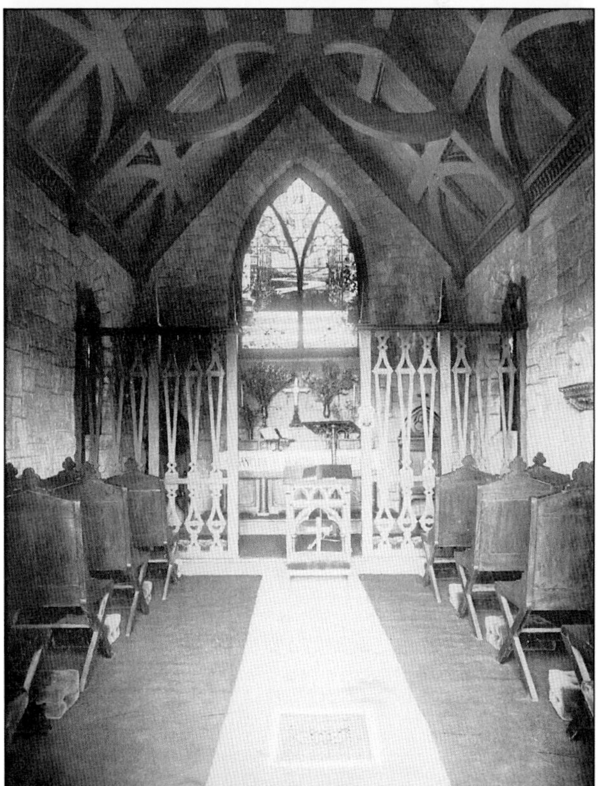

The interior of the Smith Chapel, 1907.

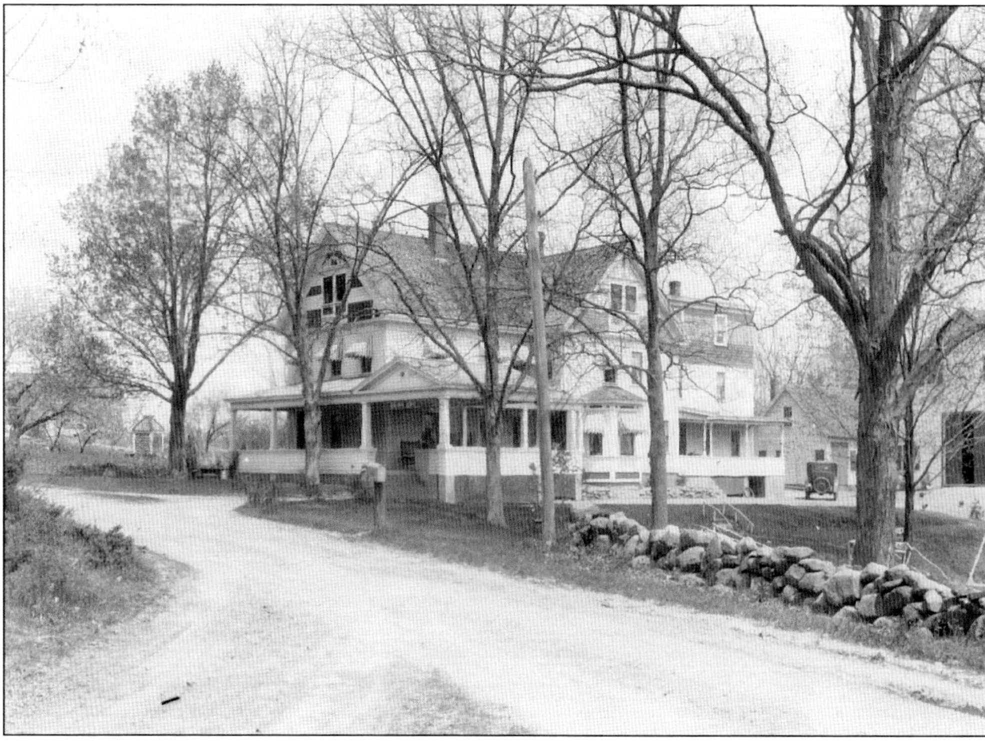

The Colony Cove House, *c.* 1924. Charles and Mary Langley operated this boarding house situated on a cove near Little Bay. The Langleys offered guests many activities including dancing, tennis, and excursions on Great Bay in their gasoline launch.

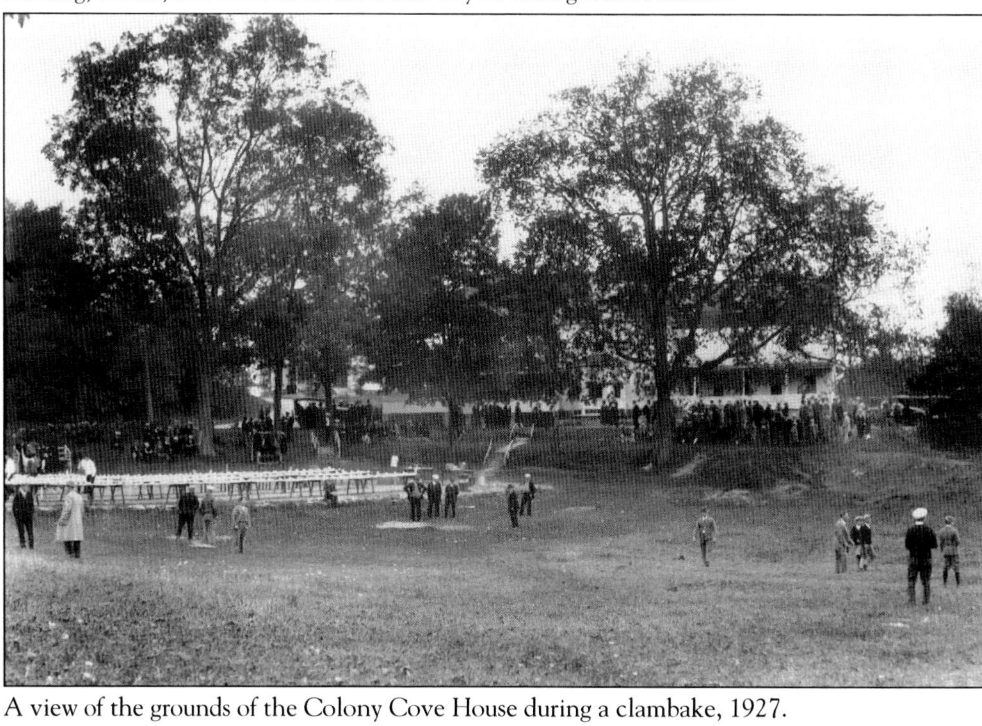

A view of the grounds of the Colony Cove House during a clambake, 1927.

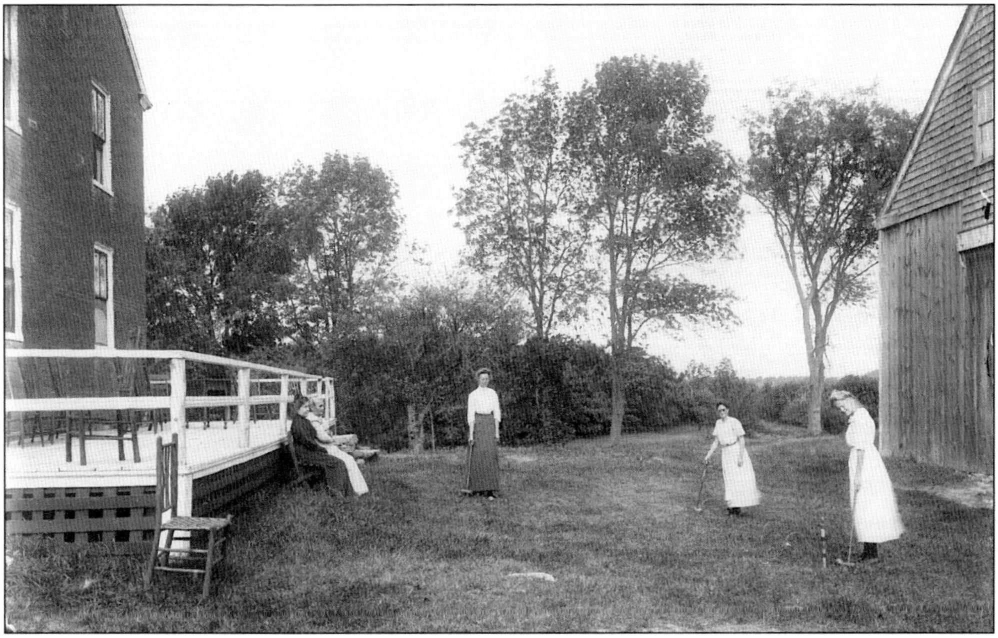

The Comfort Mathes Camp, *c.* 1914. Located at Durham Point and in operation from 1911 to 1914, the camp, run by Fannie Mathes, was a summer retreat for young women. One of the activities available to campers was croquet. (Durham Historic Association.)

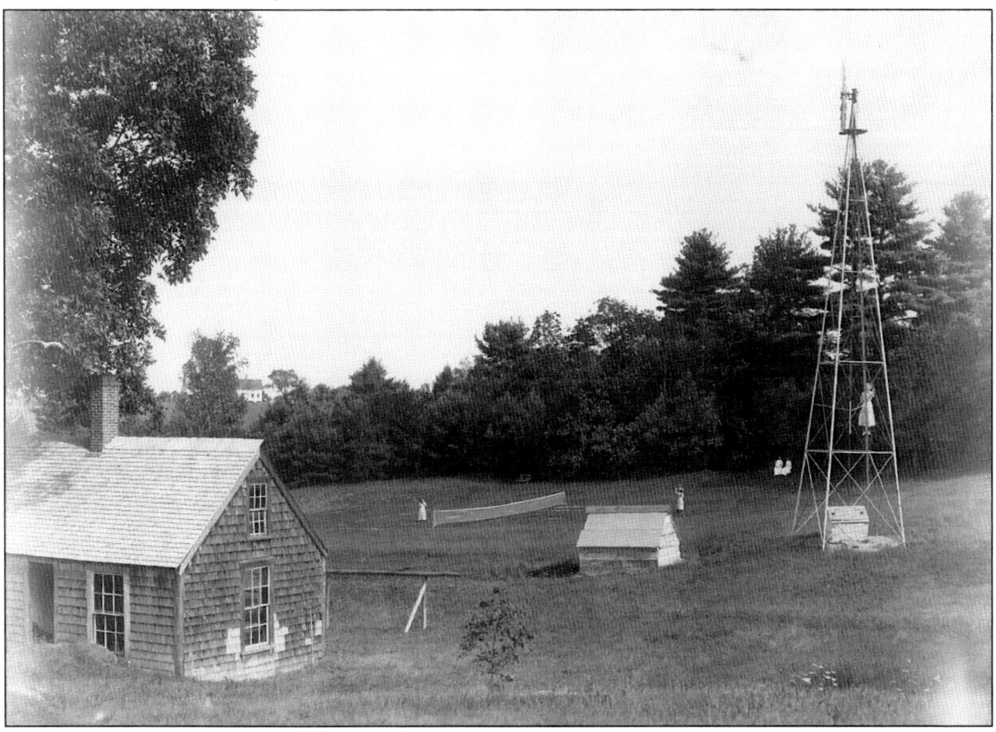

Lawn tennis, another activity offered at Camp Comfort, *c.* 1914. A postcard advertisement for the camp mentioned the "Star Spangled Meadows" where "happy girls roam and revel in more vigorous life." (Durham Historic Association.)

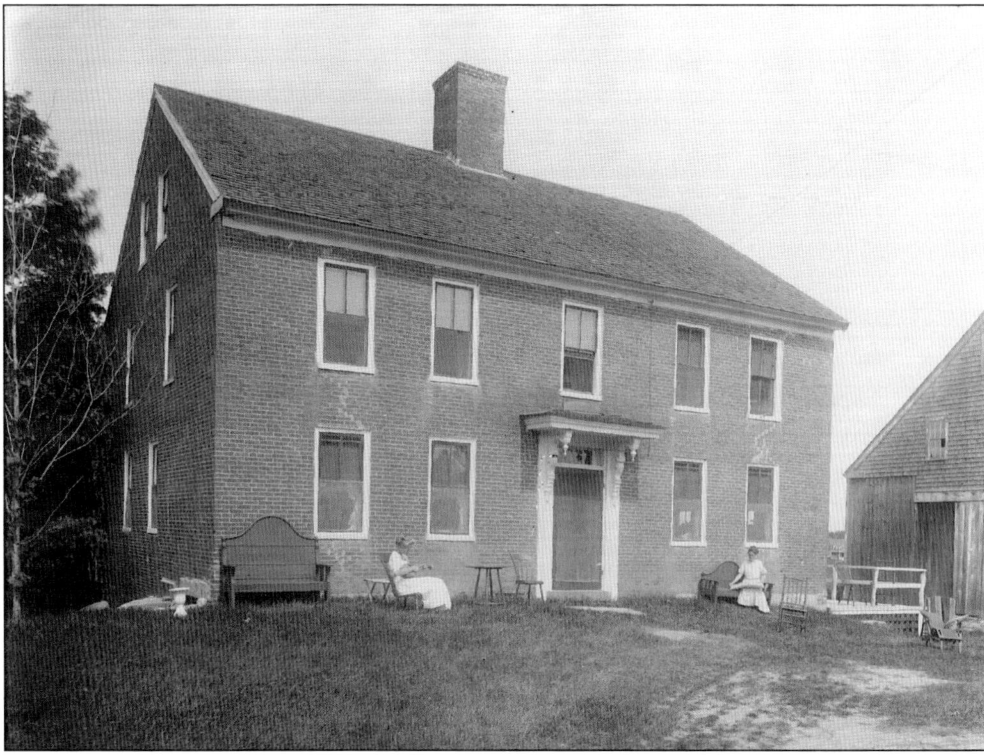

The main building at Camp Comfort, *c.* 1914. This was one of the "roomy old farm buildings amid the trees" mentioned in another postcard advertisement. (Durham Historic Association.)

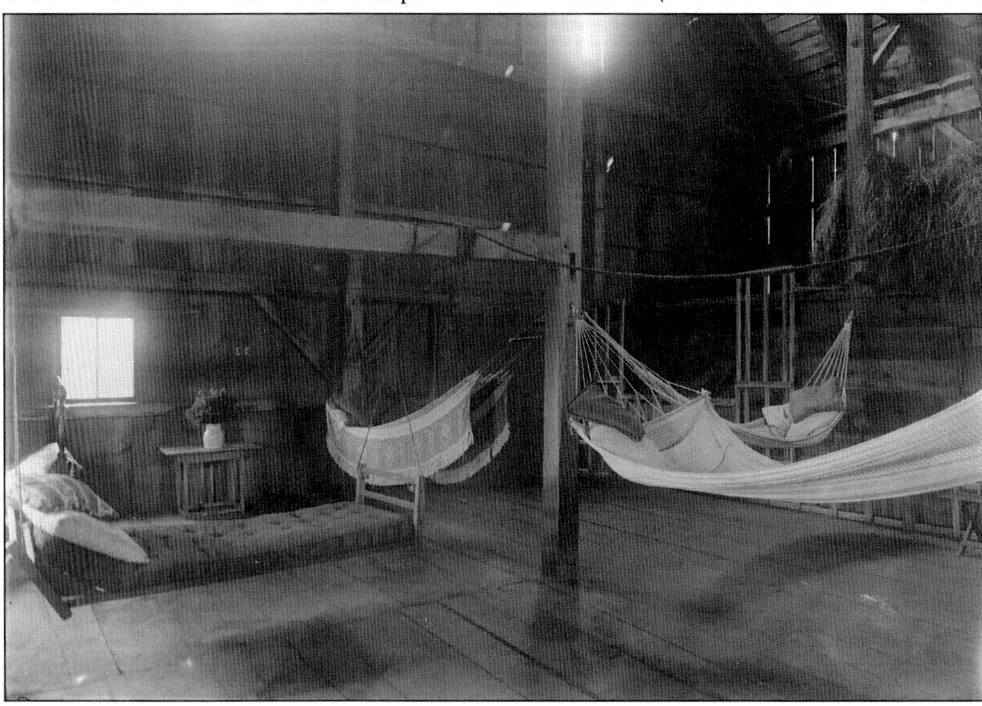

The interior of one of the buildings at Camp Comfort, *c.* 1914. (Durham Historic Association.)

Three

A College Comes to Town

On March 5, 1891, Governor Hiram A. Tuttle signed the act accepting the conditions of Ben Thompson's will. His will gave the state of New Hampshire his farm and assets of more than $400,000 to be used to establish an agricultural college in Durham. The New Hampshire College of Agriculture and Mechanic Arts had been established in 1866 in Hanover, New Hampshire, and was operating as part of Dartmouth College. On April 10, 1891, Governor Tuttle signed another act providing for the separation of the New Hampshire College of Agriculture and Mechanic Arts from Dartmouth, and the relocation of the Agricultural College to Durham. Major changes were in store for the town as the twentieth century approached.

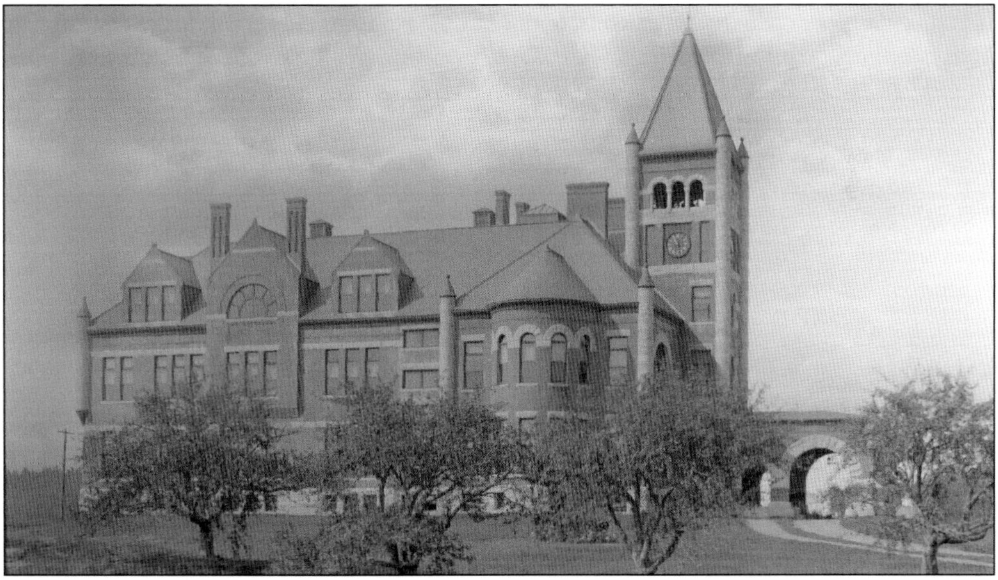

Thompson Hall, c. 1894. Named for Benjamin Thompson, this was the main building on the new campus. It housed offices, classrooms, the library, and an auditorium.

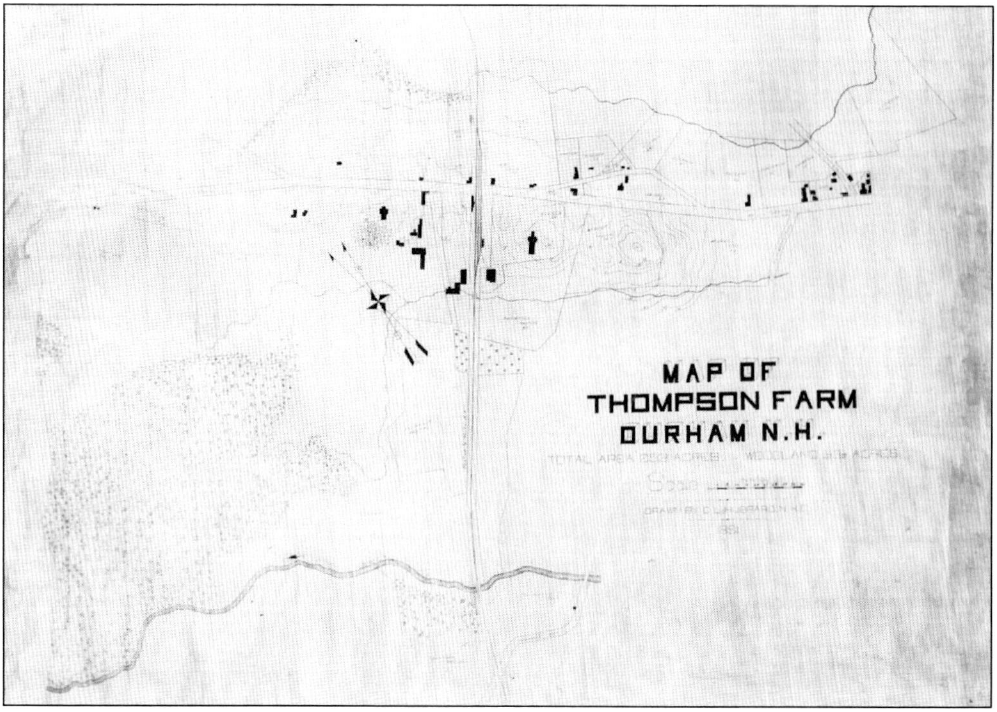

A map of Thompson Farm. Some of the college buildings constructed in 1892 and 1893 have been added to this map, which was originally drawn in 1891.

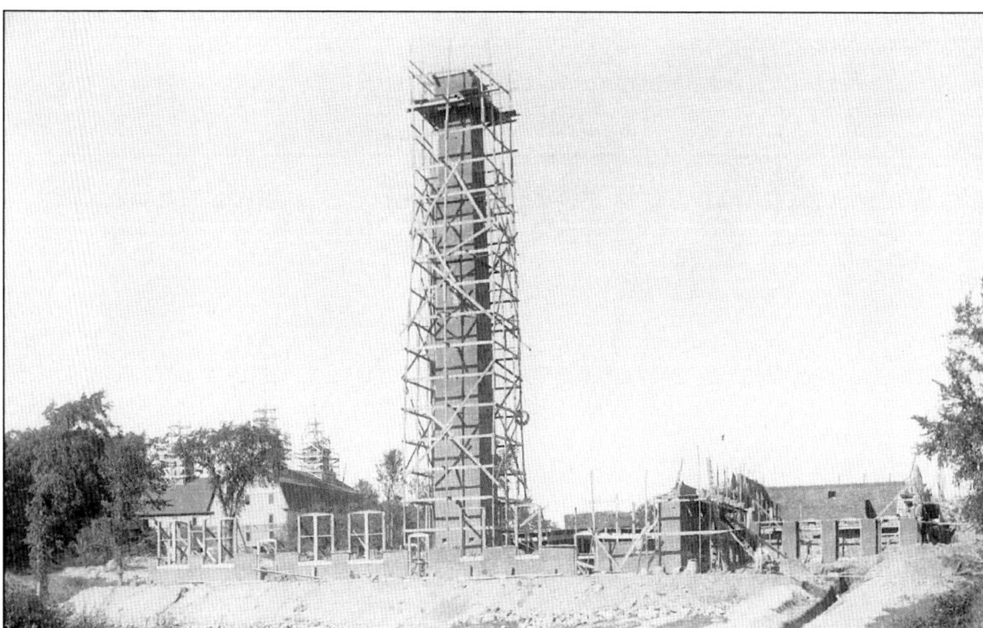

The construction of College Barn and the Heating Plant and Shop building, c. 1892.

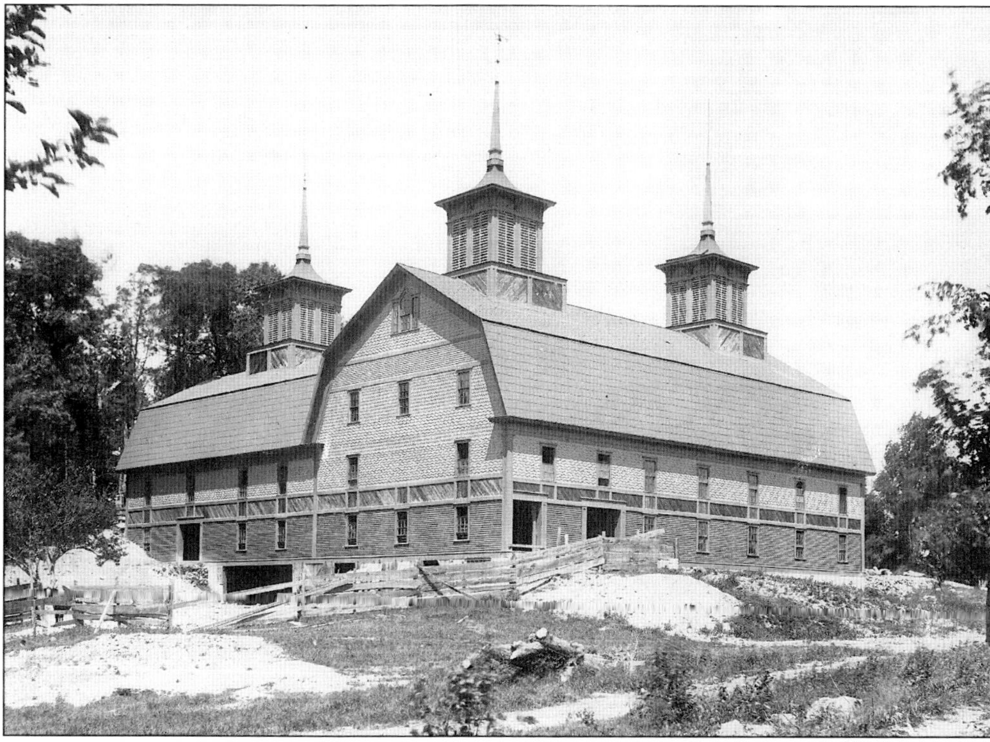

College Barn, c. 1893. The first commencement exercises on the Durham campus were held in this building. Enthusiastic about the move to Durham, the Class of 1892 held their commencement in the partially completed College Barn, even though they had never taken classes on the new campus.

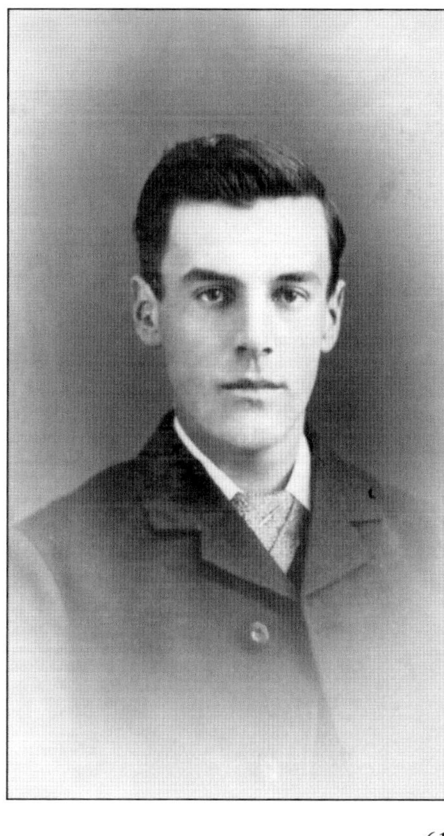

George H. Whitcher, an 1881 graduate of the college, and director of the Agriculture Experiment Station, c. 1881. In addition to designing College Barn, which was considered a model for buildings of its kind, Whitcher did much to help alleviate the housing shortage facing the students, faculty, and staff of the college. He built several houses for faculty, as well as the building that later came to be known as the Pettee Block.

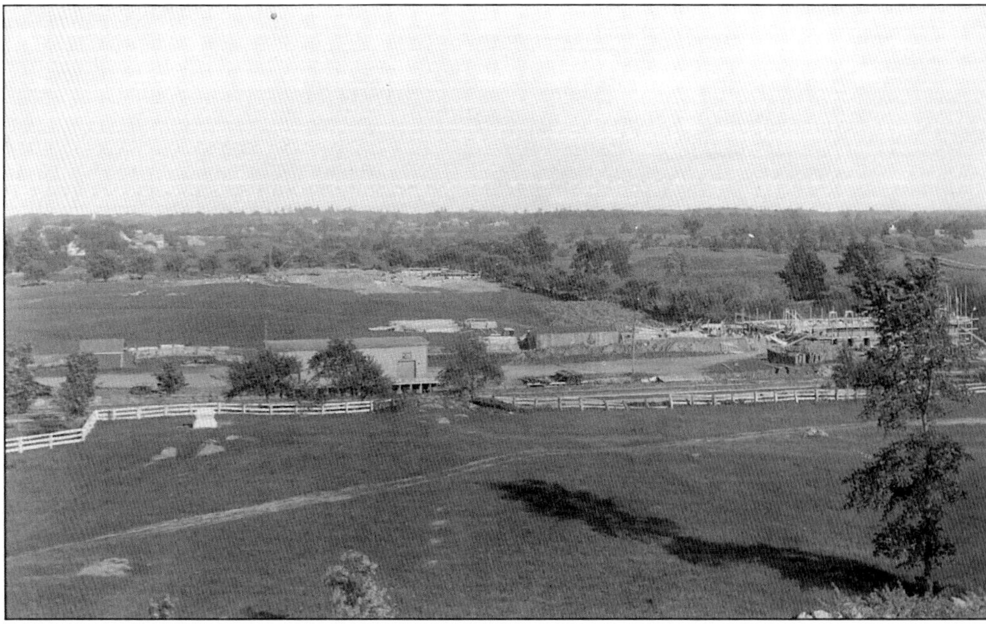

The campus in 1892, as seen from College Barn. Work has begun on the foundations of Thompson Hall (in the background) and Conant Hall (at right). The monument to Benjamin Thompson, erected by the executors of his estate, can be seen in the lower left near the fence bordering the Boston and Maine railroad tracks.

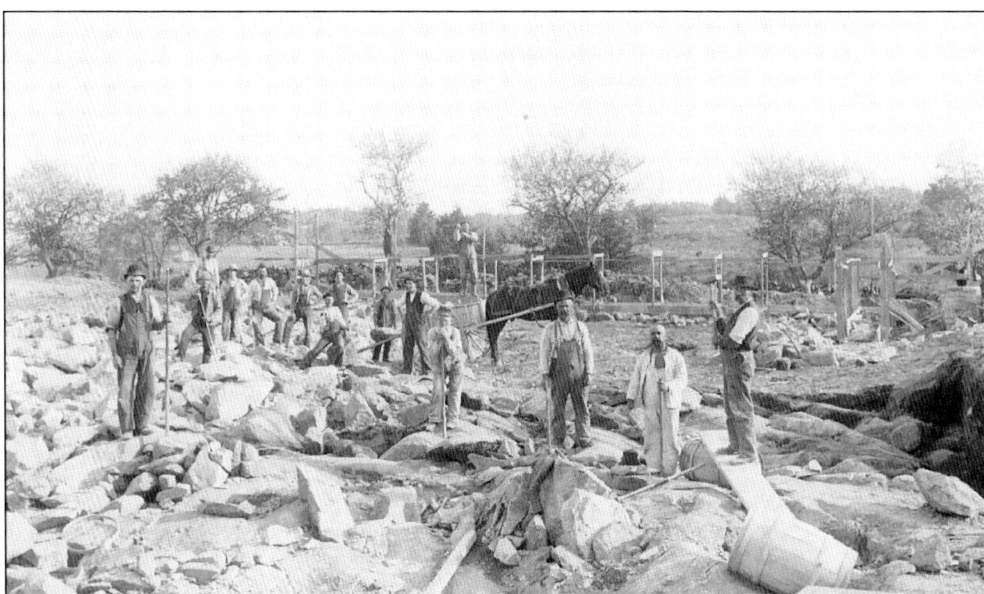

Work on the foundation of Thompson Hall, 1892.

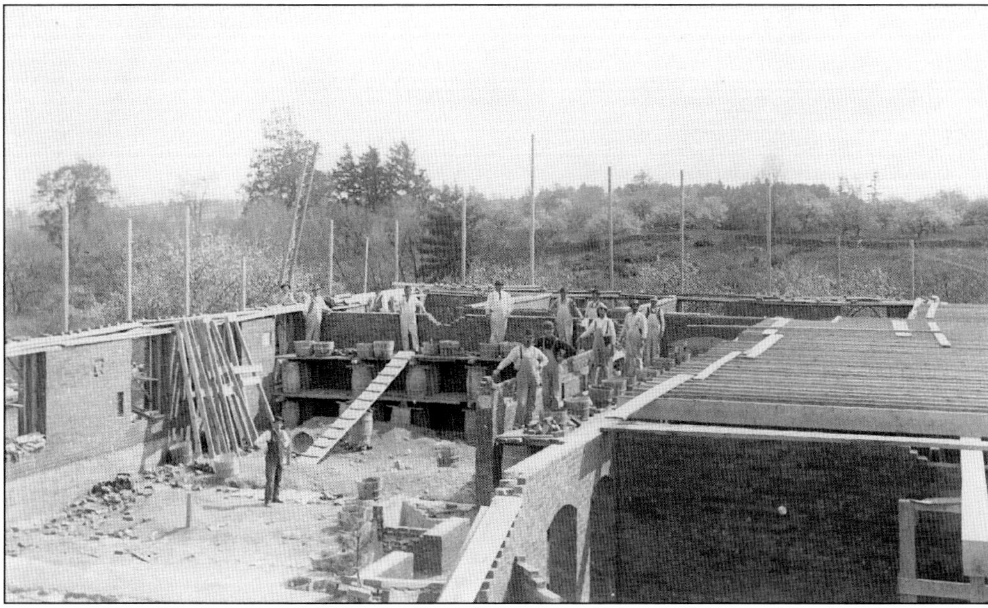
Work on the Conant Hall foundation, 1892.

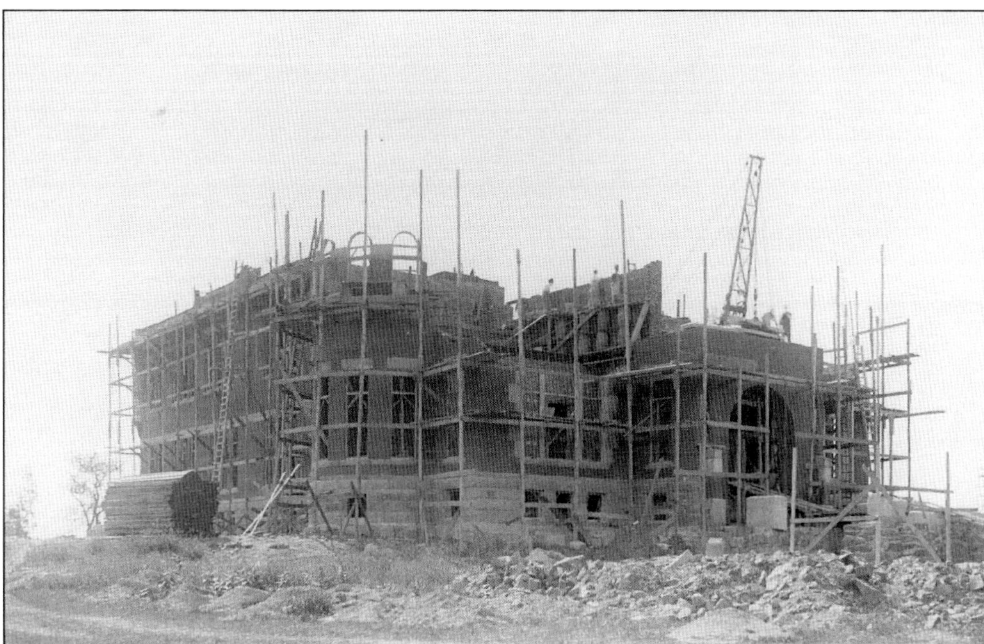
Work continues on Thompson Hall in 1892. The Concord firm of Dow and Randlett was chosen to design Thompson Hall and Conant Hall. Mr. Randlett oversaw the construction.

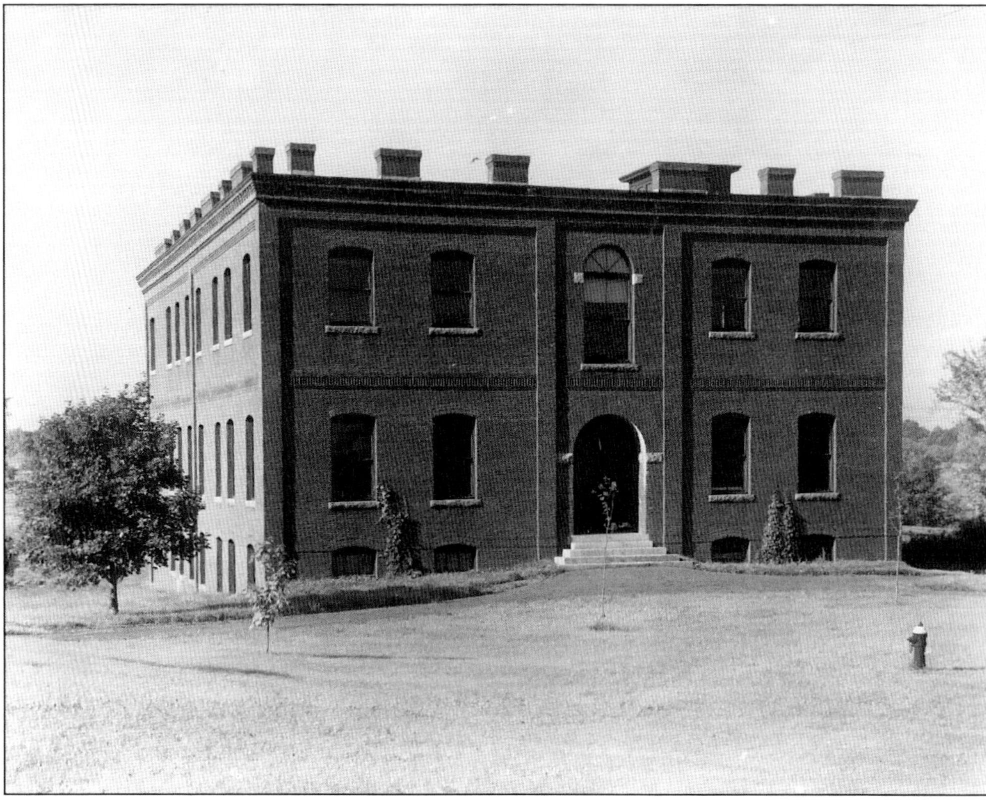

Conant Hall, *c.* 1893. Named for John Conant of Jaffrey, Conant Hall served as the science building on the new campus.

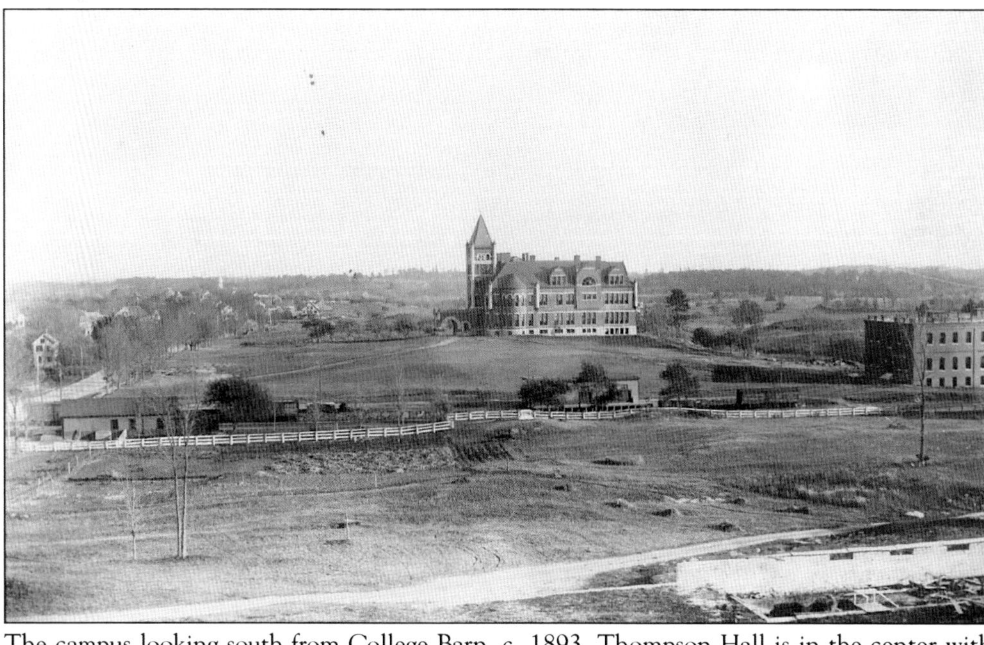

The campus looking south from College Barn, *c.* 1893. Thompson Hall is in the center with Conant Hall to the right.

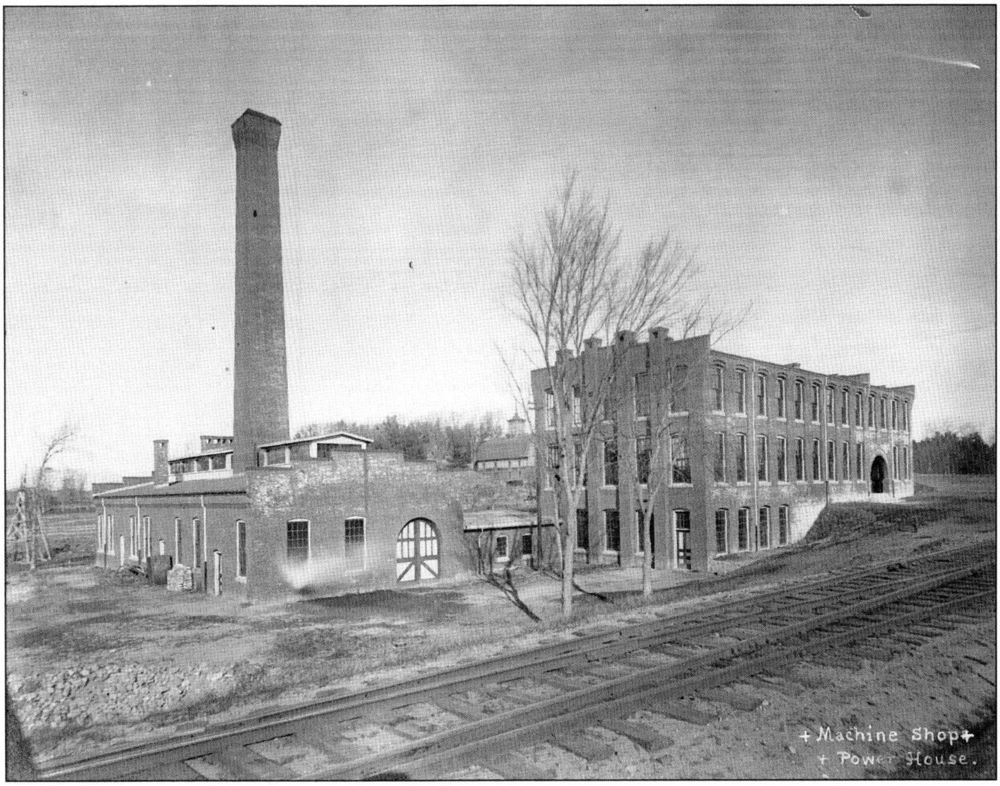

The completed Heating Plant and Shop building, *c.* 1893. The Heating Plant was designed to serve the other buildings on campus.

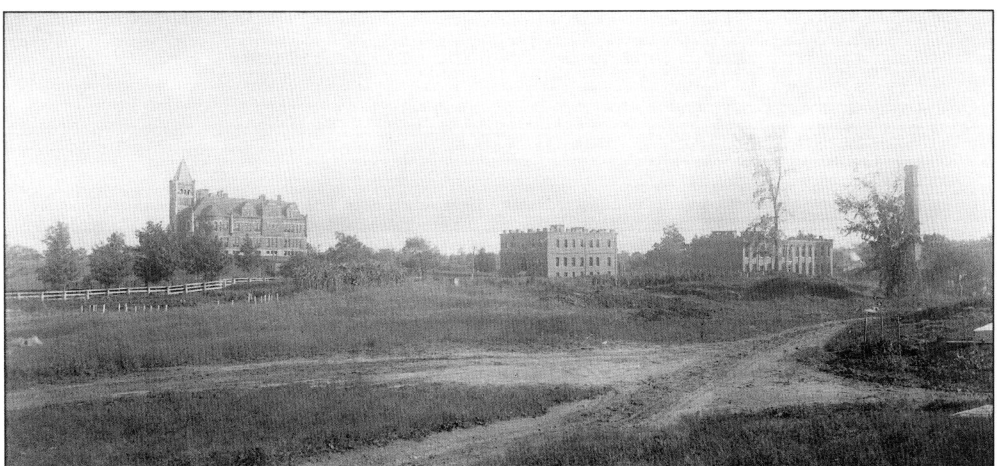

Another view of campus showing Thompson Hall, Conant Hall, and the Heating Plant and Shops, *c.* 1893. The Class of 1893 held its commencement in the third-floor auditorium of the partially completed Thompson Hall.

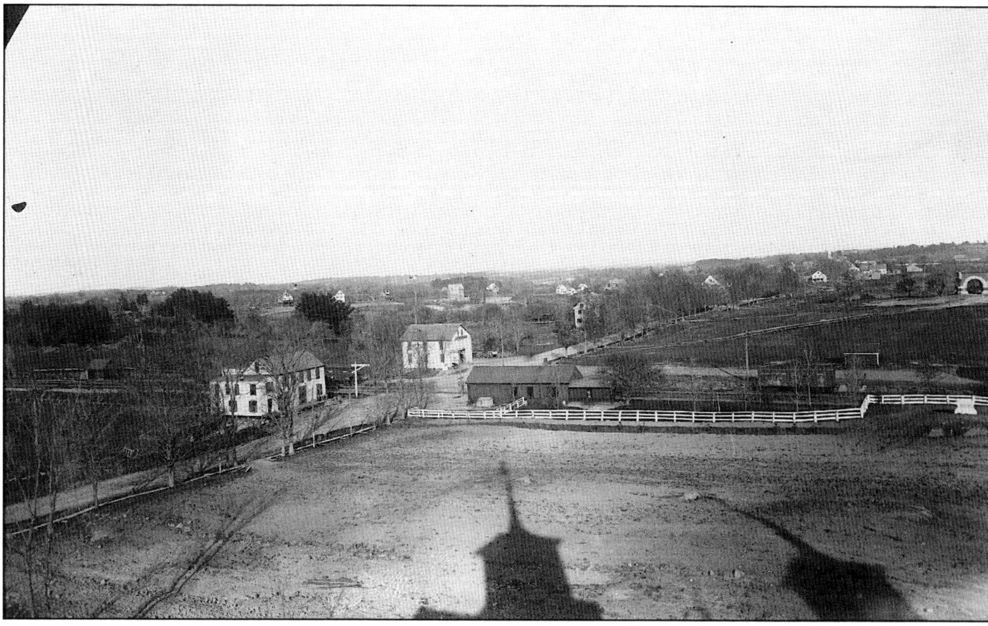

The intersection of Main Street and the Boston & Maine Railroad as seen from College Barn. Runlett's Store is on the left, and the B&M depot is on the right, *c.* 1893.

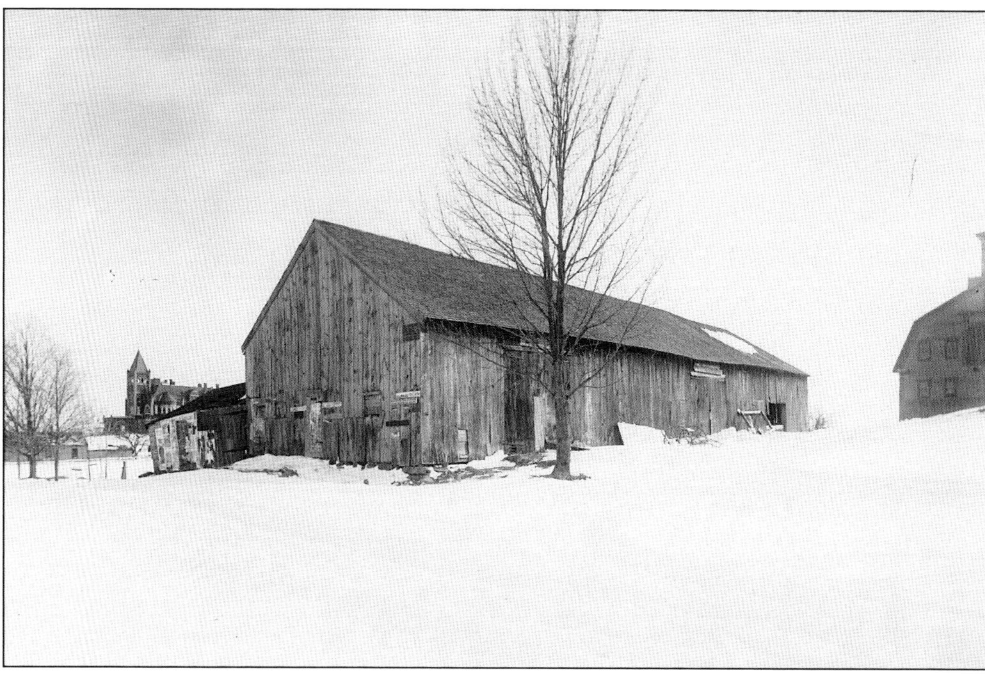

Thompson Barn in the winter of 1893. The college made use of existing buildings like this one on the land given by Benjamin Thompson.

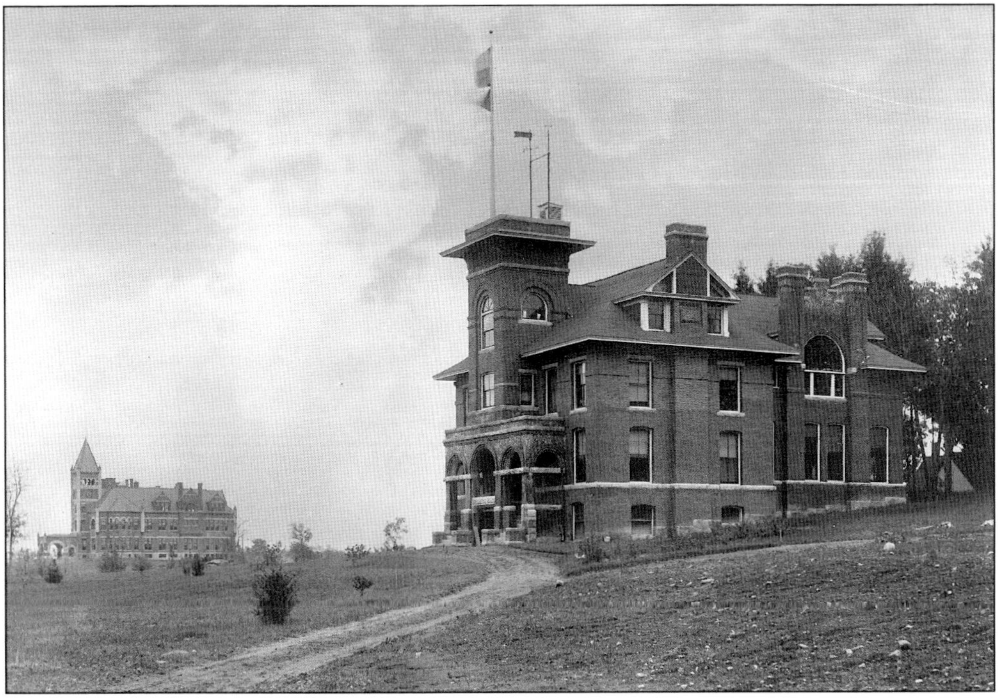

Nesmith Hall, the Agriculture Experiment Station building designed by William M. Butterfield of Manchester, *c.* 1894. Nesmith was one of the five main buildings constructed when the college first moved to Durham. The bricks used in the construction of Nesmith Hall were made in Durham.

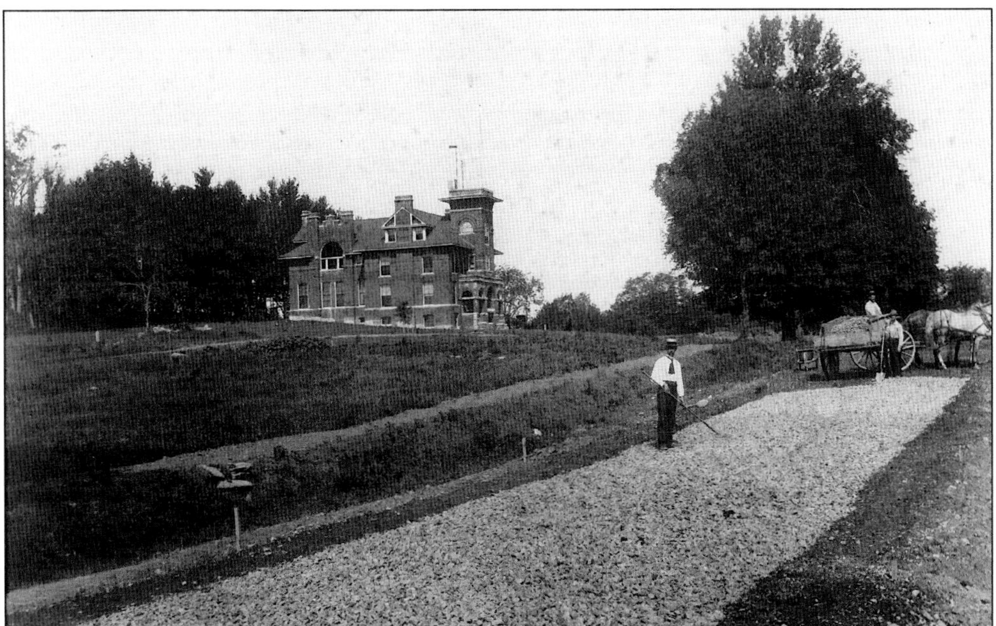

Dean Charles H. Pettee supervising work on Main Street in front of Nesmith Hall, *c.* 1895. In addition to constructing new buildings and a reservoir, the college also made improvements to the roads.

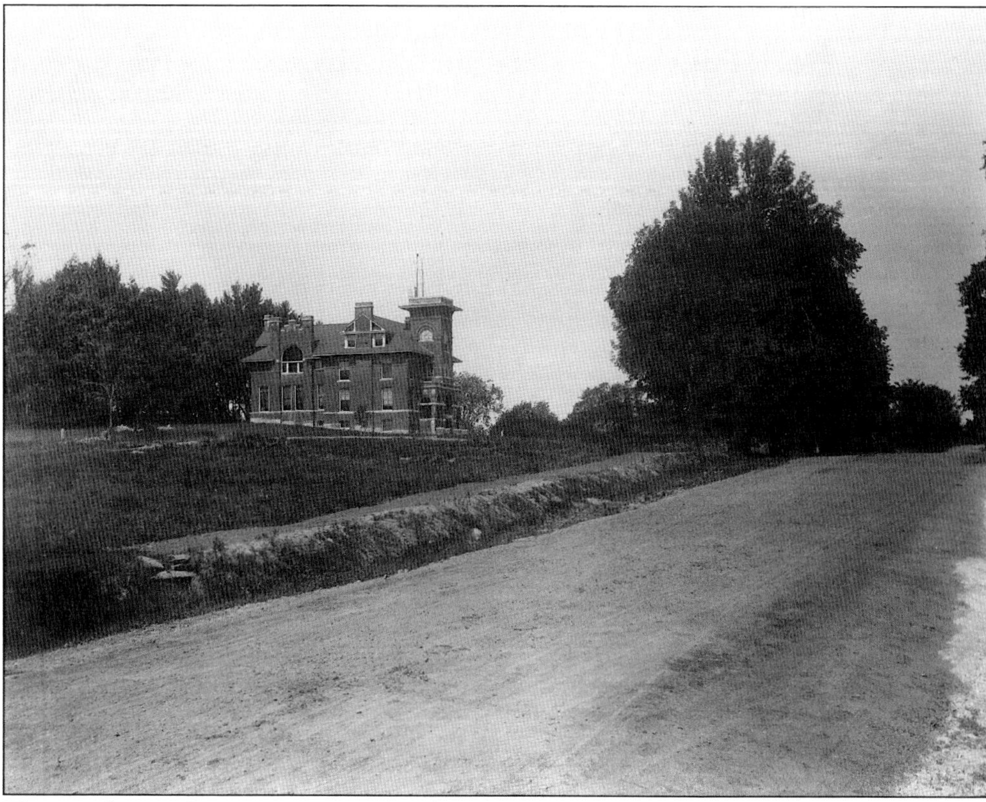

The resurfacing of Main Street completed, *c.* 1895.

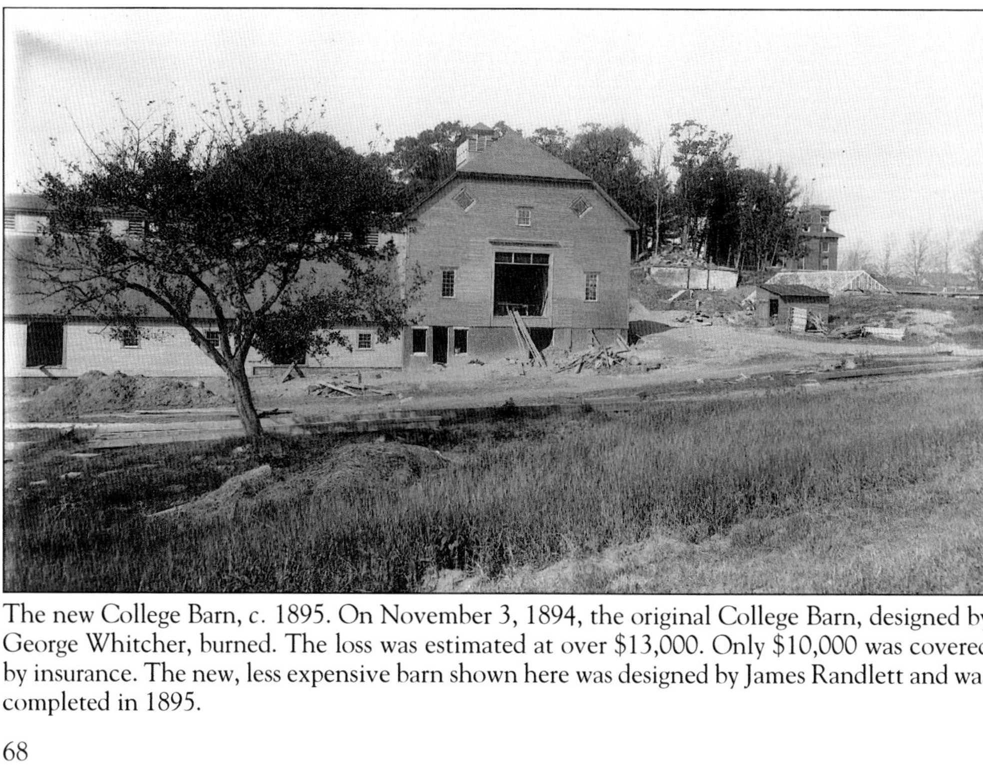

The new College Barn, *c.* 1895. On November 3, 1894, the original College Barn, designed by George Whitcher, burned. The loss was estimated at over $13,000. Only $10,000 was covered by insurance. The new, less expensive barn shown here was designed by James Randlett and was completed in 1895.

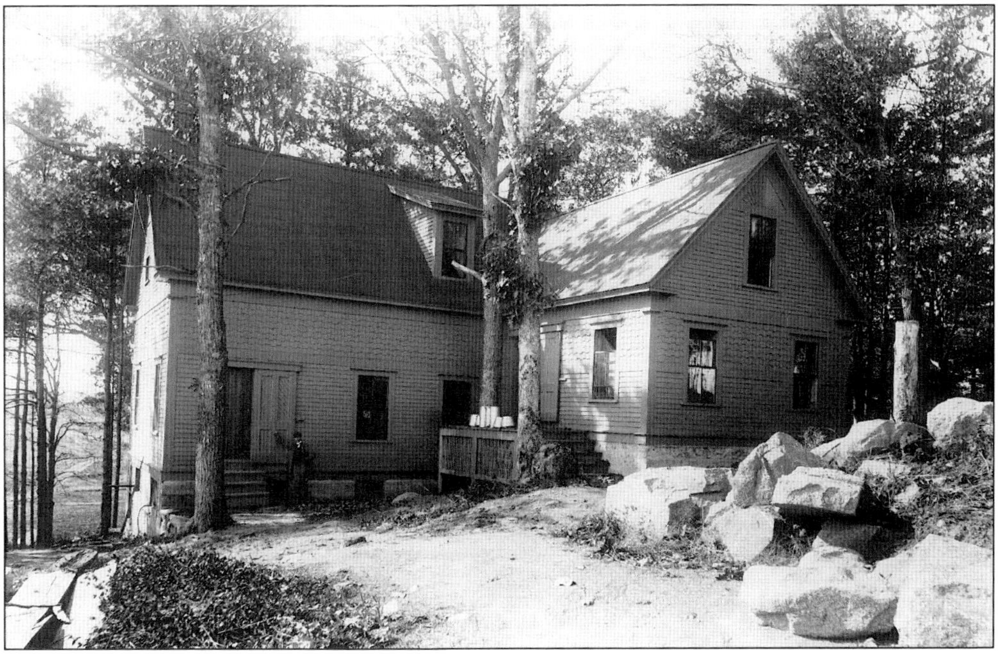

The creamery, c. 1894. This small creamery building stood near Nesmith Hall and College Barn. It narrowly escaped being burned when the original College Barn was destroyed by fire in 1894.

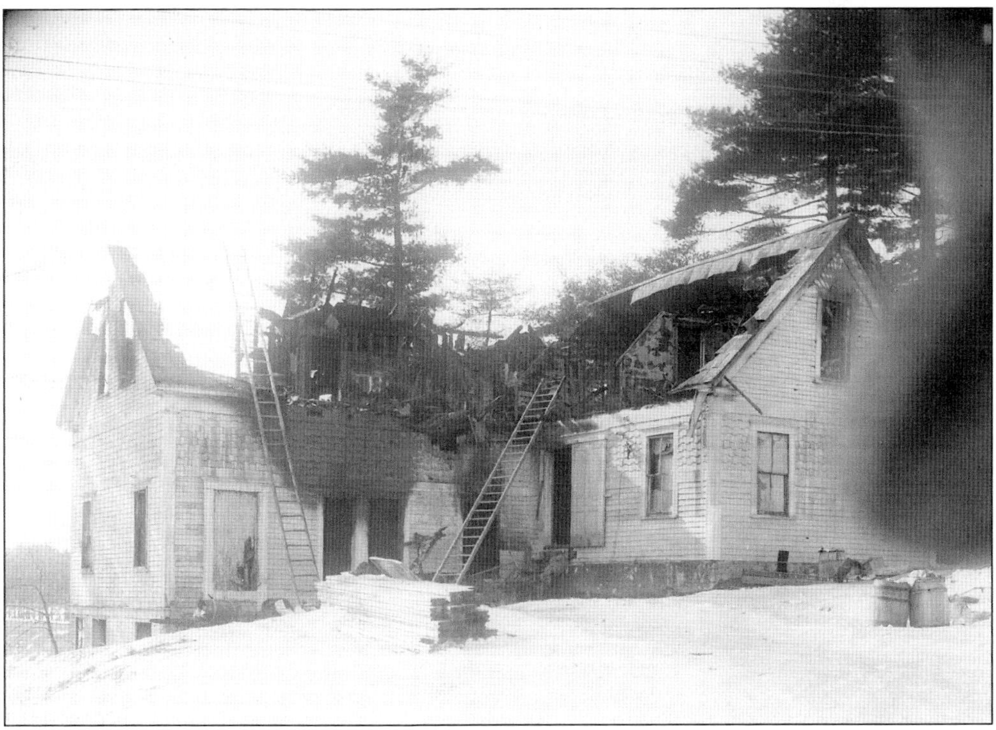

Fire at the creamery. Unfortunately, on February 3, 1922, the old creamery, being used as a dormitory for students working for the farm department, was destroyed by fire.

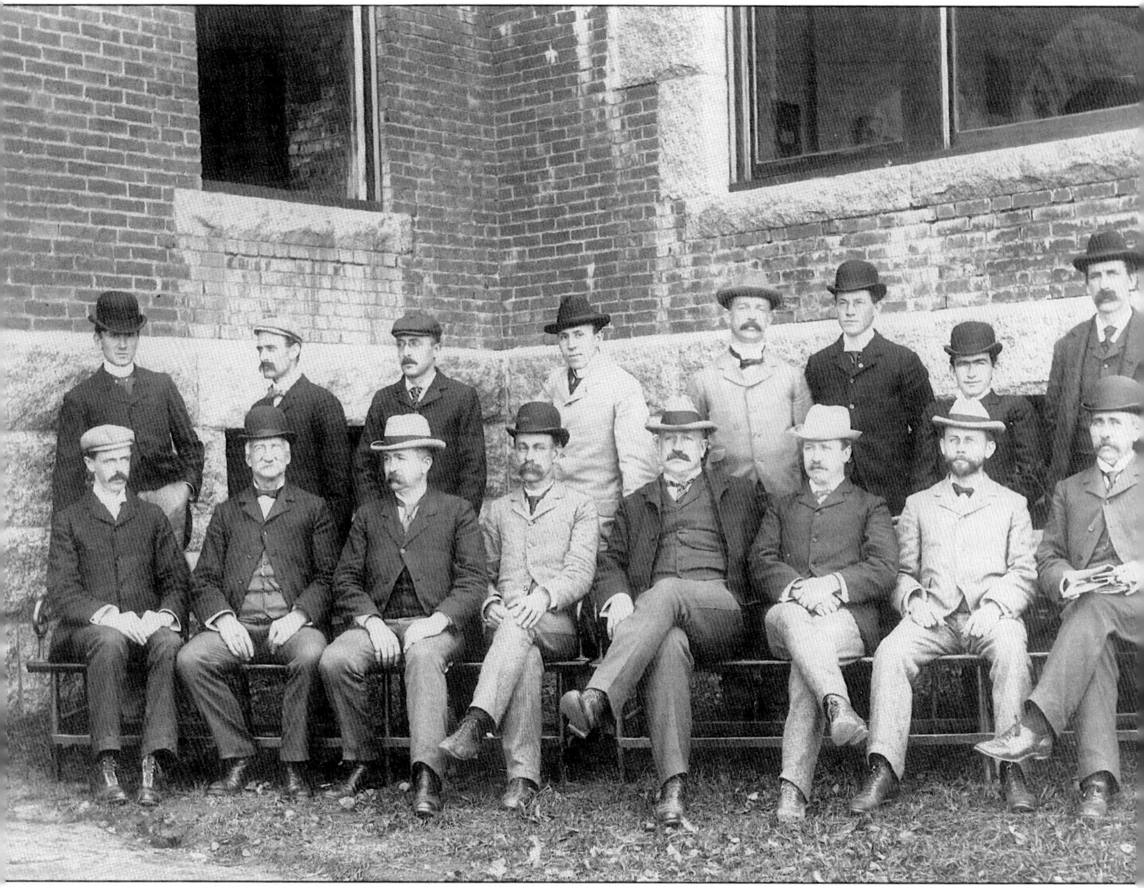

The faculty of the college in 1899. From left to right are: (seated) Fred W. Morse, professor of organic chemistry; Charles H. Waterhouse, instructor in dairying; Herbert H. Lamson, associate professor of botany; Charles H. Pettee, dean and professor of mathematics and civil engineering; President of the College Charles Sumner Murkland, professor of English language and literature; Clarence M. Weed, professor of zoology and entomology; Frank W. Rane, professor of horticulture; and Clarence W. Scott, professor of history and political economy; (standing) Frederic S. Johnston, assistant professor of agriculture; Irving A. Colby, instructor in wood work; Arthur F. Nesbit, associate professor of physics and electrical engineering; Charles W. Burkett, professor of agriculture; Charles L. Parsons, professor of general and analytical chemistry; Joseph H. Hawes, associate professor of drawing; Richard Whoriskey Jr., assistant professor of modern languages; and Edward E. Russell, engineer and curator of buildings.

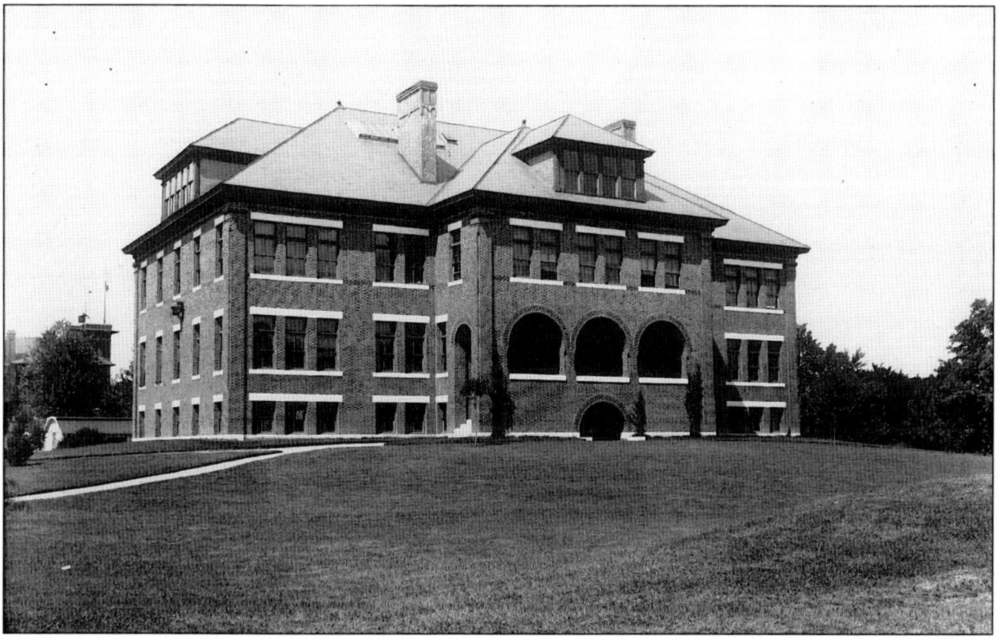

The agricultural building, Morrill Hall, *c.* 1906. Morrill Hall was completed in June of 1903, and was dedicated at the inauguration of President Gibbs in October of that year. Morrill Hall was named for Justin Morrill, the senator from Vermont who introduced the bill establishing the land grant college system. The Morrill Act was signed by President Lincoln on July 2, 1862.

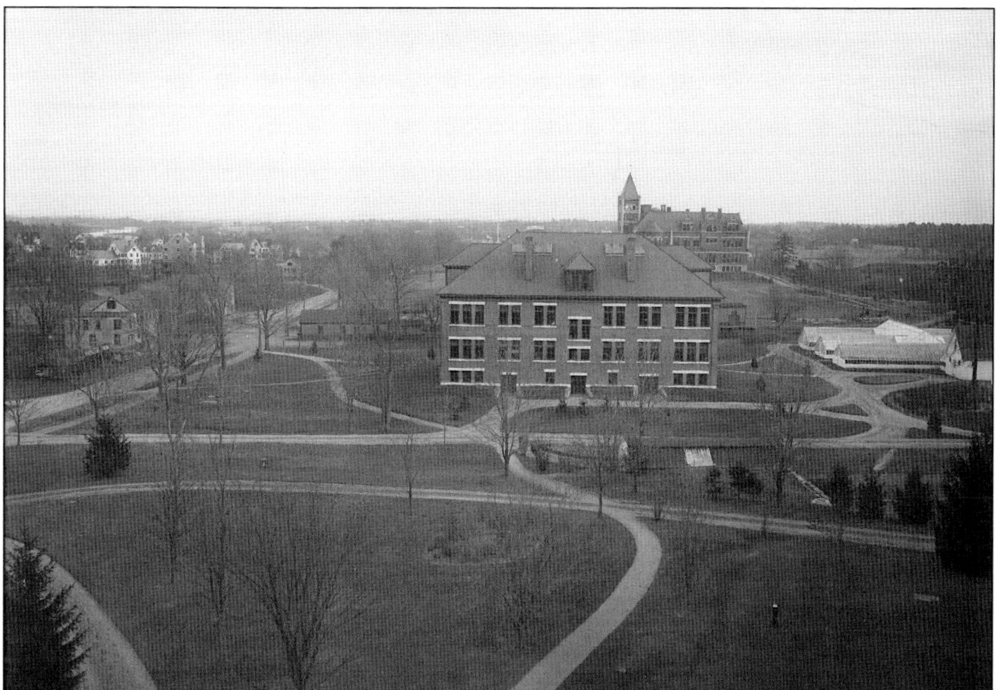

A view from College Barn showing the campus after Morrill Hall was completed, *c.* 1905. Some of the lumber used in the construction of Morrill Hall was cut from the college woods.

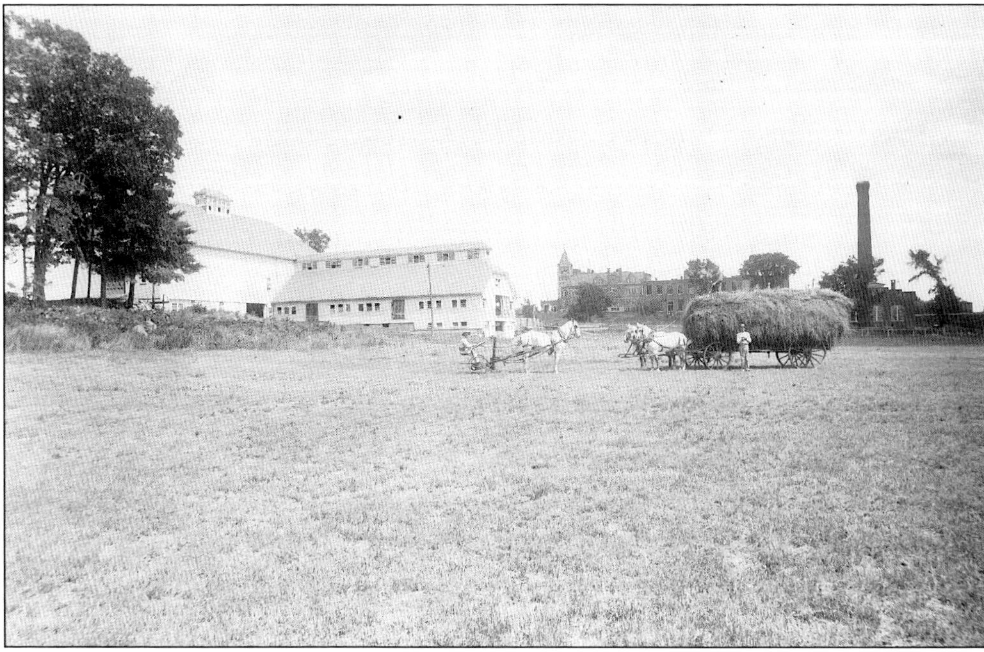

Haying behind the new College Barn, *c.* 1895. Thompson Hall can be seen in the background.

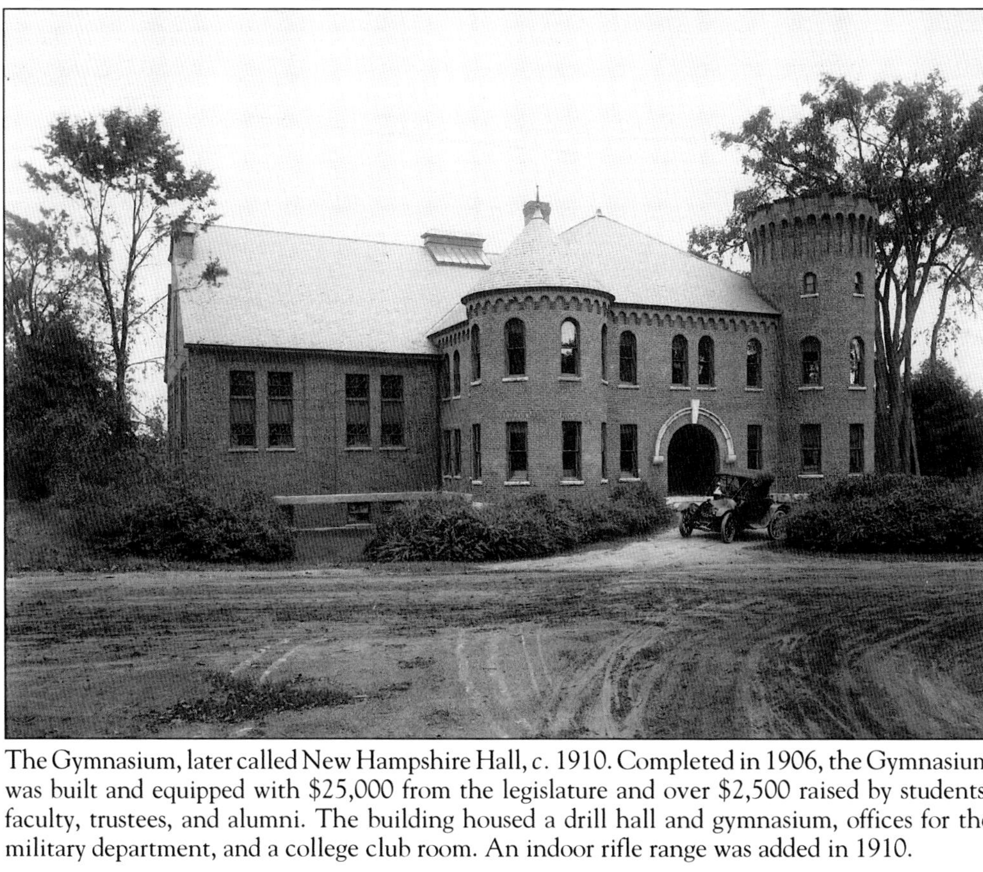

The Gymnasium, later called New Hampshire Hall, *c.* 1910. Completed in 1906, the Gymnasium was built and equipped with $25,000 from the legislature and over $2,500 raised by students, faculty, trustees, and alumni. The building housed a drill hall and gymnasium, offices for the military department, and a college club room. An indoor rifle range was added in 1910.

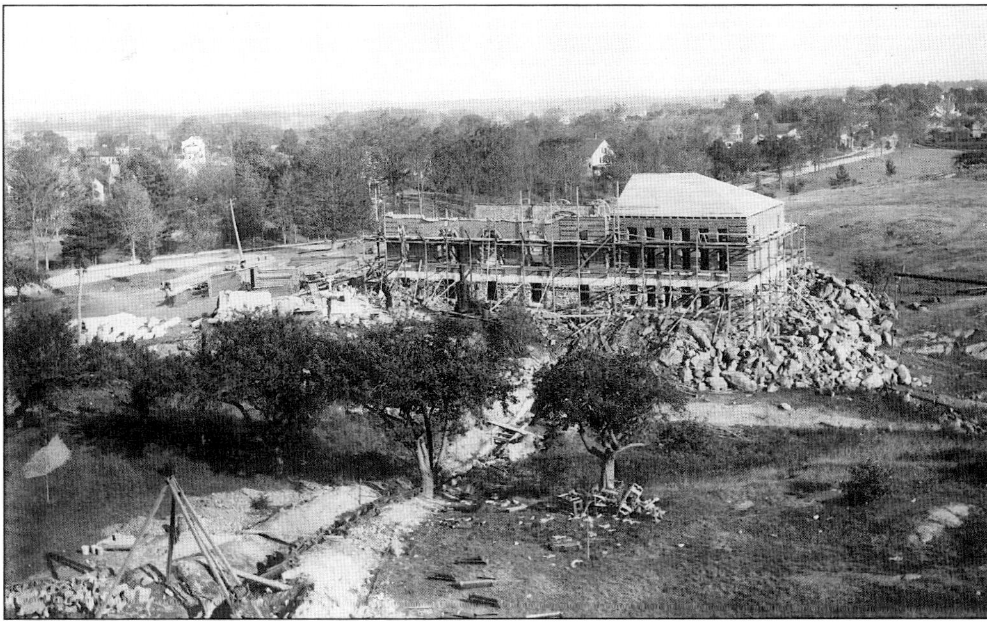

Construction of the Hamilton Smith Library, *c.* 1906. On January 13, 1906, an agreement was signed combining the libraries of the college, the Durham Library Association, and the Durham Public Library. In 1900, Hamilton Smith left $10,000 to the town of Durham for a new library building. The Smith money was left in trust and by 1906 the sum had grown to $12,888. With an additional $20,000 from Andrew Carnegie, construction began on the Hamilton Smith Library.

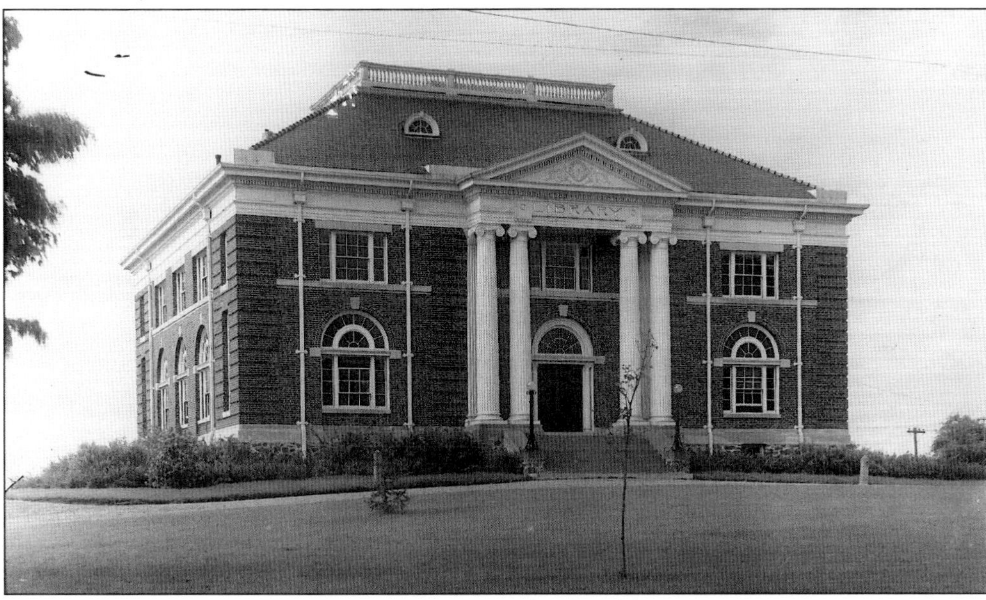

The Hamilton Smith Library. The new library was dedicated during commencement ceremonies, on June 3, 1907, although the building was not ready for use until November, and the relocation of the books from the town library was not complete until early in 1908. Gertrude Whittemore was appointed the first librarian under this new arrangement. Former town librarian Charlotte Thompson became the assistant librarian.

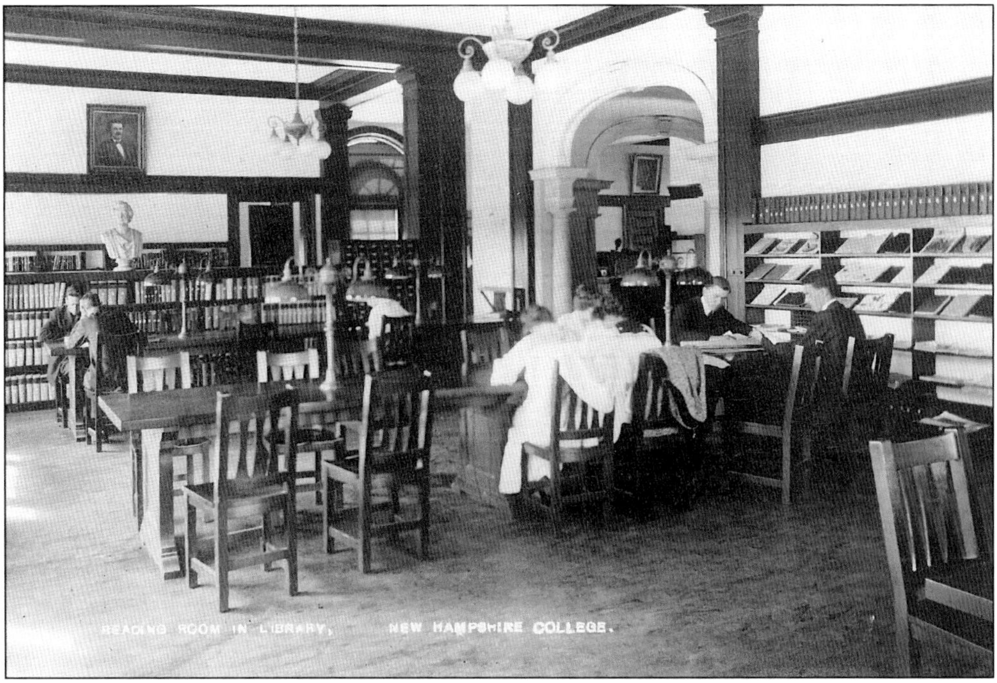

The interior of the Hamilton Smith Library, c. 1907.

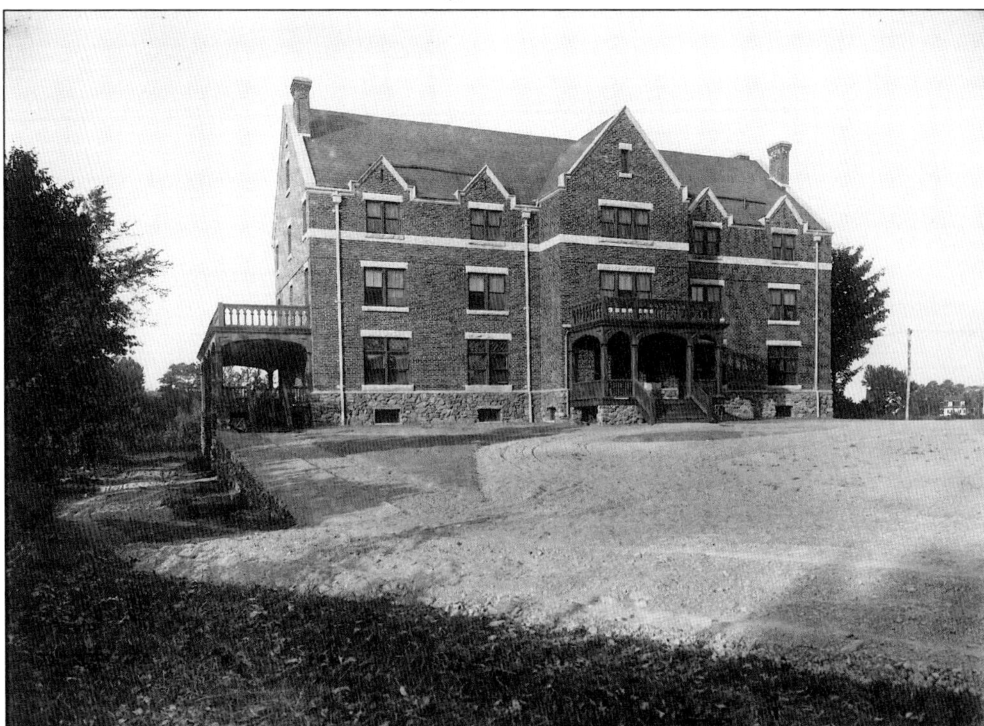

Smith Hall, c. 1908. Angela Congreve Onderdonk, stepdaughter of Hamilton Smith, following the wishes of her mother, gave $16,000 to be used to help pay for the construction of a women's dormitory. Smith Hall, named for Mrs. Hamilton Smith, was completed in 1908.

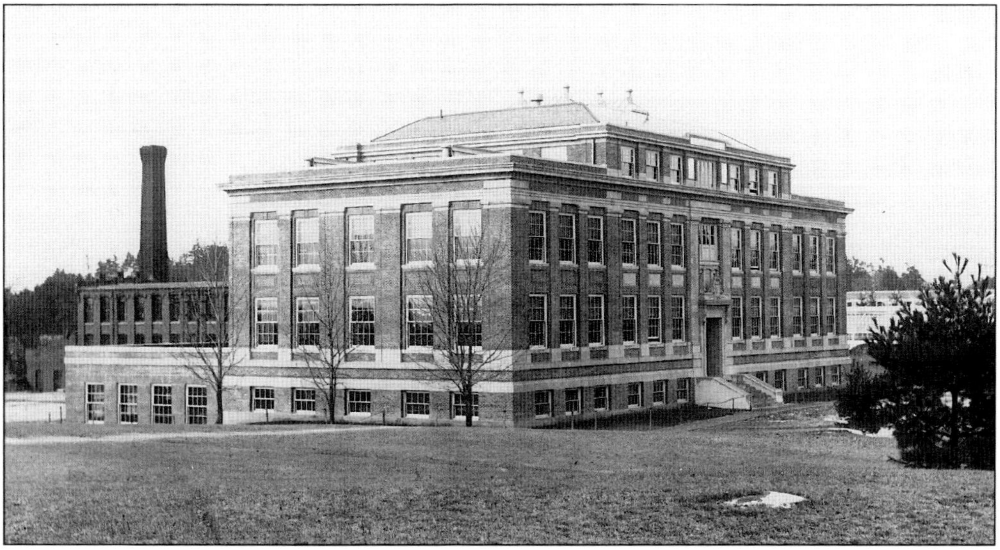

DeMeritt Hall, the engineering building, completed in 1914. The building was named for Albert DeMeritt of Durham. DeMeritt, the Durham representative to the 1913 legislature and a strong supporter of the college, helped secure $80,000 in state funds for the construction of the engineering building. He died in a hunting accident before the building that bears his name was completed. Until 1912, when they were moved several hundred feet to the west, the Boston & Maine Railroad tracks ran through the site of DeMeritt Hall.

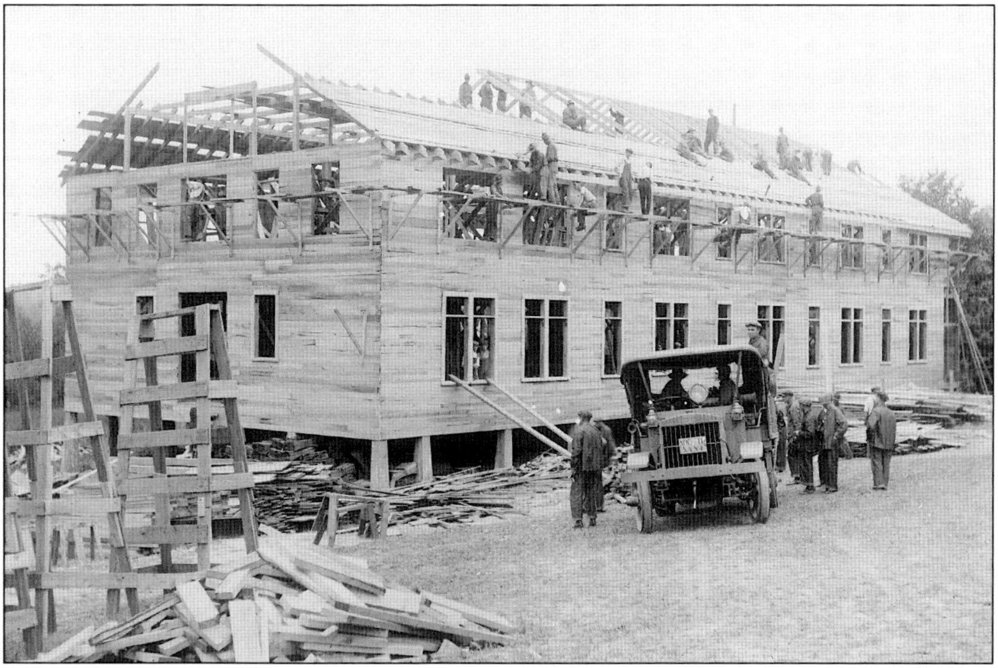

The East-West Barracks were constructed in the summer of 1918 by men participating in vocational training at the college. The land grant colleges had been assigned the task of training 300,000 men to help alleviate the labor shortage caused by the war. On the Durham campus, between May 16, 1918, and December 21, 1918, 1,269 men were trained as mechanics, carpenters, electricians, blacksmiths, concrete workers, machinists, cooks and bakers, or clerks.

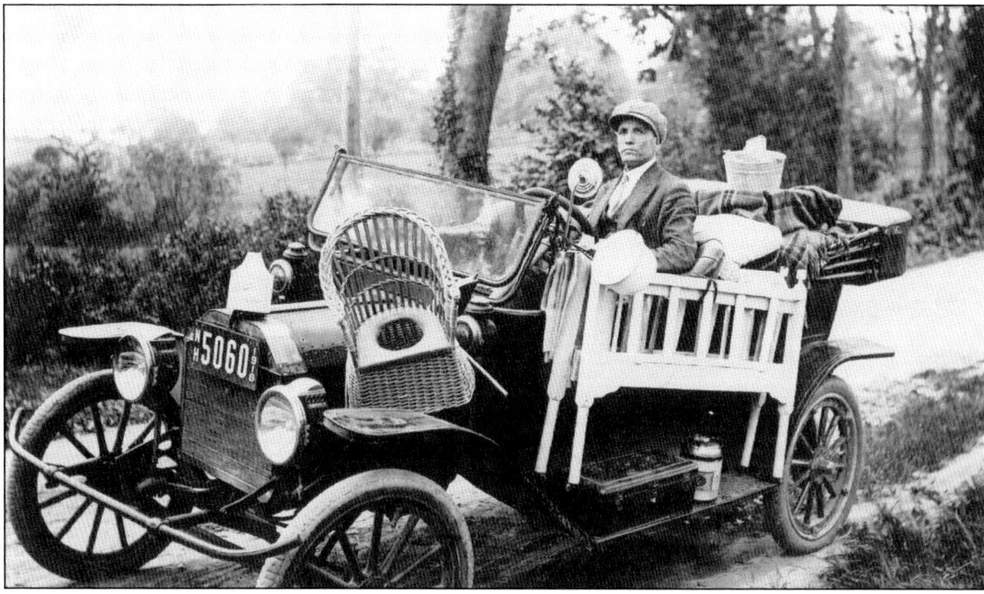

Oren V. "Dad" Henderson, business secretary for the college and purchasing agent for the Experiment Station, in a car loaded for a trip to the Mathes House, 1918. Seeking refuge from the flu epidemic which struck the campus in 1918, "Dad" Henderson and Eric T. Huddleston moved their families to the Mathes House on Durham Point.

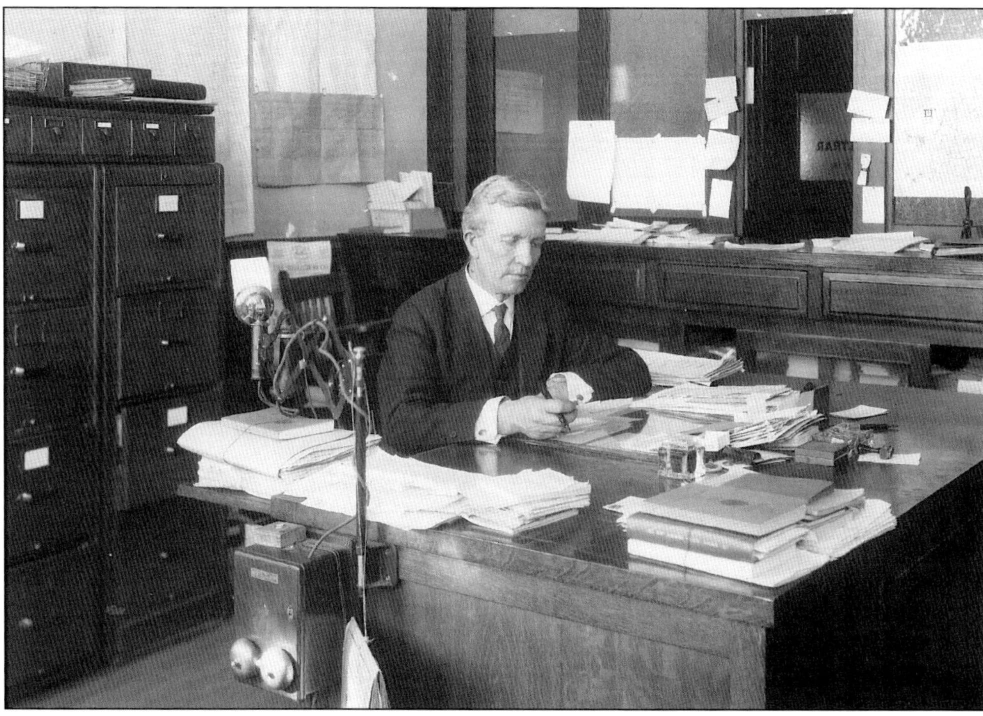

Oren V. "Dad" Henderson in his campus office, *c*. 1924. Henderson was promoted to executive secretary of the college in 1920, and from 1925 to 1939 he served as registrar. "Dad" was active in the community and in state politics. He served on the Durham Board of Selectmen, in the New Hampshire House of Representatives, and on the Governor's Council.

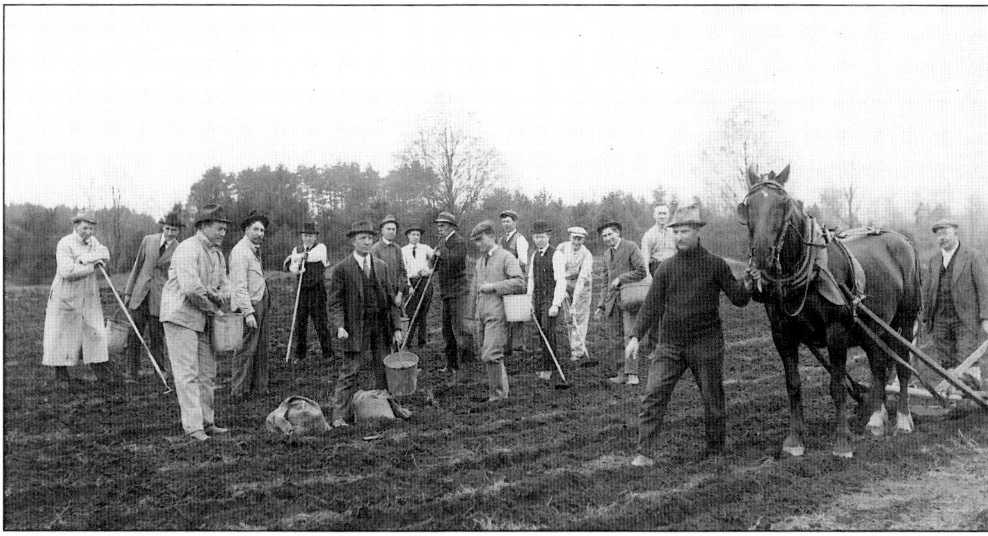

The Factato Club planting their first crop, May 1917. Food production was important during the war years and the Factato Club was one effort by the faculty to demonstrate methods of increasing production through cooperation. Twenty-eight faculty members joined together in the spring of 1917 to raise a 1.5-acre potato crop. Dean of Agriculture Frederick W. "Pa" Taylor, leading the horse, supervised the effort. Oren V. Henderson, second from left in the front row, served as the club's Factatum (secretary-treasurer).

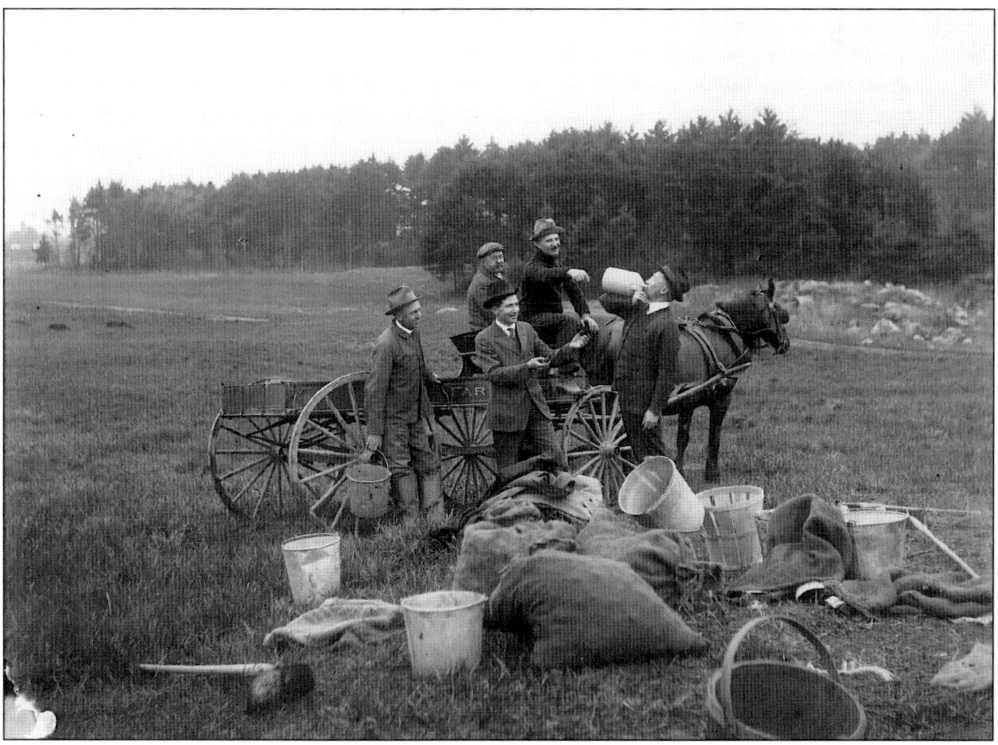

"Pa" Taylor, Factator (chairman) of the Factato Club, dispensing refreshment to club members preparing to plant the potato crop, May 1917. The efforts of the Factaters, as the club members were known, produced 260 bushels of potatoes in 1917, and 324 bushels the following year.

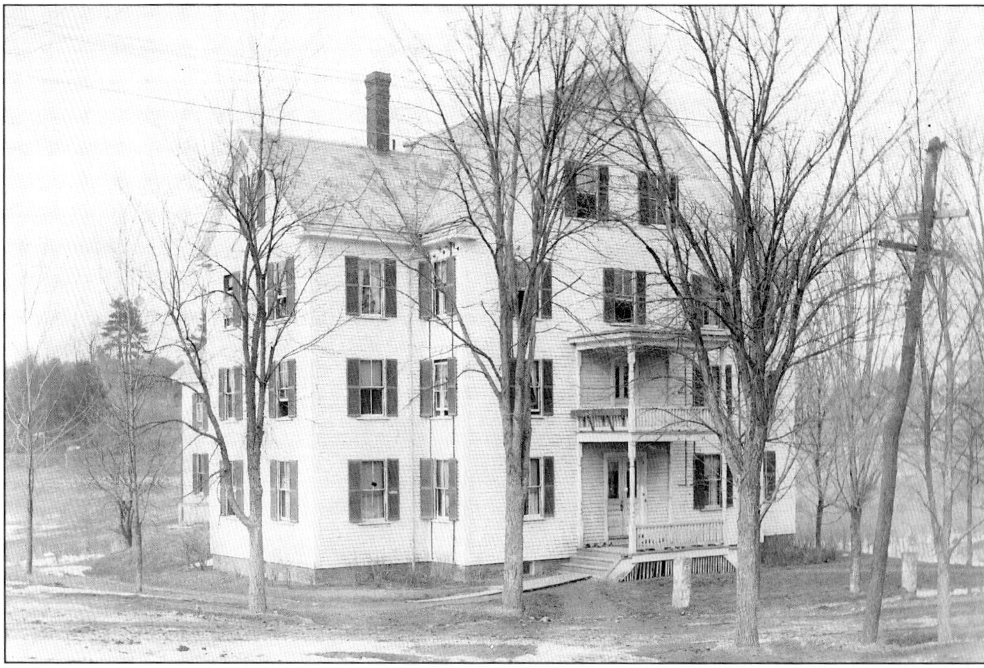

Ballard Hall, *c.* 1918. This building, situated on Garrison Avenue, just off of Main Street, was built by Albert DeMeritt in 1894 to be used as a dormitory and boarding house for students. It was purchased by the college in 1915 and named Ballard Hall.

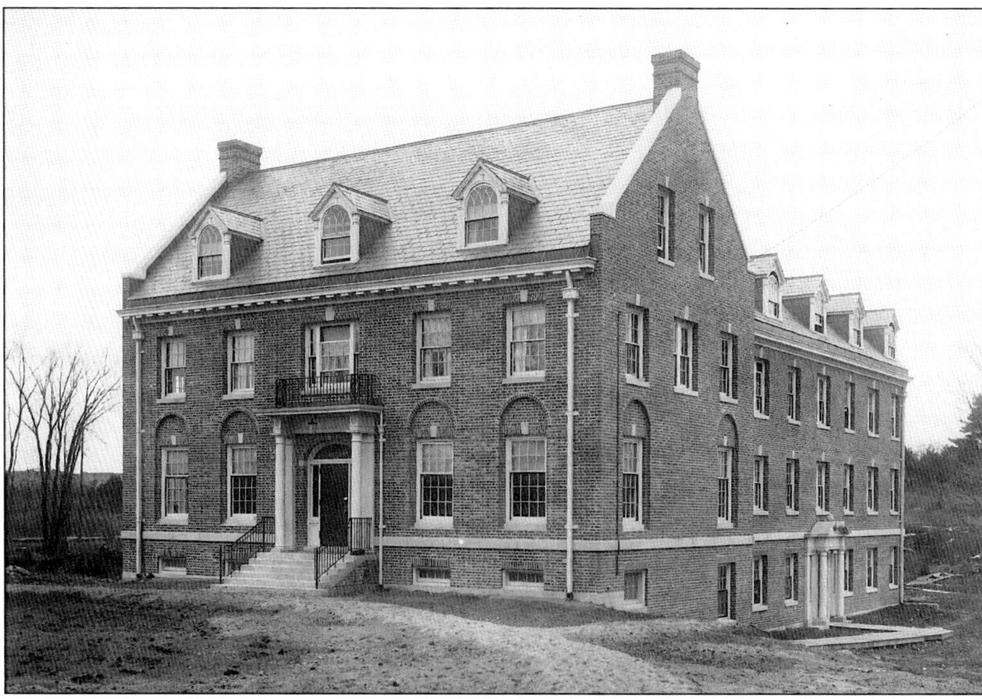

Congreve Hall, *c.* 1920. A second women's dormitory was built with additional funds from the estate of Mrs. Hamilton Smith. Congreve Hall, named for Mrs. Smith's daughter, Angela Congreve Onderdonk, was completed in 1920.

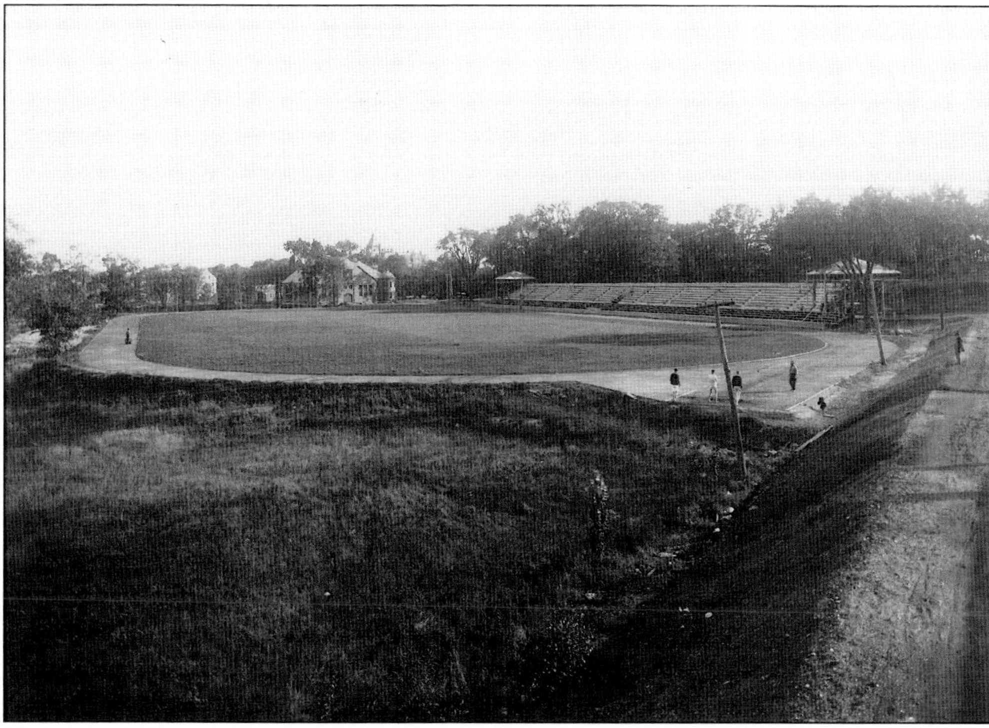

The construction of Memorial Field, 1921. Built with funds raised by the alumni, the field was a memorial to eighteen men who had been closely associated with the college and who had lost their lives in military service during the war.

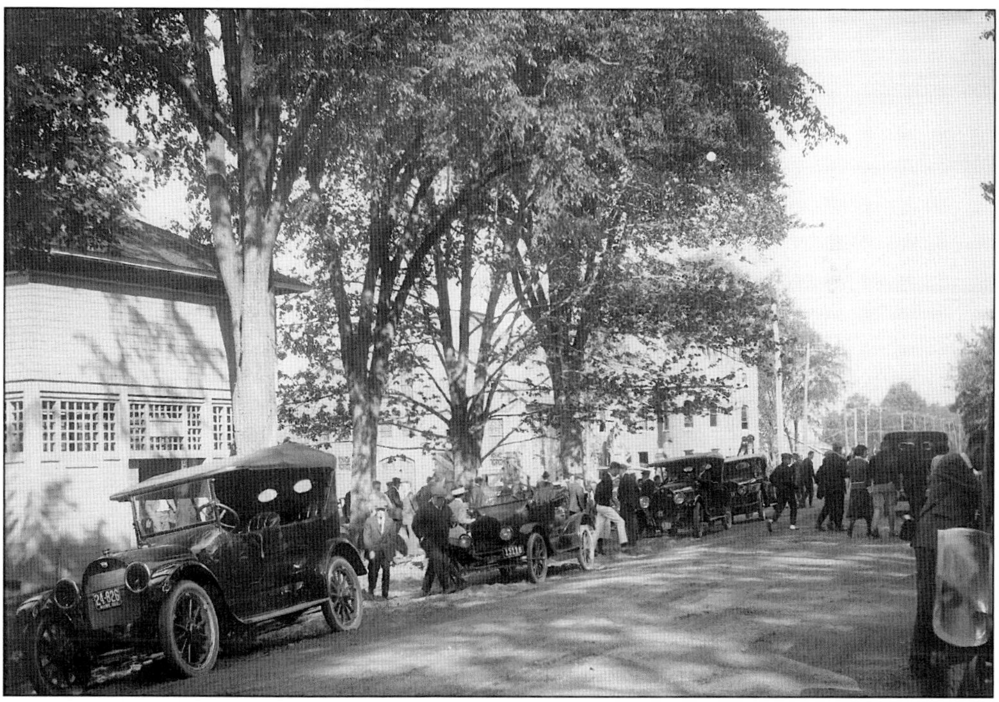

A crowd leaving Memorial Field in 1922.

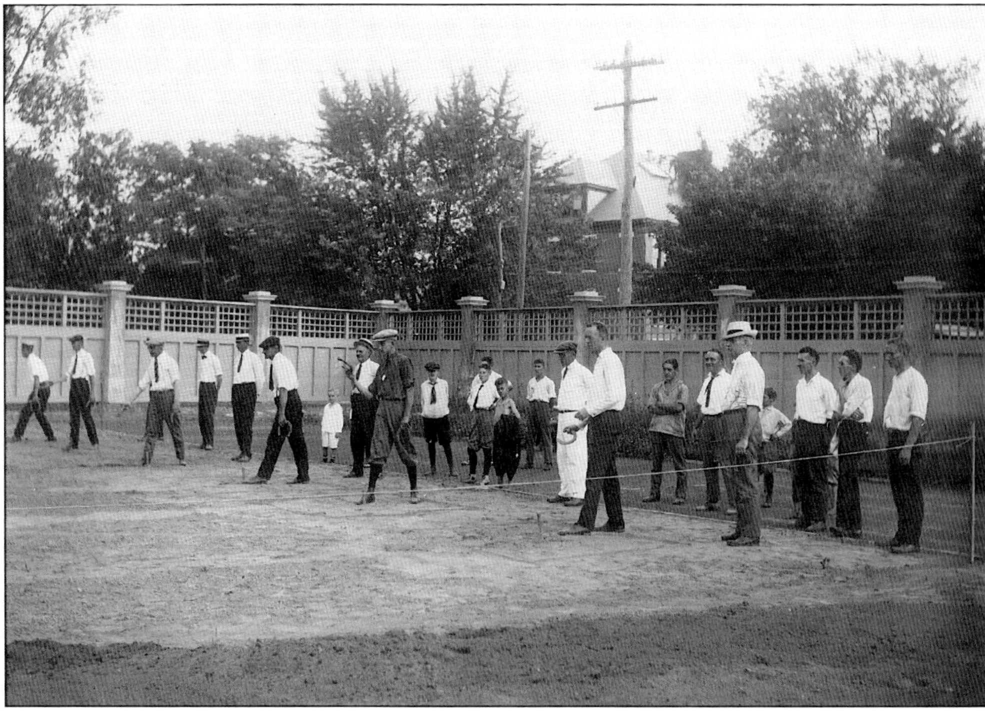

Horseshoe pitching in the corner of Memorial Field during Farmers' and Home-Makers' Week, 1922. Farmers' and Home-Makers' Week, athletic events, and other college activities brought many visitors to Durham.

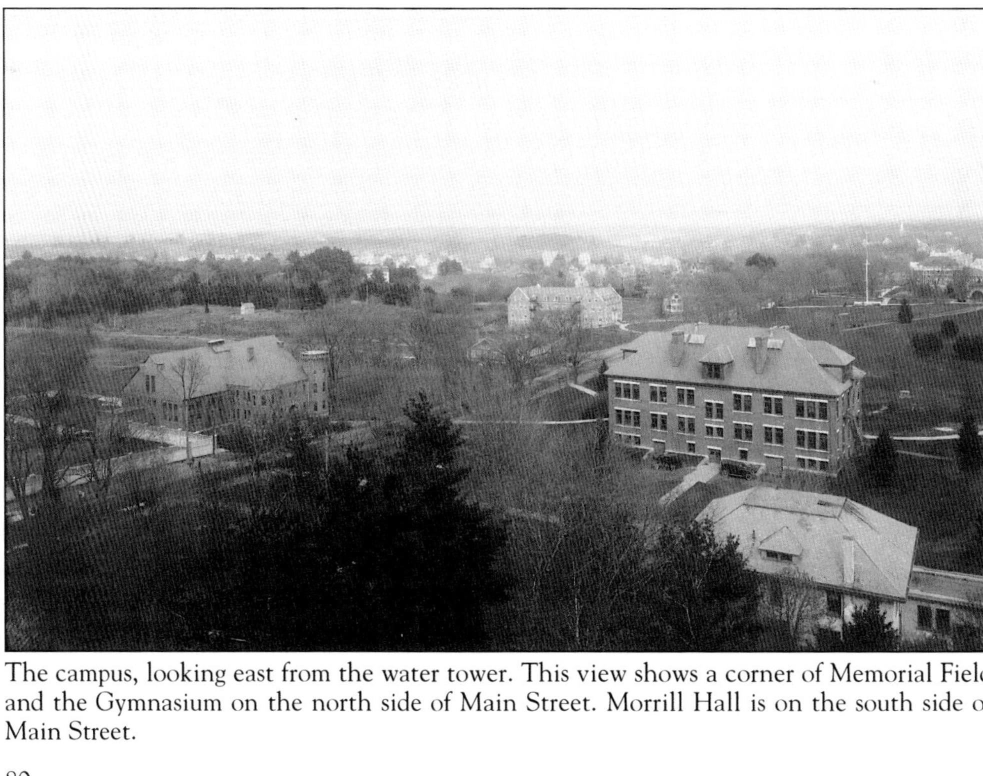

The campus, looking east from the water tower. This view shows a corner of Memorial Field and the Gymnasium on the north side of Main Street. Morrill Hall is on the south side of Main Street.

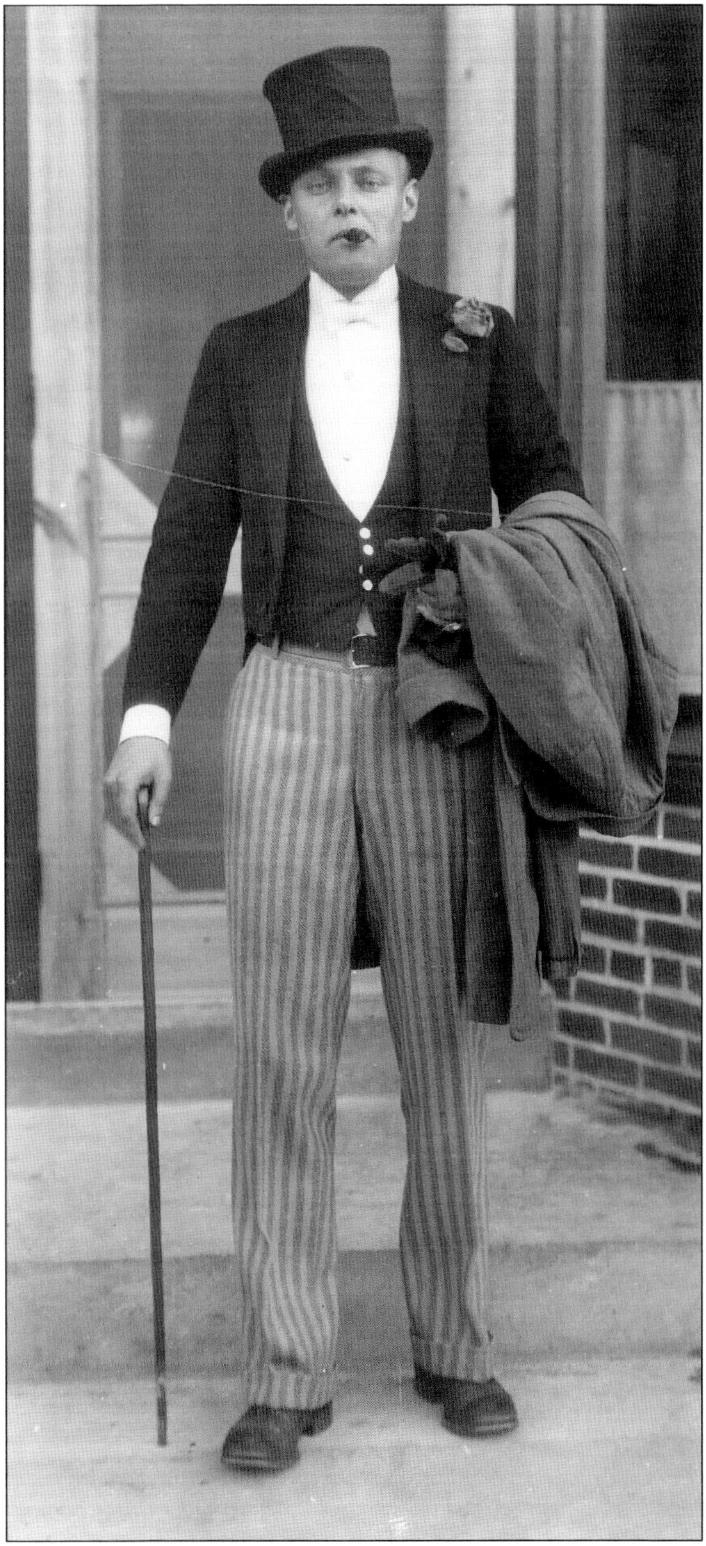

Laurence V. Jensen, the first "Mayor of Durham," 1926. In 1926, the Blue Key, a senior honorary society, sponsored the first "mayoralty" campaign. Jensen's platform promoted individual liberty and was against allowing female matrons in male dormitories.

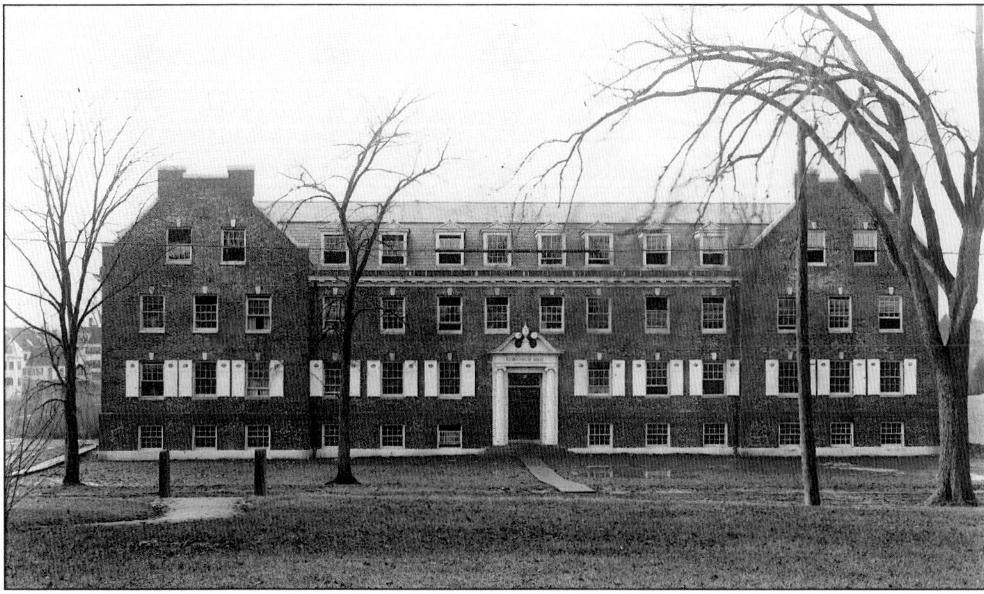

Fairchild Hall, *c.* 1916. In the spring of 1915, construction started on Fairchild Hall, a men's dormitory. It was hoped that the building would be ready for occupancy by the beginning of the fall term. Although part of the building was opened in October, construction was not completed until after Thanksgiving.

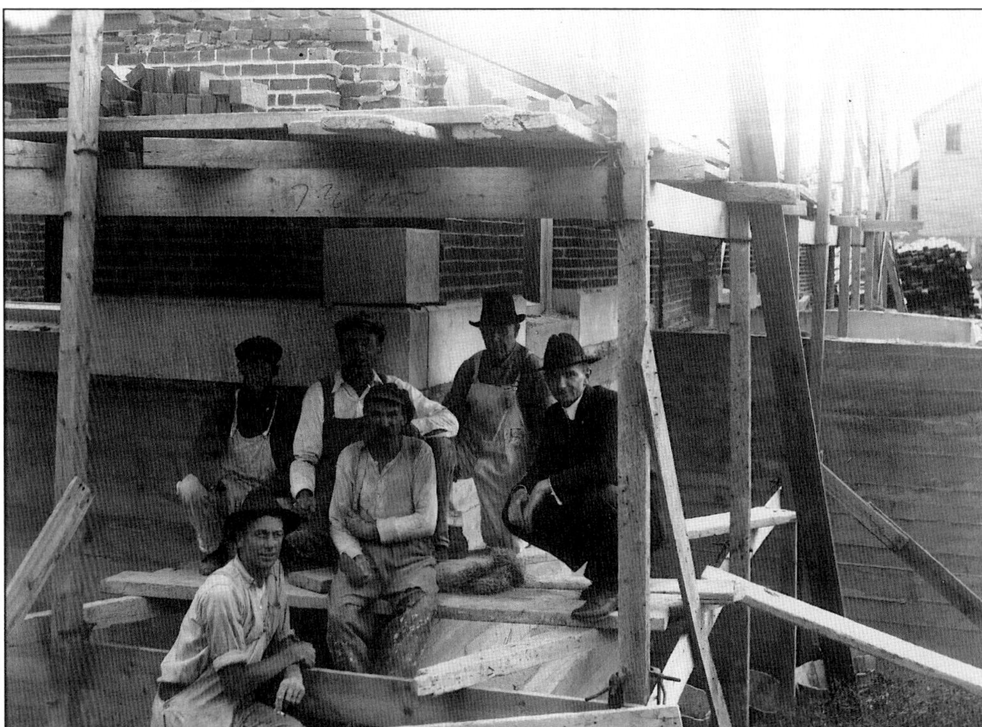

Professor Eric T. Huddleston and workers laying the cornerstone of the Commons, *c.* 1919. Professor Huddleston designed many of the buildings on campus, including the Commons, Fairchild Hall, and Hetzel Hall. The Commons was later renamed Huddleston Hall.

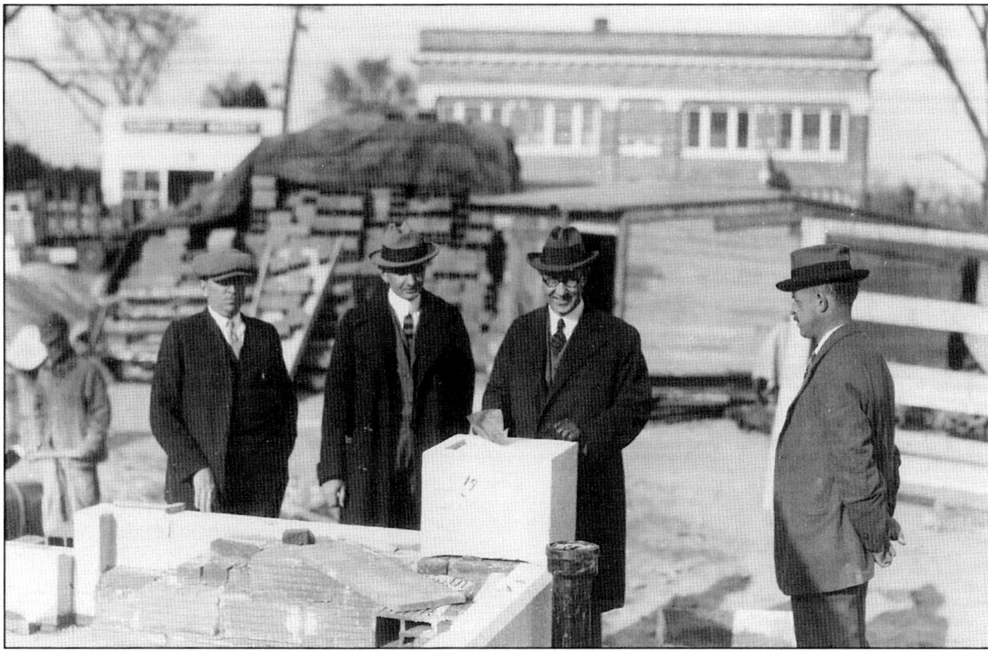

Eric Huddleston (second from left) and University President Ralph D. Hetzel laying the cornerstone for Hetzel Hall, October 23, 1925. Hetzel served as president from 1917 until 1927. It was during his tenure as president that the college became a university. In 1923 Governor Fred H. Brown signed the bill changing the name of the New Hampshire College of Agriculture and Mechanic Arts to the University of New Hampshire. The change took effect on July 1, 1923.

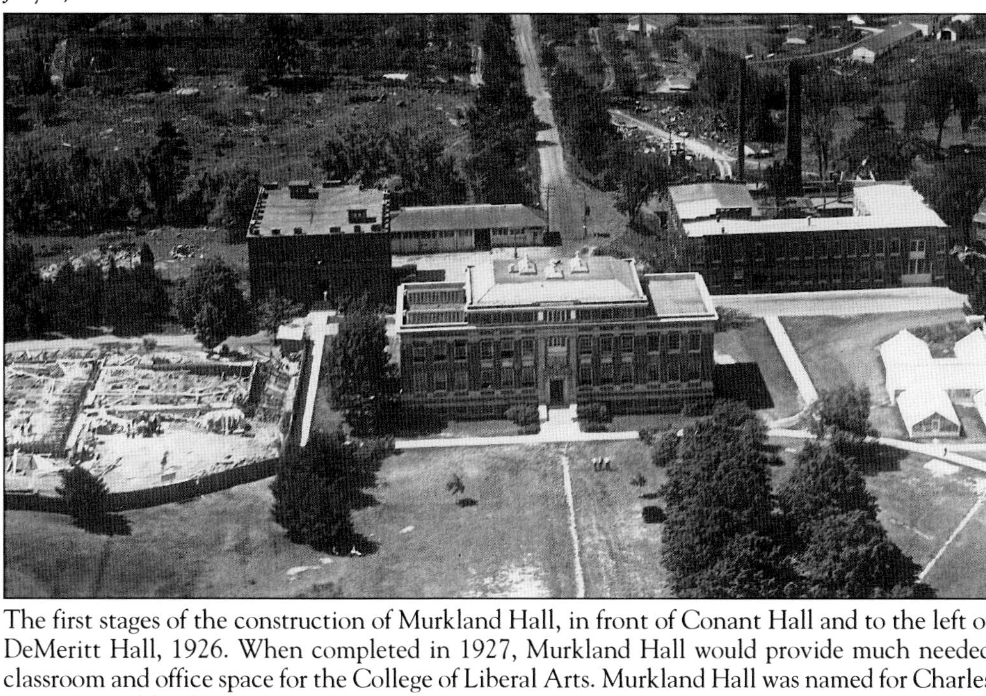

The first stages of the construction of Murkland Hall, in front of Conant Hall and to the left of DeMeritt Hall, 1926. When completed in 1927, Murkland Hall would provide much needed classroom and office space for the College of Liberal Arts. Murkland Hall was named for Charles Sumner Murkland, president of the college from 1893 to 1903.

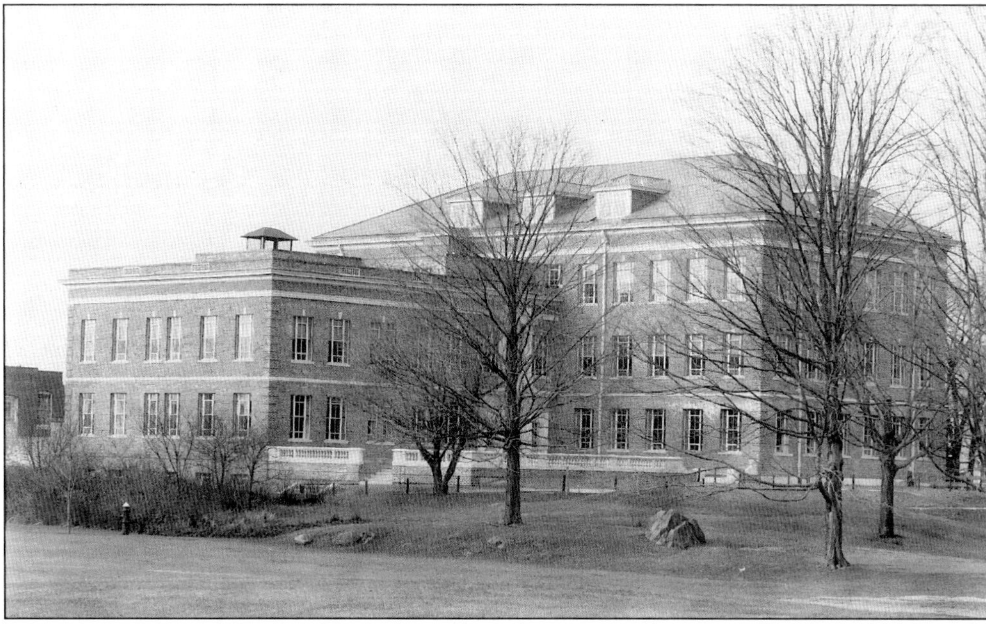

James Hall, *c.* 1929. This building was completed in 1929 with dedication ceremonies held on November 9. James Hall was named for Chemistry Professor Charles James who had served the university since 1906. He died unexpectedly in December 1928, at the age of forty-seven.

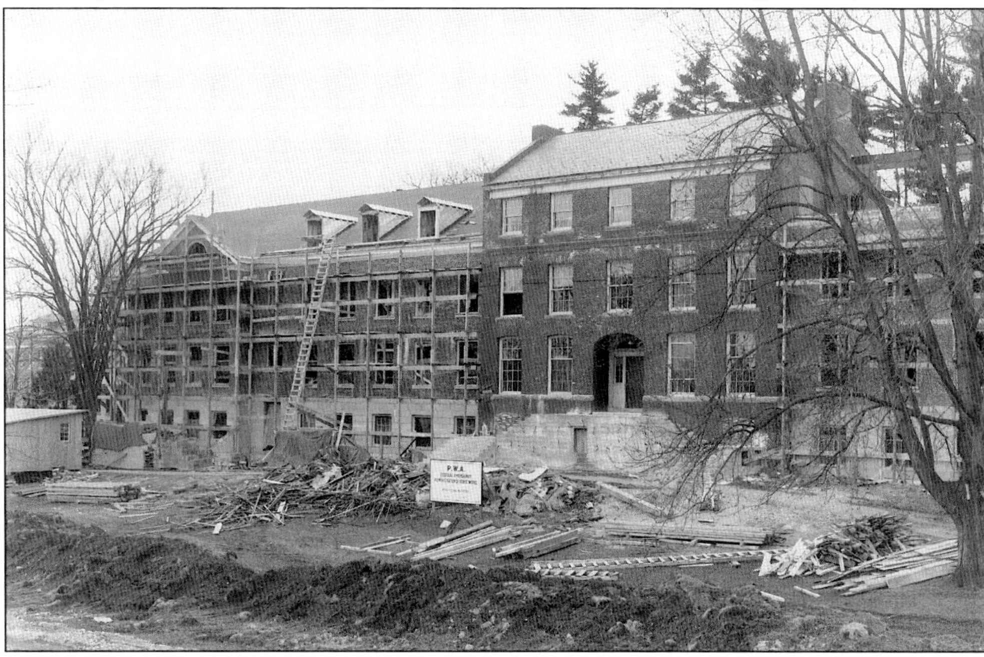

Construction underway on an addition to Nesmith Hall, April 17, 1939. The 1930s saw much construction activity on campus. Hood House, Pettee Hall, and the Field House were among the new buildings completed. Several projects were made possible by the Civil Works Administration, the Emergency Relief Administration, and the Public Works Administration. Among them were the construction of Lewis Fields, a reservoir, a swimming pool, and additions to several buildings.

Four

Durham Village

Even with the arrival of the New Hampshire College of Agriculture and Mechanic Arts and the rapid growth that led to the college becoming the University of New Hampshire, the town of Durham managed to retain much of its rural charm.

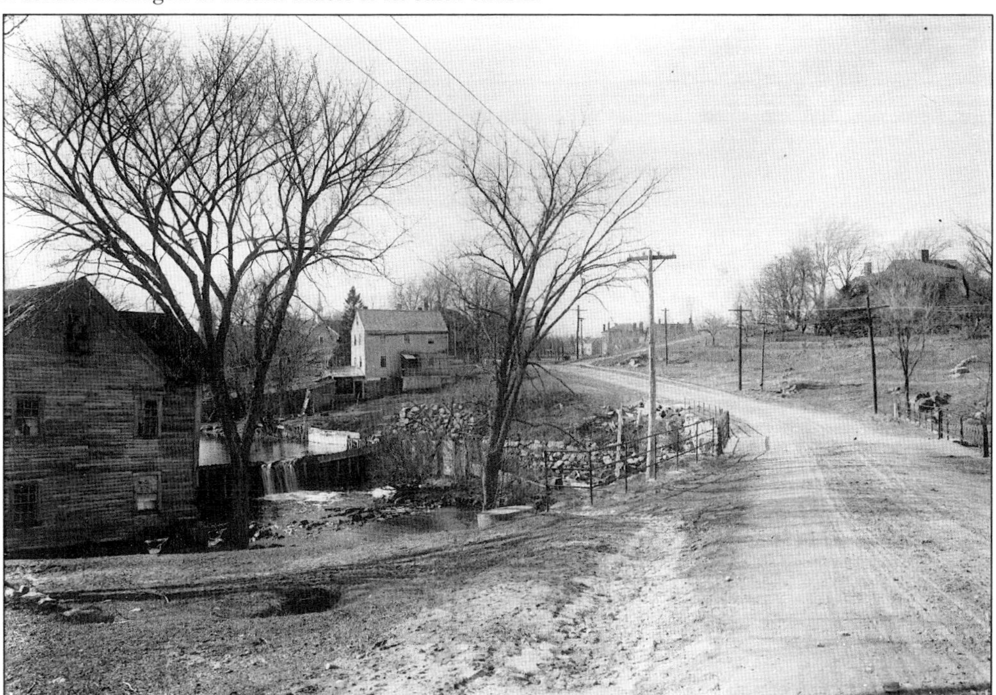

The Oyster River Bridge on Newmarket Road looking north, *c.* 1910. Jenkins Mill and the Runlett House are on the left.

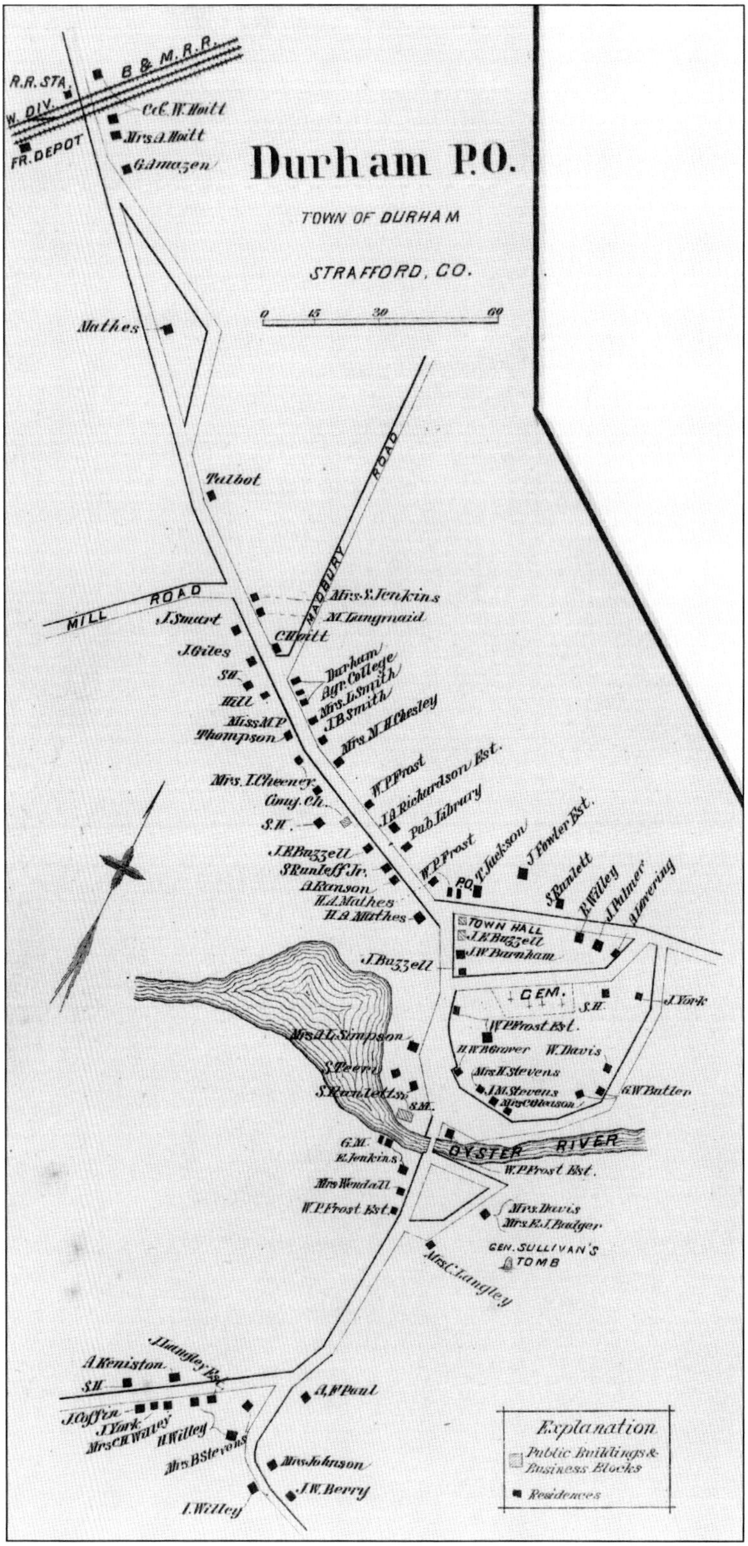

Map of Durham, 1892, from the *Town and City Atlas of the State of New Hampshire* (Boston: D.H. Hurd and Co., 1892).

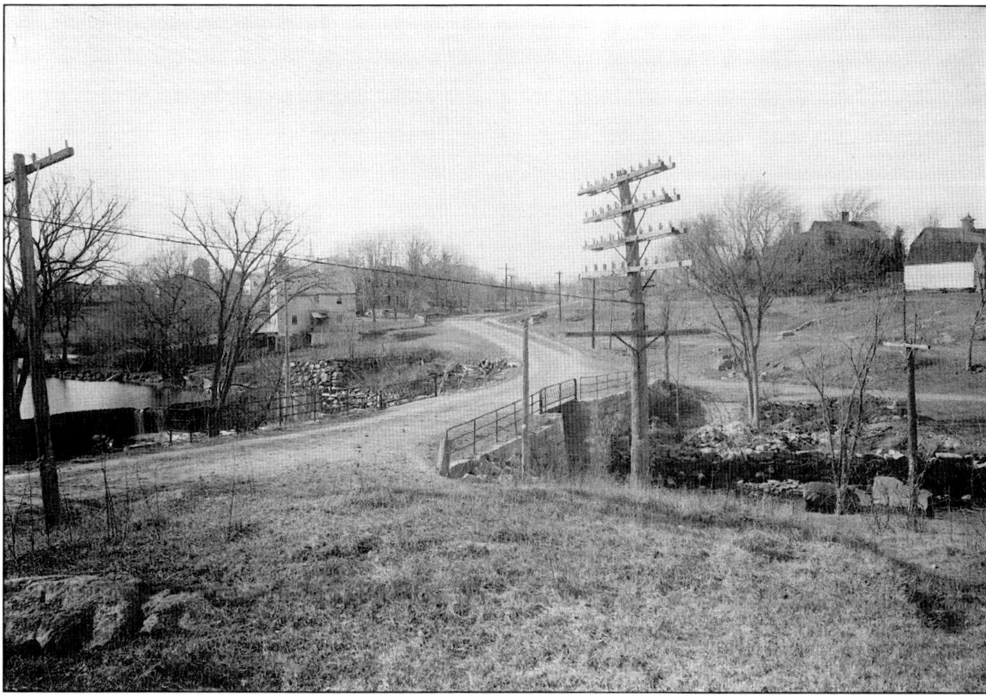

The Oyster River Bridge on Newmarket Road looking north, *c.* 1910. The Ffrost House and barn are on the hill to the right and the Runlett House is across the river on the left. The water tower on the Red Tower estate and the Community Church steeple are visible in the distance on the left.

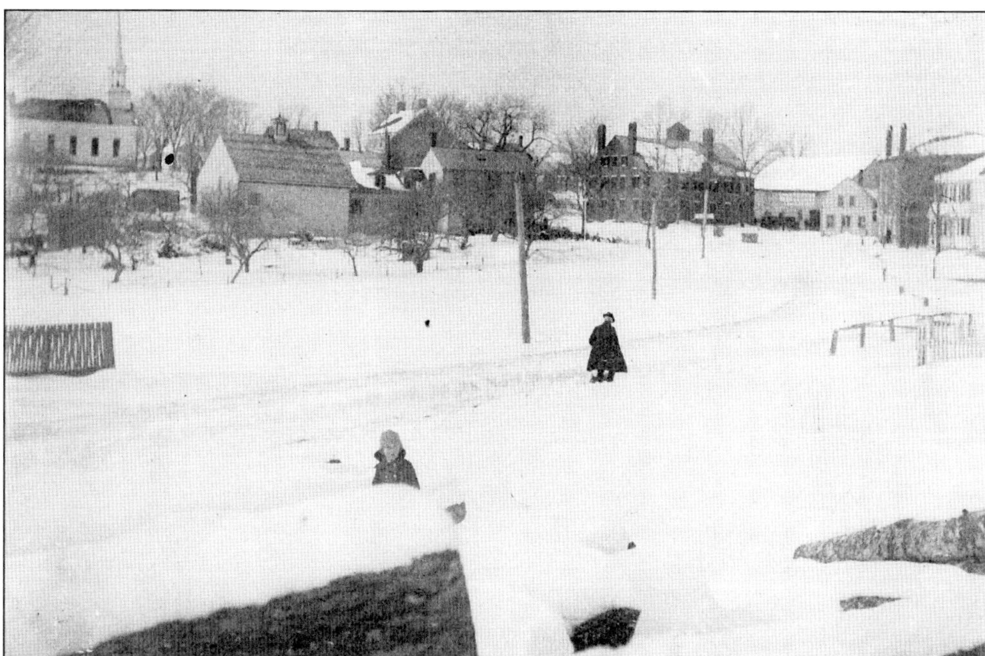

A view up Newmarket Road toward Durham Town Hall and the Oyster River Tavern from a spot just past the Oyster River Bridge, *c.* 1890. (Durham Historic Association.)

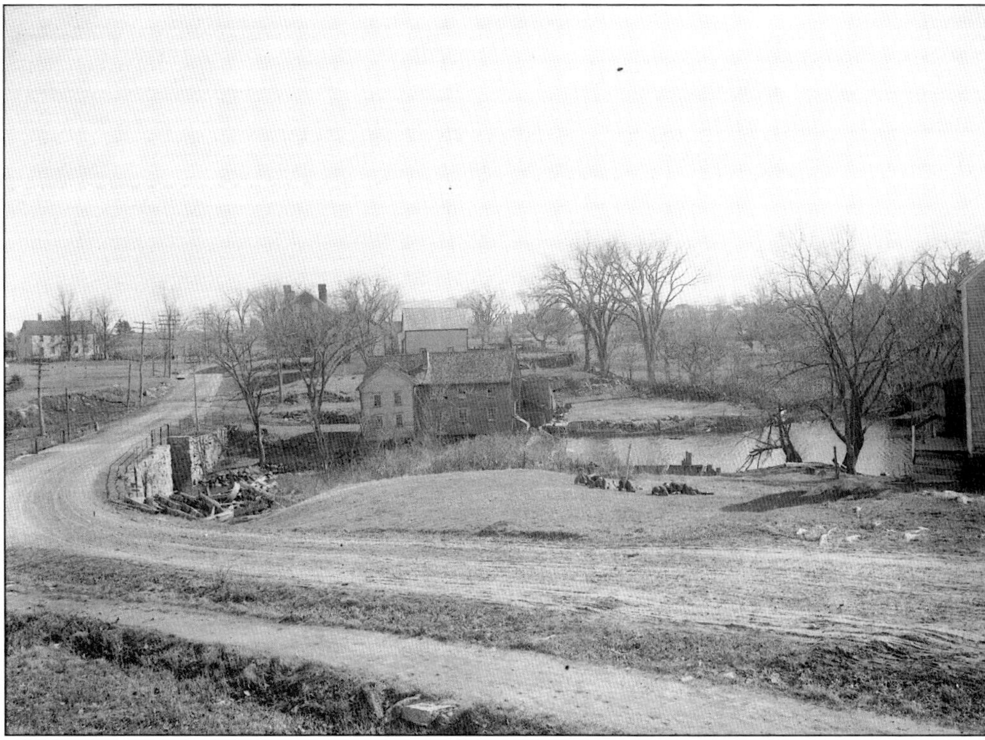

The Oyster River Bridge on Newmarket Road, looking toward Newmarket, *c.* 1910. The corner of the Runlett House is on the right. Jenkins Mill is across the river in the center, with the Winborn Adams Inn and the James Paul House behind it. The Sullivan Monument and the Sullivan House are across the road, on the left.

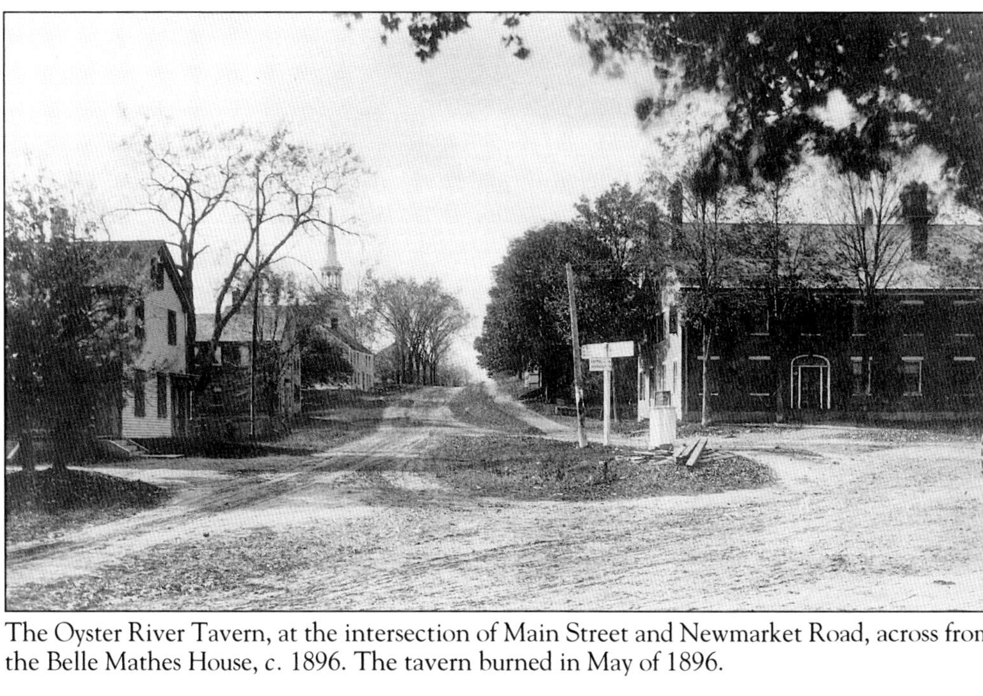

The Oyster River Tavern, at the intersection of Main Street and Newmarket Road, across from the Belle Mathes House, *c.* 1896. The tavern burned in May of 1896.

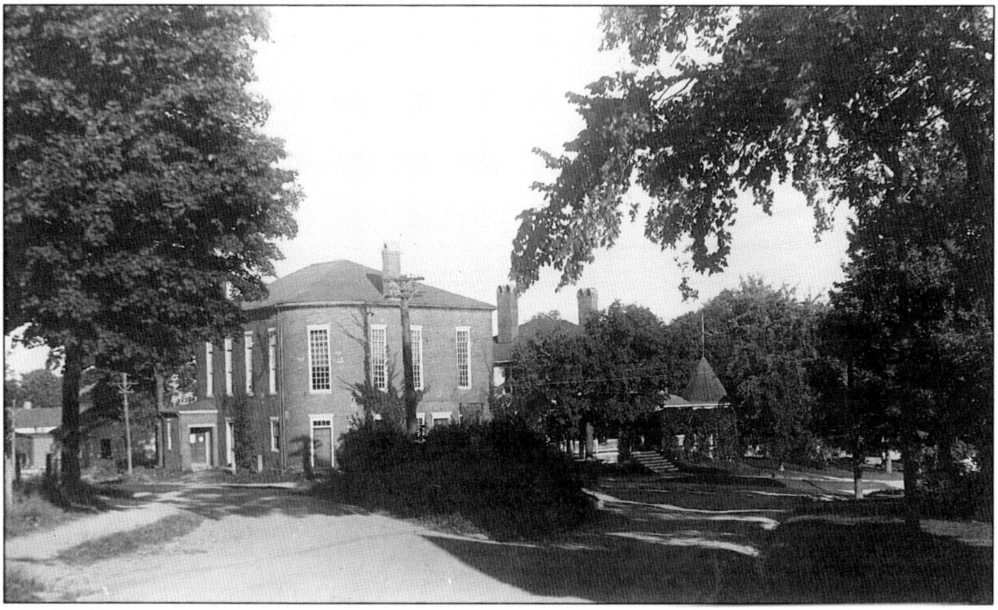

The Durham Town Hall, *c*. 1910. Built in 1825 by Joseph Coe, this building was purchased by the town in 1840.

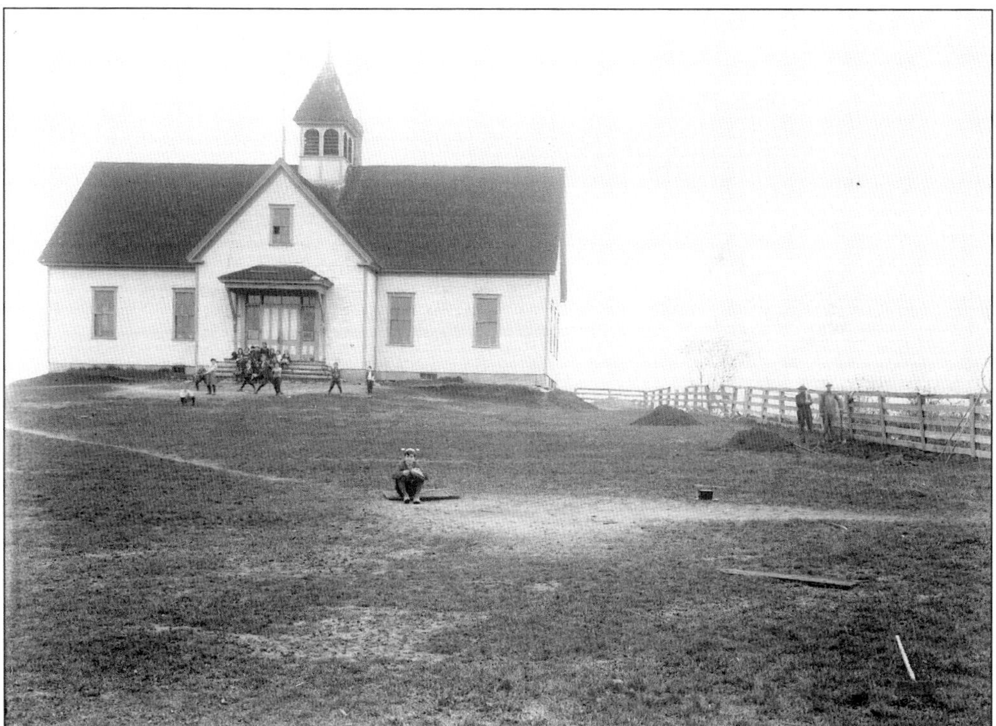

Children at play at the Village School, *c*. 1900. This school building was built in 1890.

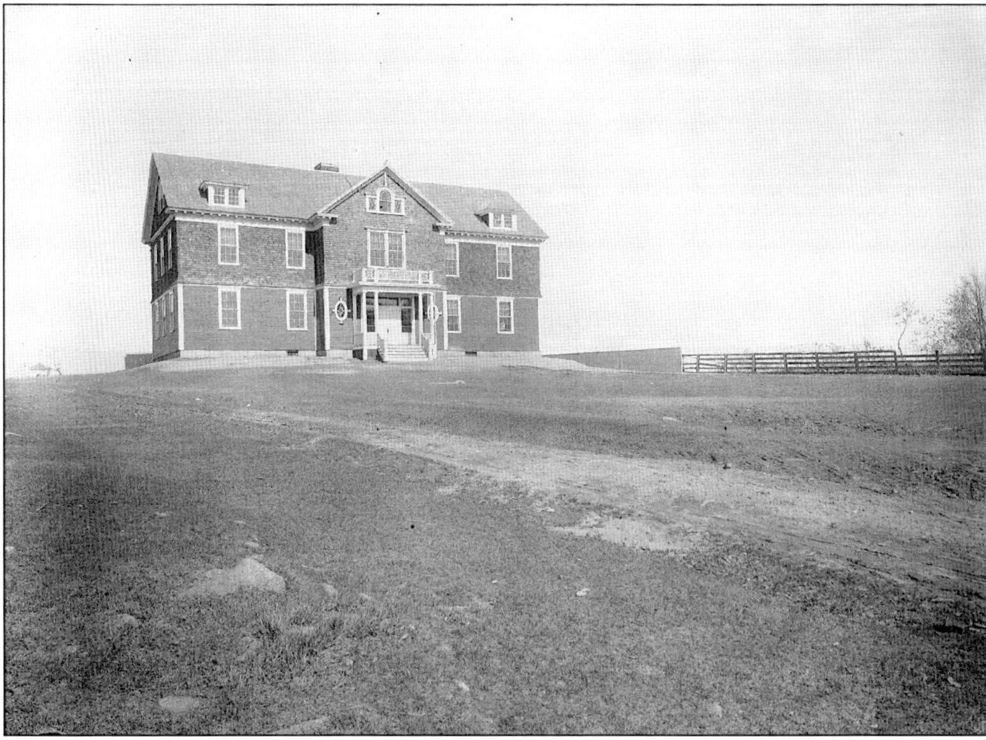

The Village School after the addition of a second story, *c.* 1917.

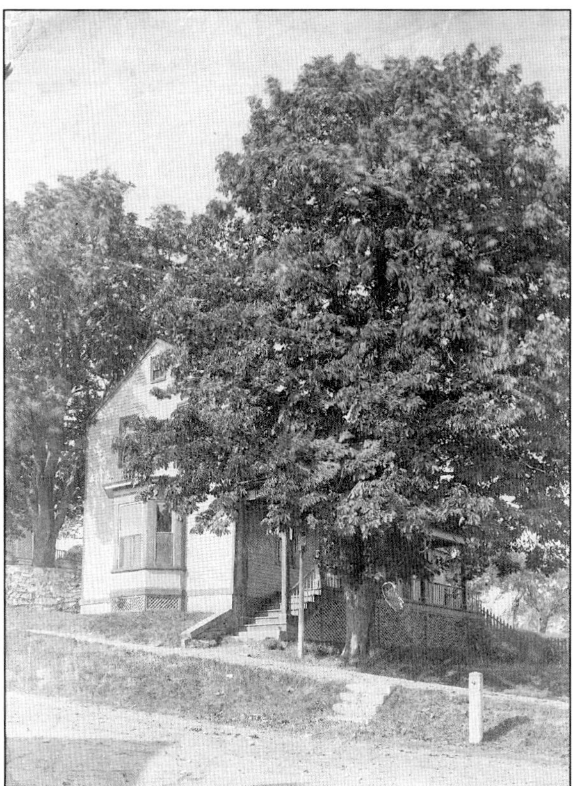

The Durham Public Library, *c.* 1893. In April 1893, the Durham Public Library opened in the Richardson Building on Main Street near the town hall. Miss Mary E. Smith was the librarian. The library remained in this location until it merged with the college library and was moved into the Hamilton Smith Library in the winter of 1907–1908.

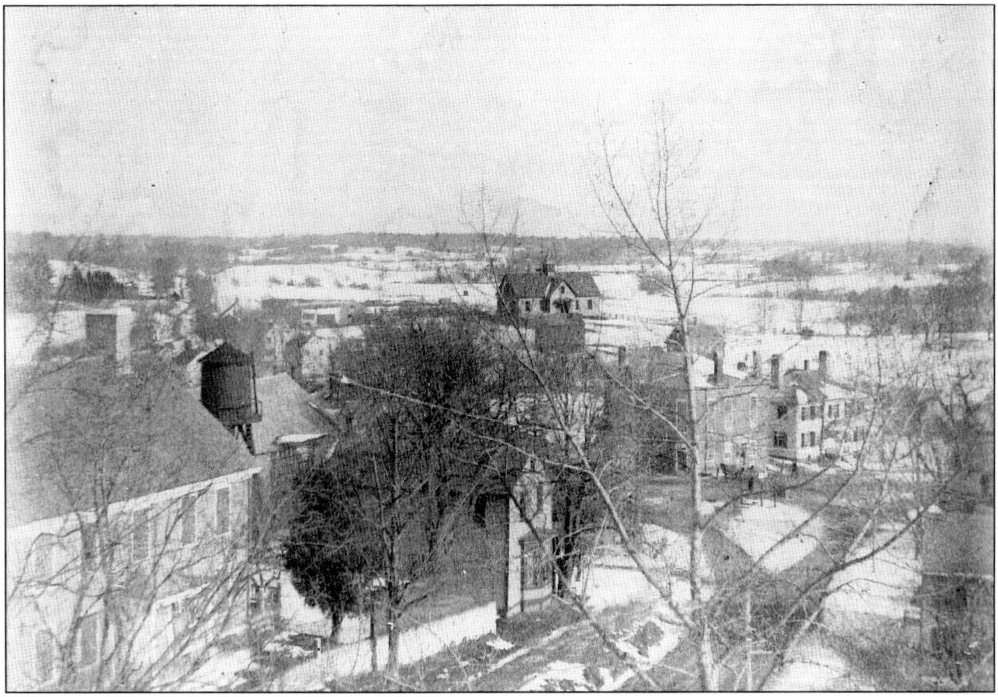

Lower Main Street at the New Market Road intersection, *c.* 1895. The Richardson Building housing the Durham Public Library is in the center foreground. The town hall is across the intersection on the eastern side of Newmarket Road. The Village School is on the hill behind the town hall. (Durham Historic Association.)

The Community Church, *c.* 1892. This structure was built in 1848 by the Congregational Society. It served as the fourth home of the society in Durham, and for many years was the only church building in the town.

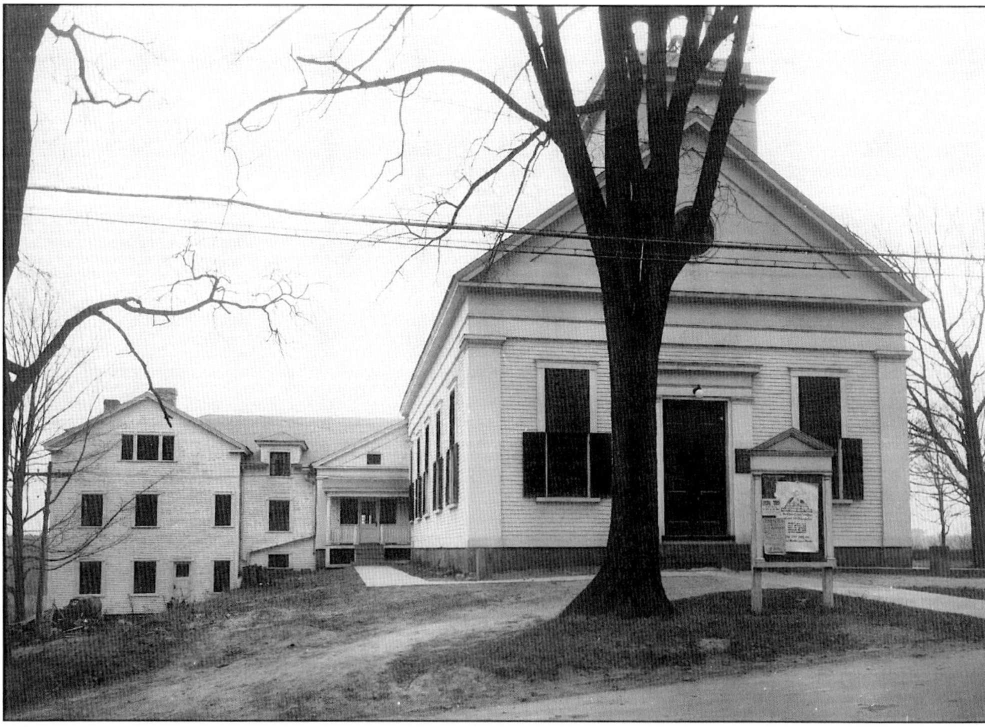

The Community Church, after the addition of an auditorium, January 1, 1924.

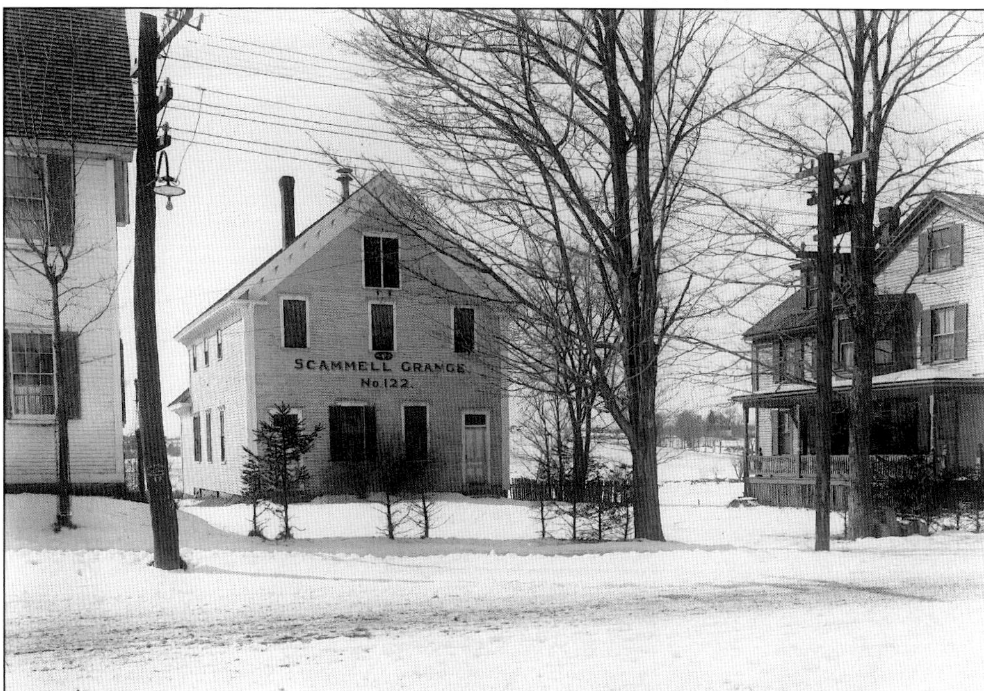

The Scammell Grange, *c.* 1918. In 1893, the Scammell Grange No. 122 purchased the old schoolhouse on Main Street for use as a Grange hall.

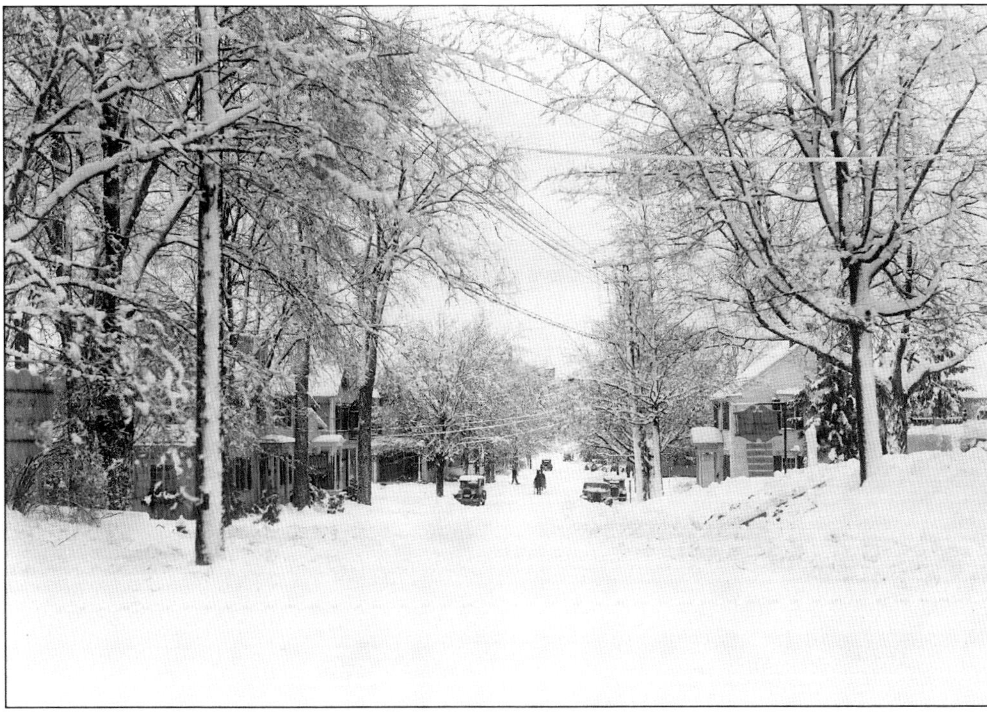

Main Street looking northwest from near Red Tower, *c.* 1935.

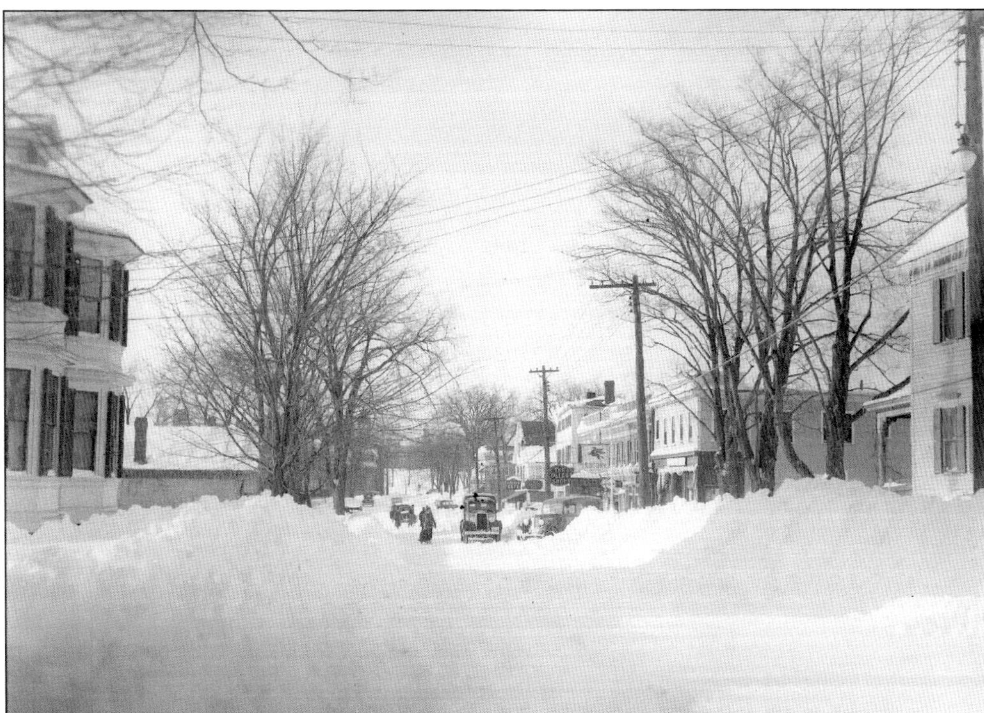

Main Street looking northwest from the Madbury Road intersection, *c.* 1935.

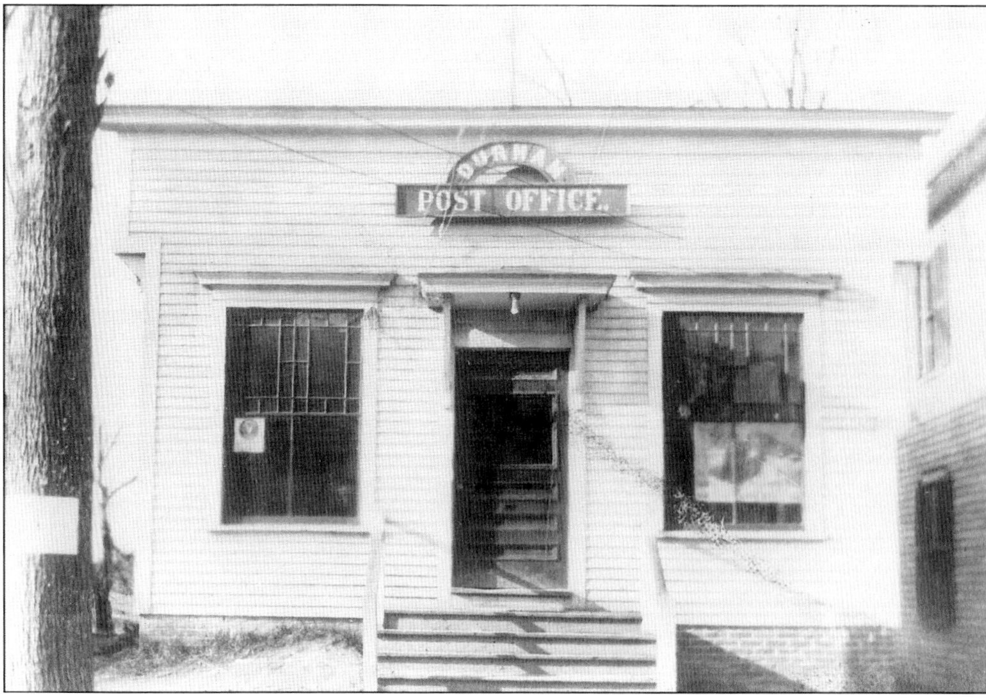

The first Durham Post Office building, *c.* 1907. Prior to 1907, the post office was located in a variety of homes and stores along Main Street. In 1907 it moved into this building on the south side of Main Street, near the Madbury Road intersection. The building was built specifically to house the post office. (Durham Historic Association.)

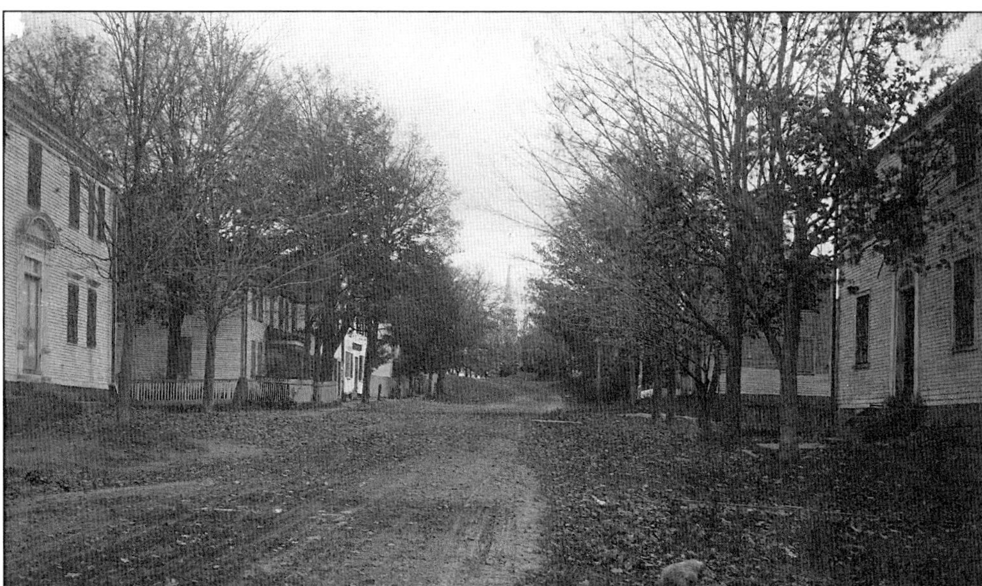

The Main Street and Madbury Road intersection, *c.* 1895. The Ballard House and the Benjamin Thompson House (with fence) are at left; the Community Church is in the center.

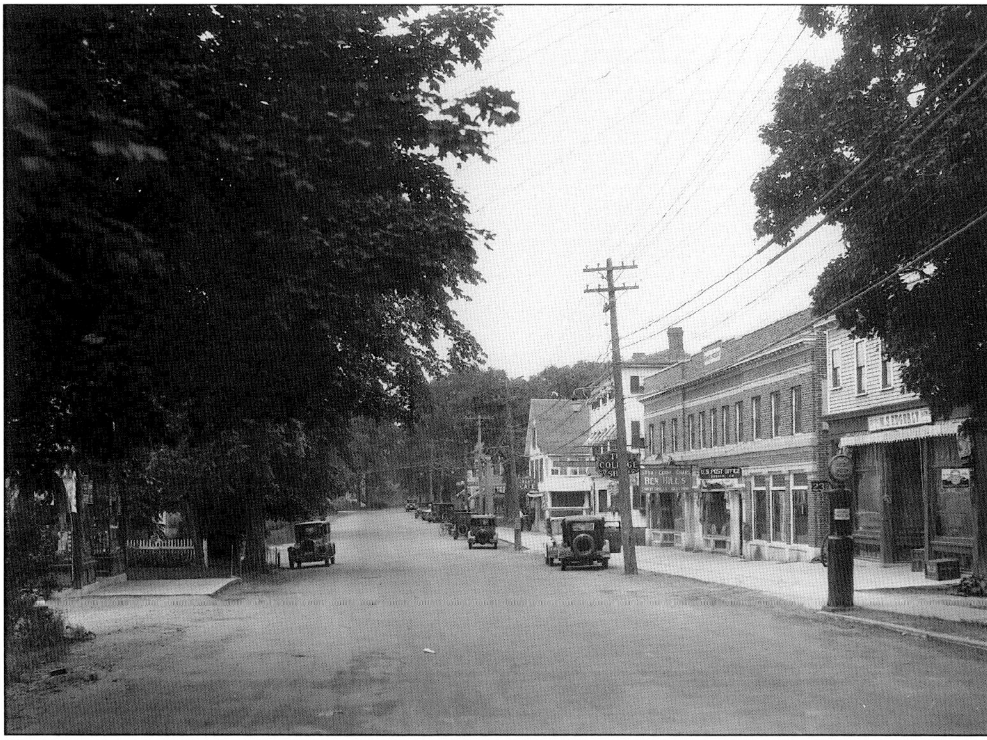

Main Street looking northwest, 1928.

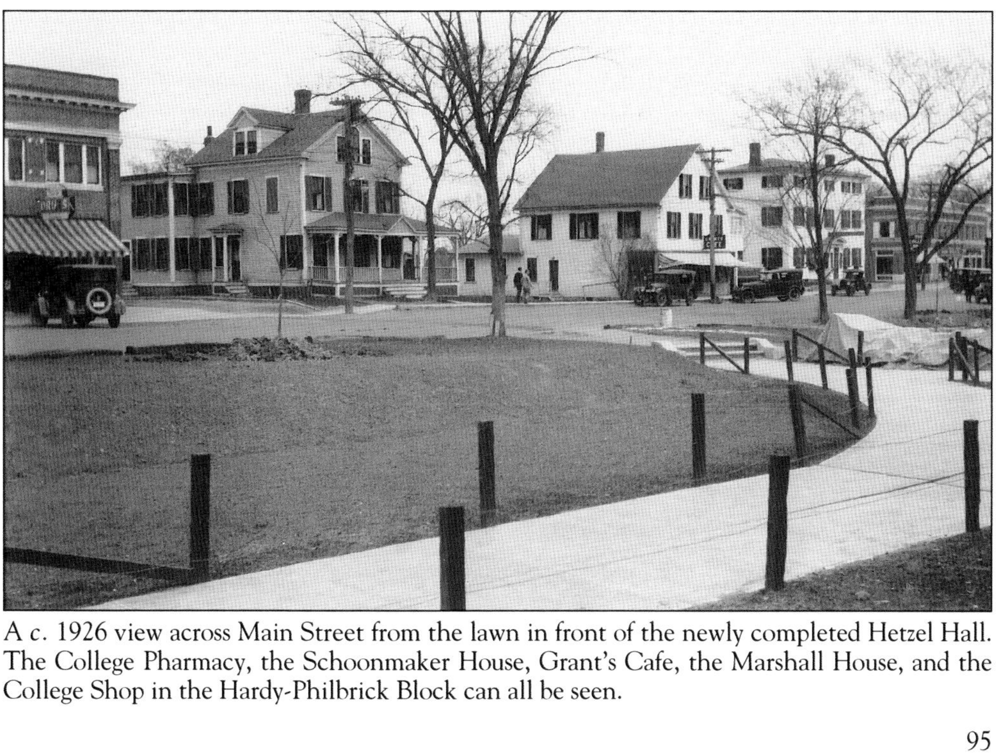

A c. 1926 view across Main Street from the lawn in front of the newly completed Hetzel Hall. The College Pharmacy, the Schoonmaker House, Grant's Cafe, the Marshall House, and the College Shop in the Hardy-Philbrick Block can all be seen.

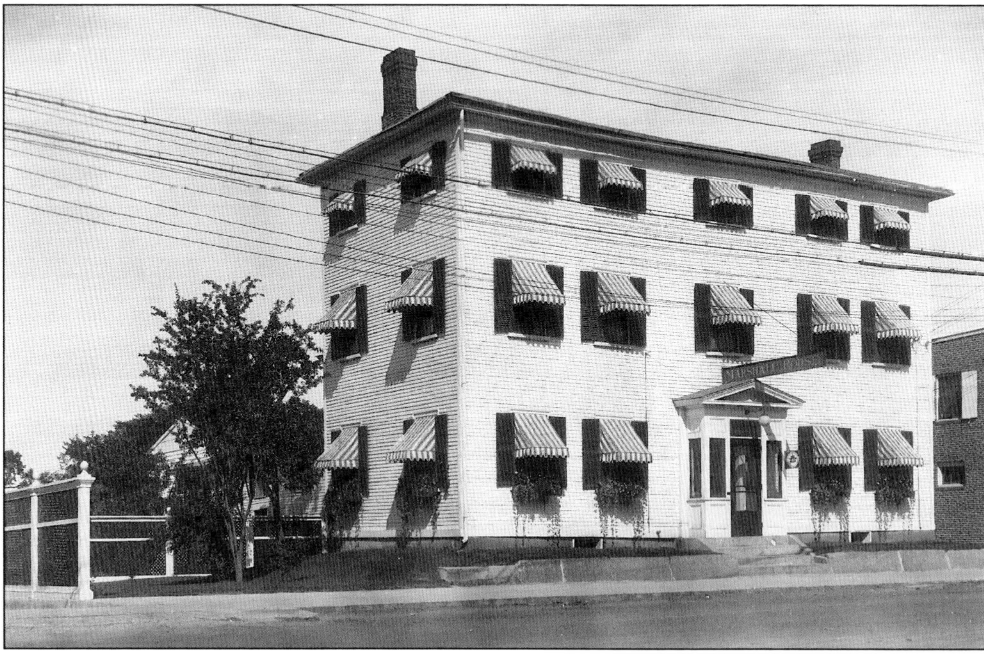

The Marshall House, 1926. Built in 1806 and originally owned by Stephen Mitchell, this building was a private residence until *c.* 1895. Over the years it housed various businesses, served as a boarding house, and was known as the College Inn, the Hotel, and the Hi-Hat-Club.

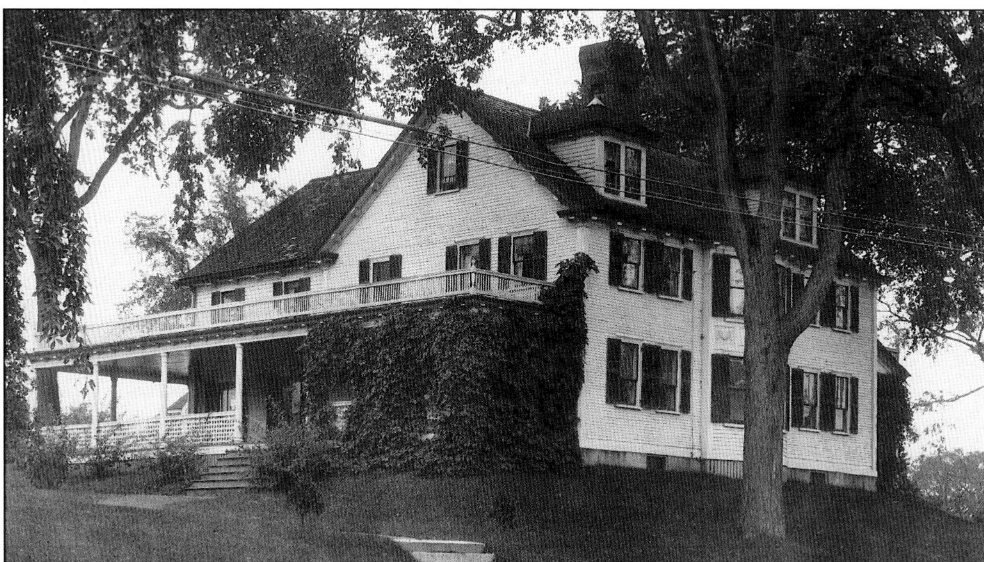

Professor Charles Parsons' House on Main Street, *c.* 1911. This house is thought to have been built by Daniel Mathes around 1806. In 1912, Professor Parsons, an award-winning chemistry professor, resigned from his position at the college. His letter of resignation indicated that the main reason for his leaving was the governor's veto of a bill for a new engineering building at the college. He felt his research would suffer without the new facility. When Professor Parsons left the college his house was purchased by the Gamma Theta fraternity. Gamma Theta later became Alpha Tau Omega.

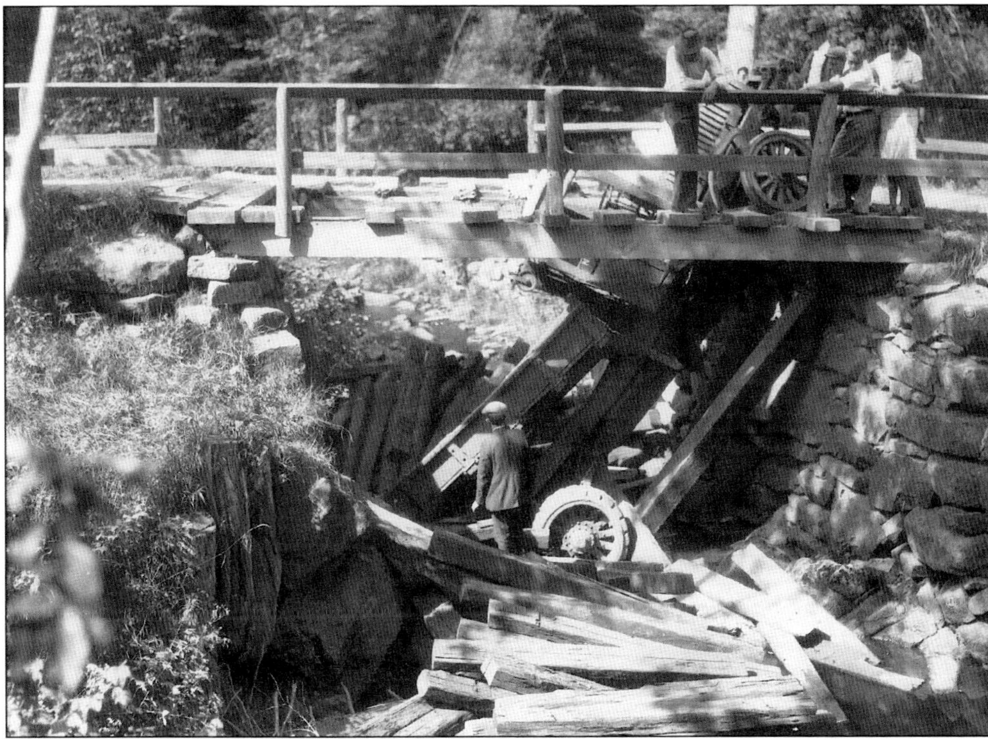

An accident on Mill Road, *c.* 1926. A state highway truck transporting railroad ties broke through the bridge over the Oyster River on Mill Road. (Durham Historic Association.)

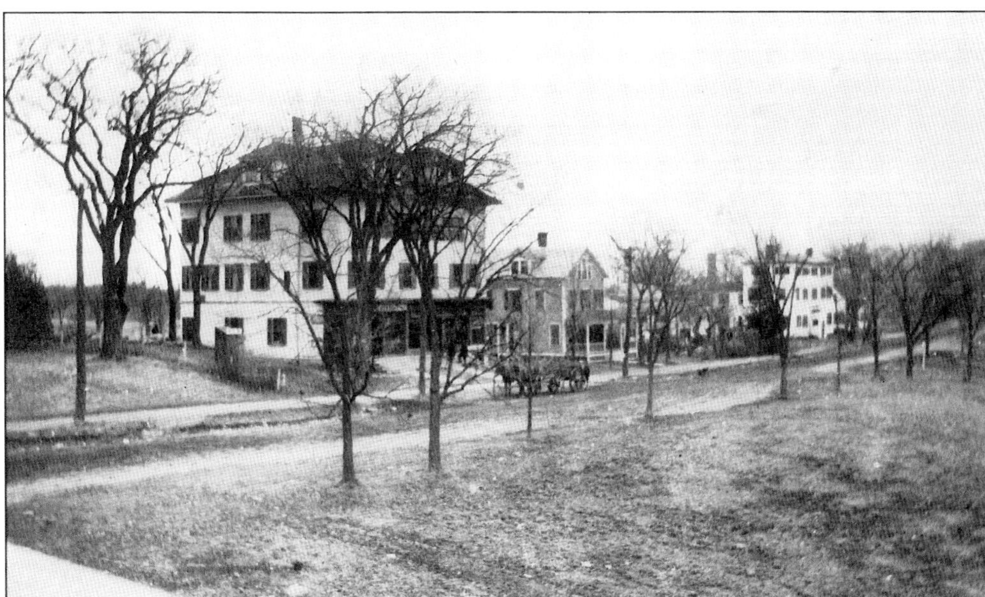

The Pettee Block, *c.* 1910. George Whitcher built this four-story building on Main Street in 1897. Some rooms on the top floors were rented to students to help alleviate the student housing shortage. Whitcher sold the building to Dean Charles H. Pettee in 1900, after which the building was known as the Pettee Block. (Durham Historic Association.)

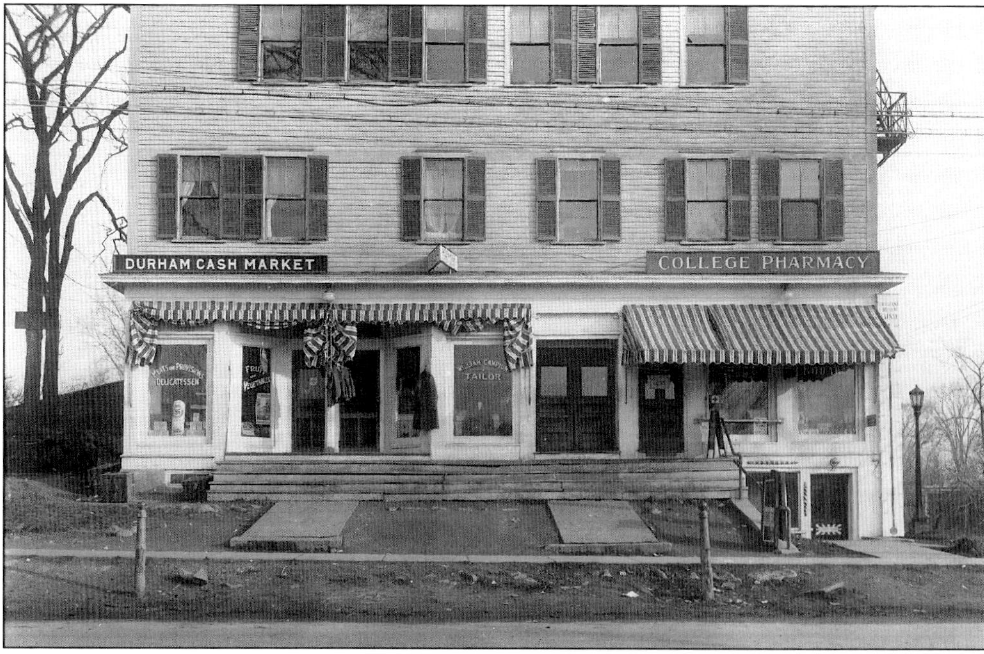

The Pettee Block, *c.* 1920. The main floor and basement of the Pettee Block housed various businesses over the years. W.S. Edgerly's general store was located in this building for a time and was the site of Durham's first ice-cream parlor. At the time of this photograph, the main floor housed the Durham Cash Market, William Campion's Tailor Shop and the College Pharmacy. A barber shop was in the basement.

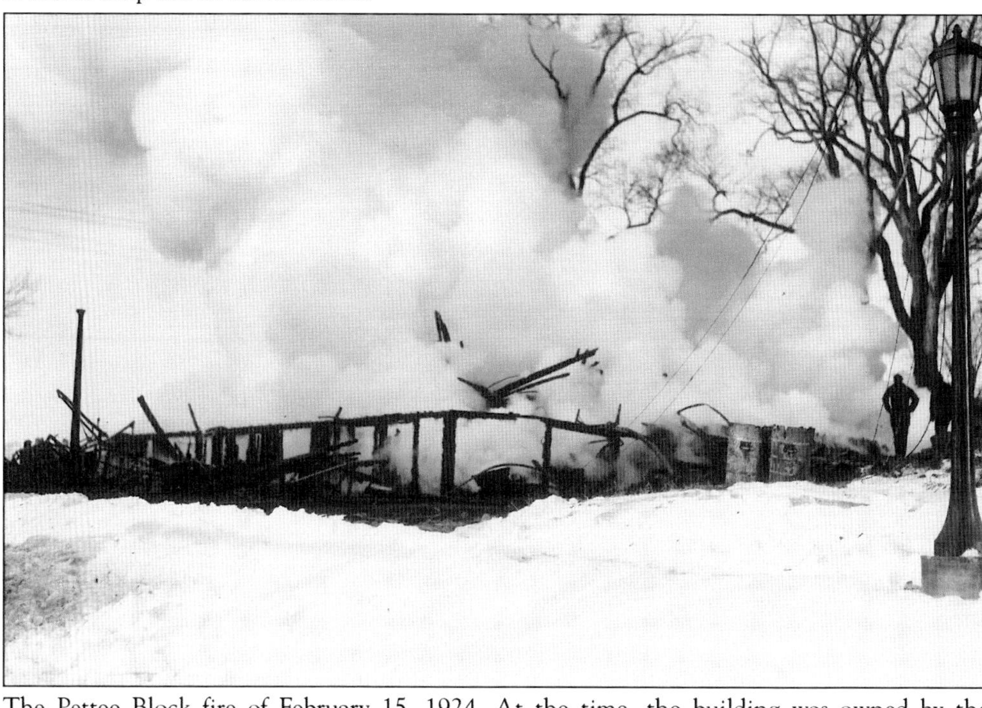

The Pettee Block fire of February 15, 1924. At the time, the building was owned by the proprietors of the College Pharmacy, brothers James and Joseph Gorman.

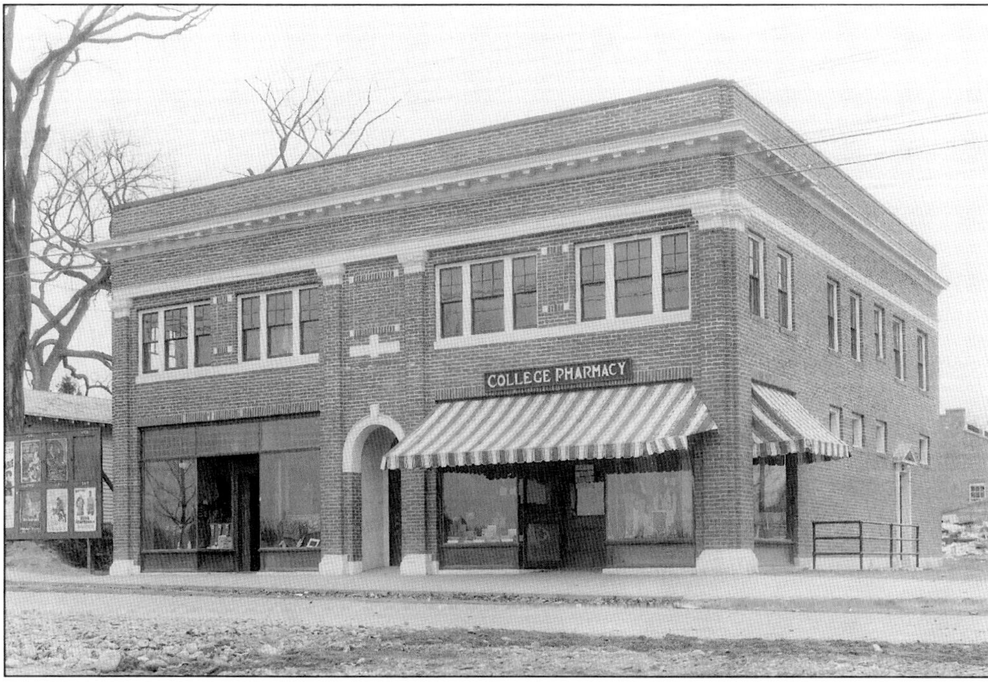

The Gorman Block, c. 1924. The Gorman brothers hired Eric T. Huddleston to design a building to replace the Pettee Block. The College Pharmacy reopened in its new home and the building became known as the Gorman Block.

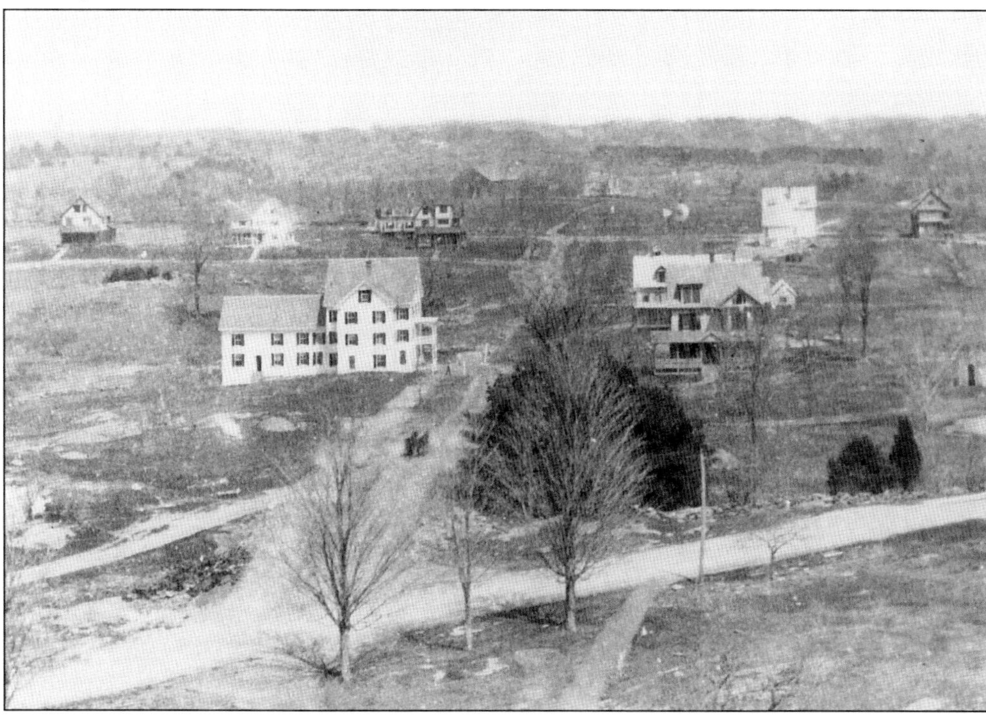

A view up Garrison Avenue from its intersection with Main Street, 1897. Ballard Hall is on the left; Dr. A.E. Grant's house is on the right.

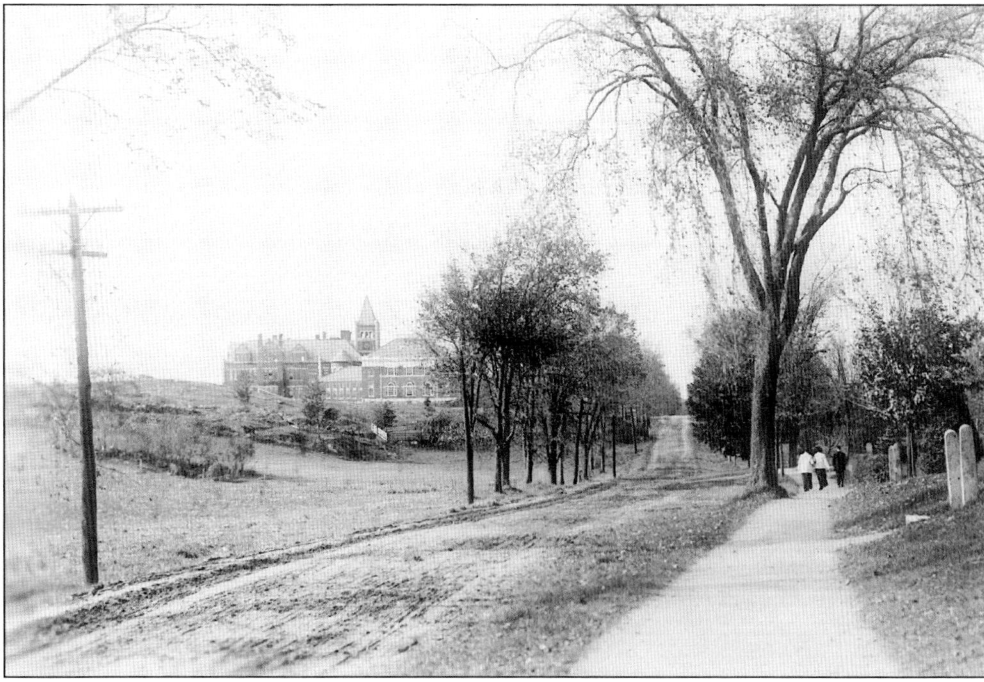

Main Street looking toward campus and the Ballard Street intersection, *c.* 1910. Thompson Hall and the Hamilton Smith Library are at the top of the hill on the left. By 1925, the area to the left of Main Street, leading up to the library, would be the site of three dormitories and the Kappa Sigma fraternity house.

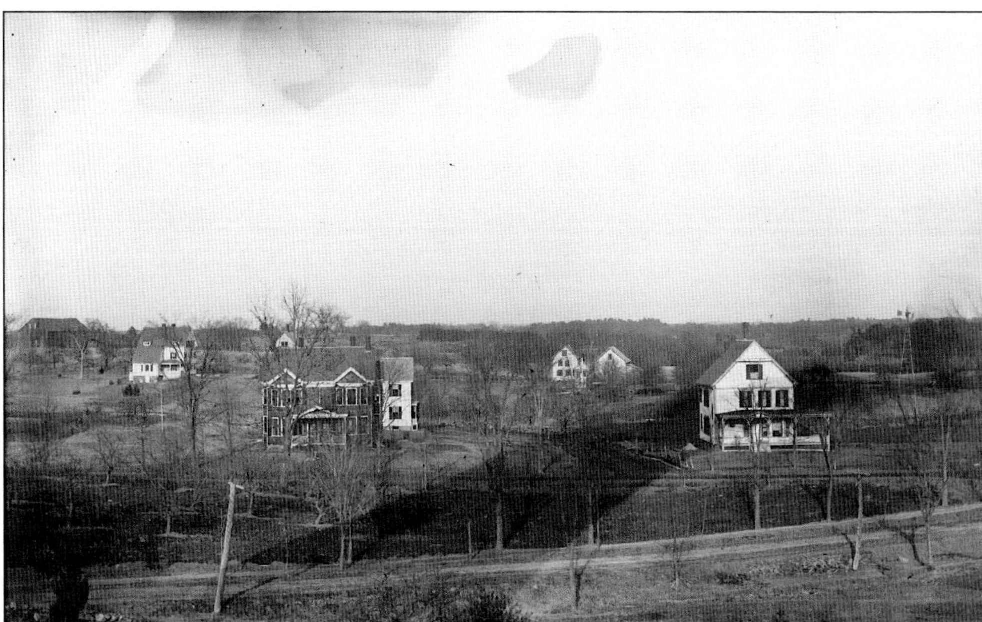

The intersection of Main and Ballard Streets, *c.* 1904.

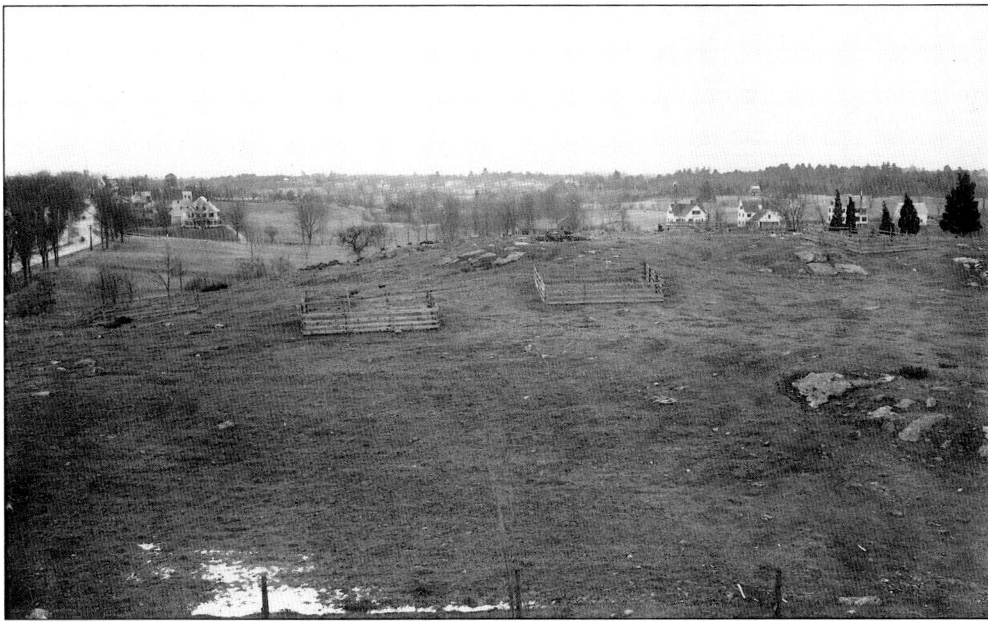

Looking southeast, *c.* 1894, from Thompson Hall toward the town prior to the construction of Fairchild Hall, Hetzel Hall, the Commons, the Kappa Sigma house, and the Hamilton Smith Library. The water tower on the Hamilton Smith estate, and the Community Church steeple are visible in the distance at left.

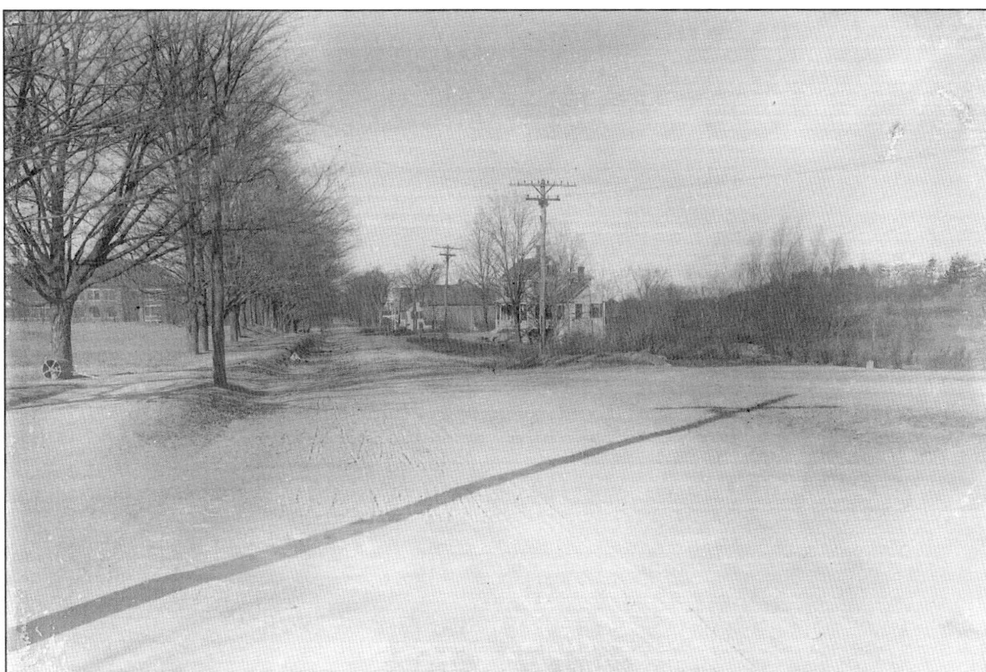

Looking northwest along Main Street from the Garrison Avenue intersection. The "Orphanage" is on the right. The Meserve barn, Runlett's store, and the Gymnasium are in the distance on the right; Morrill Hall is on the left.

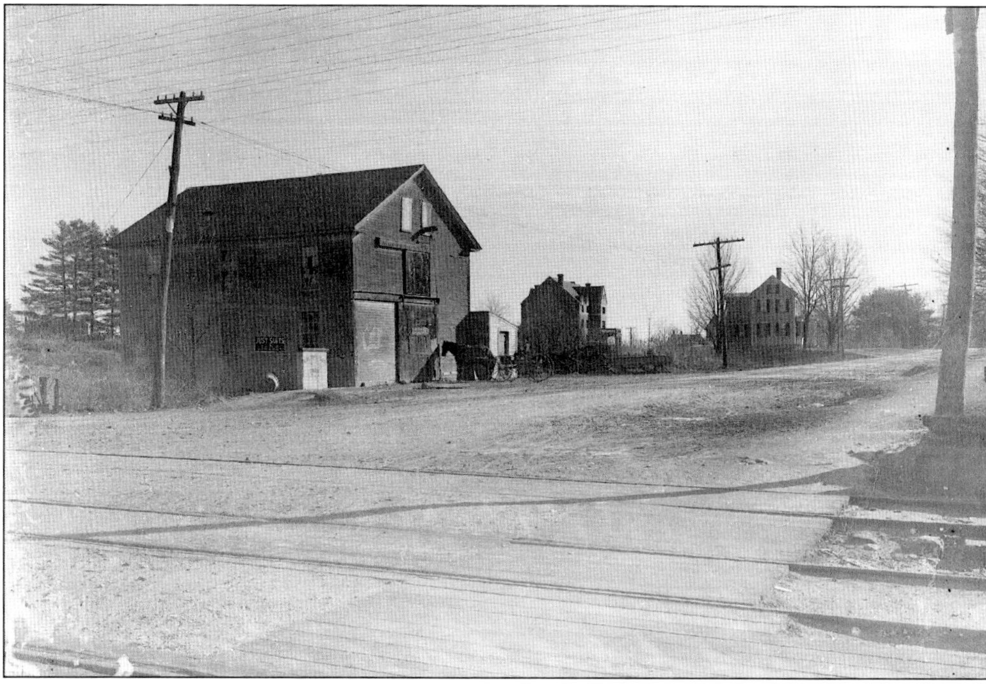

Looking southeast along Main Street from the Boston & Maine railroad tracks, *c.* 1908. The Meserve barn is at left. The house further up Main Street to the right of the picture was used by the college for various purposes. For a time it was known as the "Orphanage" and was used as a dormitory. It also served as a practice house for Home Economics. Smith Hall is in the background, behind the "Orphanage."

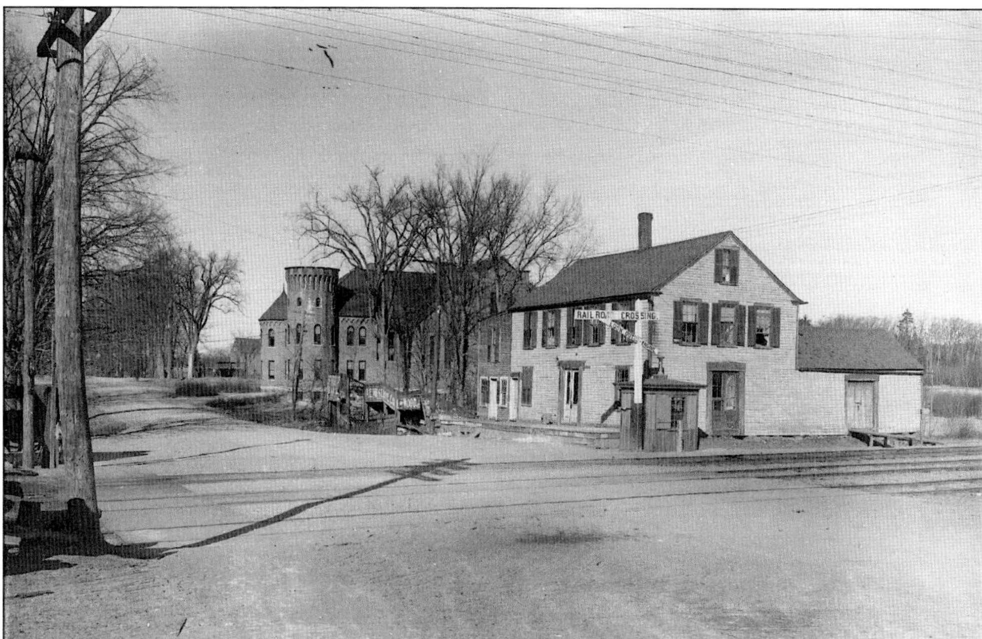

Runlett's store and the Gymnasium at the intersection of Main Street and the Boston & Maine Railroad, *c.* 1906.

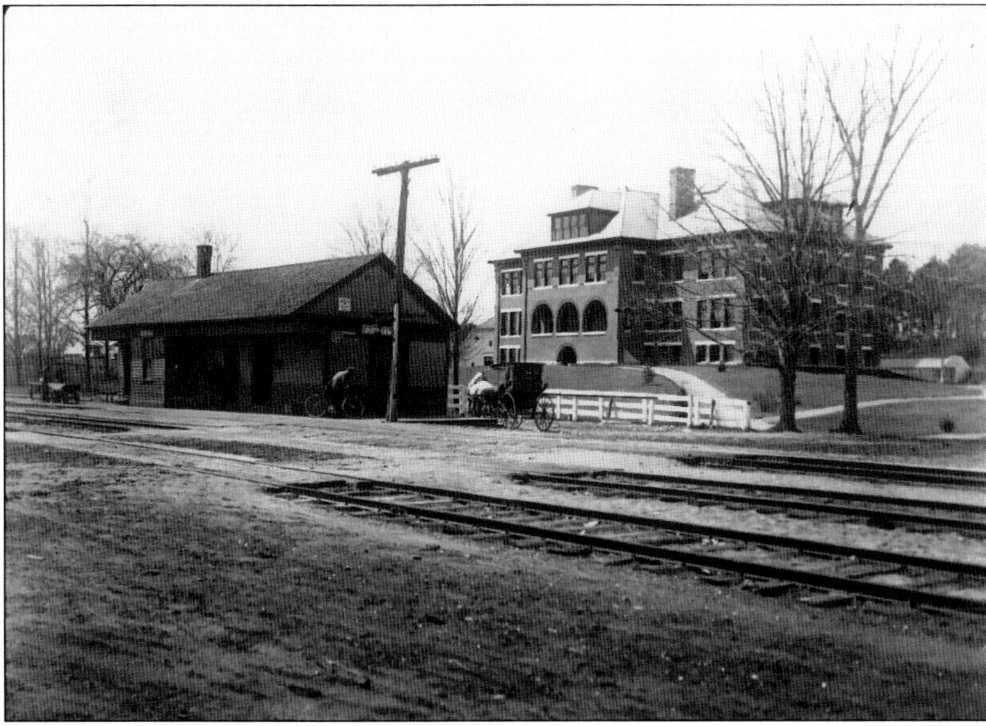

The Boston & Maine Railroad station and Morrill Hall, *c.* 1902.

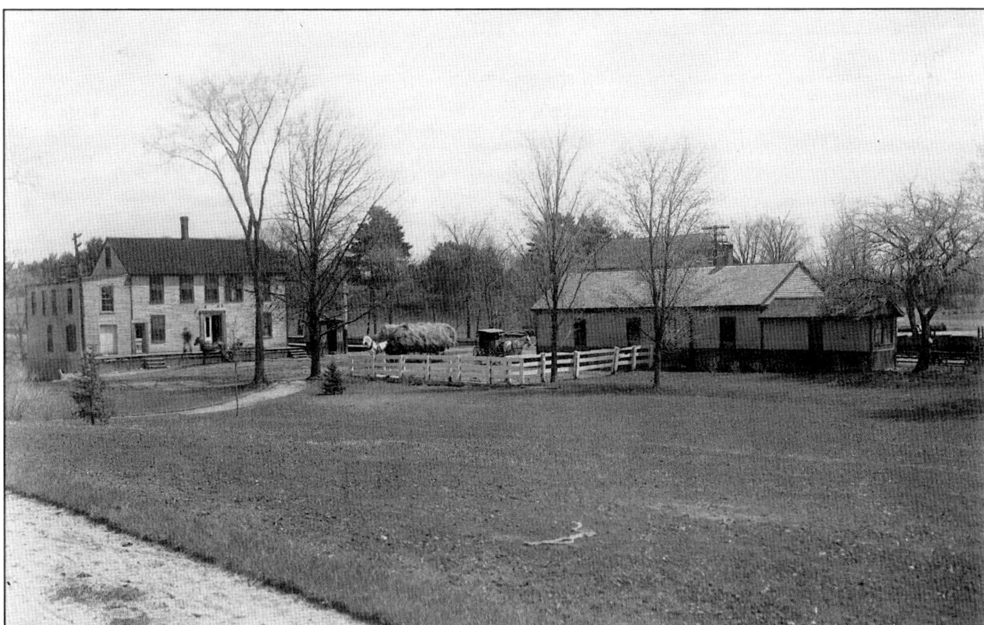

Runlett's store at left, and the Boston & Maine Railroad station at the intersection of the railroad and Main Street, *c.* 1905. When the Boston & Maine tracks were moved in 1912, the station house was moved to a lot near the corner of Main Street and Mill Road, and Sam Runlett relocated his store there. His original store building was moved from its spot near the old tracks to a location on Ballard Street and became the original Tin Palace Restaurant.

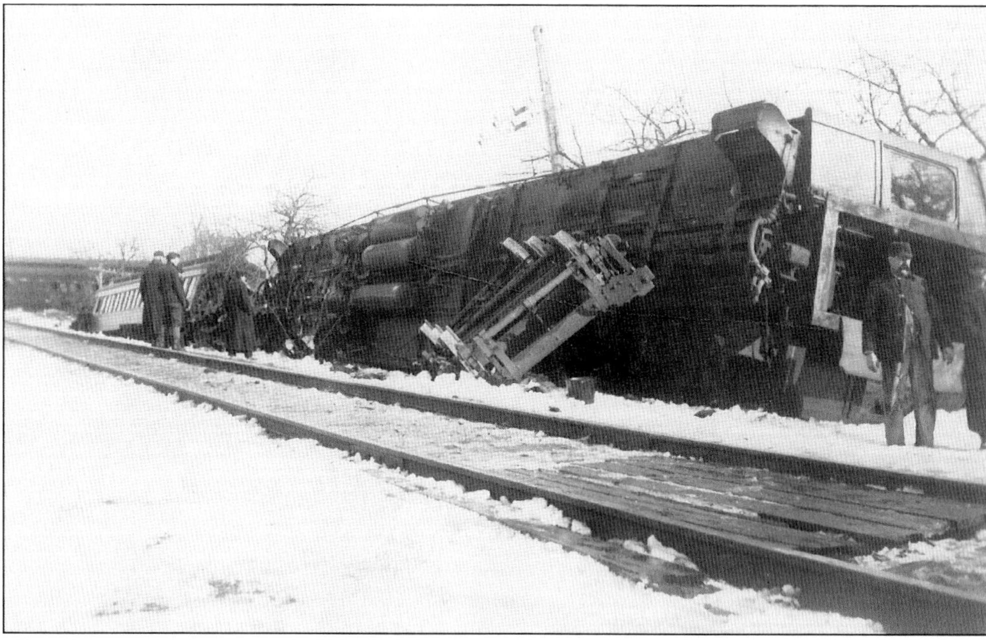

The wreck of the St. John's express, 1905. As the St. John's express, a passenger train, was going through Durham, at 7:40 am on January 20, 1905, a defect in the tracks near the college machine shop caused the last four cars of the eight-car train to derail. Three of the four cars overturned. Eighty-five passengers were on the train. Students helped the passengers from the wreckage and transported the injured to Dr. A.E. Grant's house on Garrison Avenue, and to a fraternity house where they were cared for until a train arrived from Dover carrying additional doctors and nurses.One report indicated that only eleven or so were badly hurt.

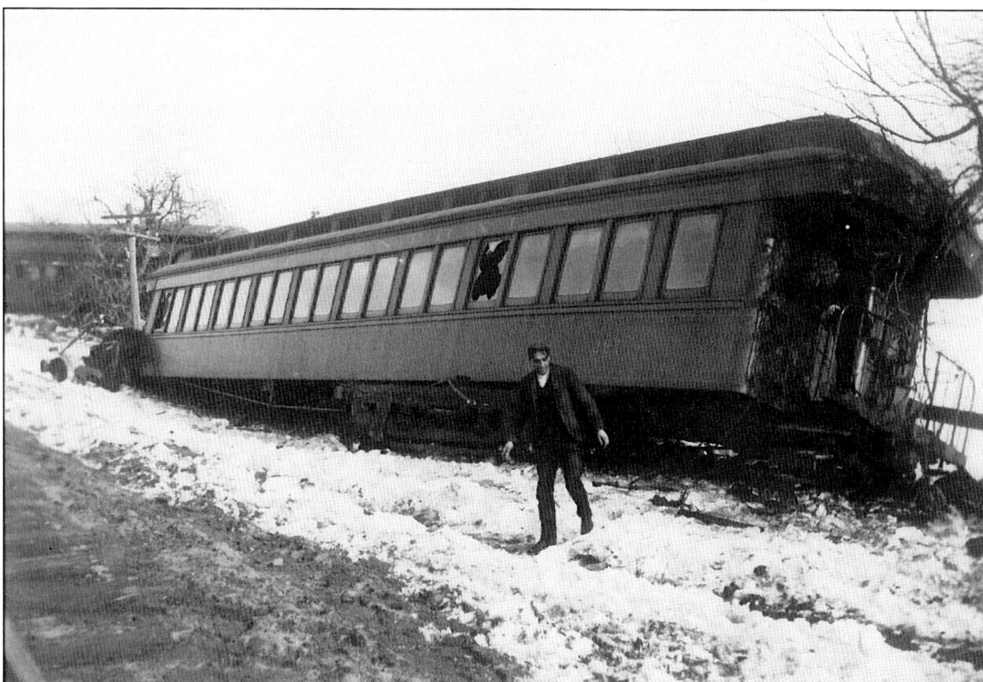

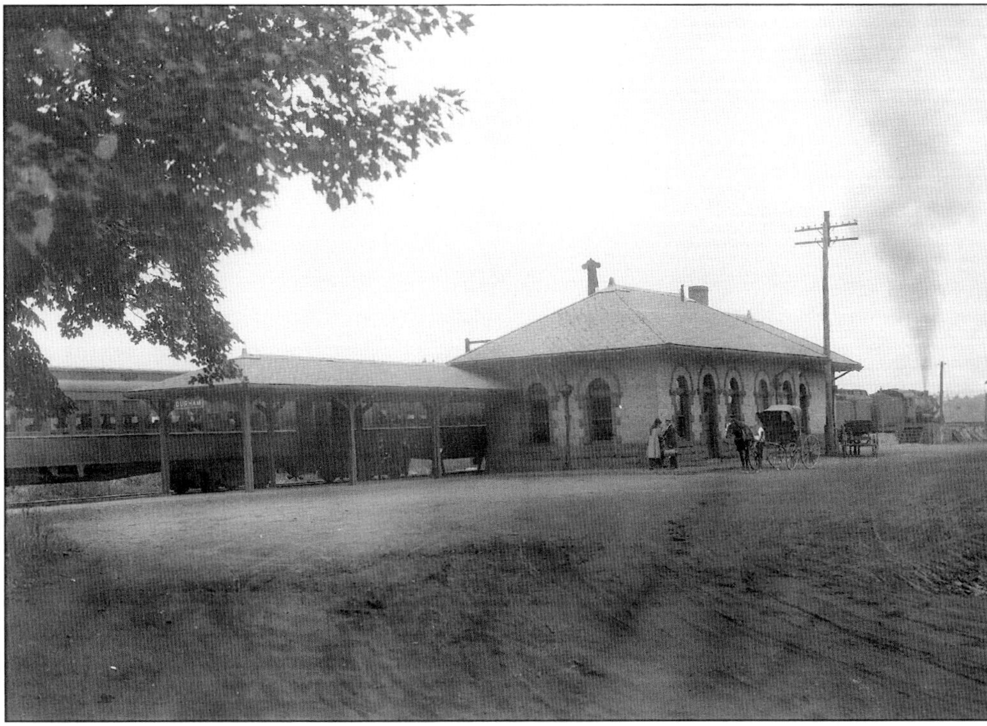

The Boston & Maine Railroad station, *c.* 1920. Originally built in Lynn, Massachusetts, *c.* 1896, this station was moved to Durham when the Boston & Maine tracks were moved in 1912.

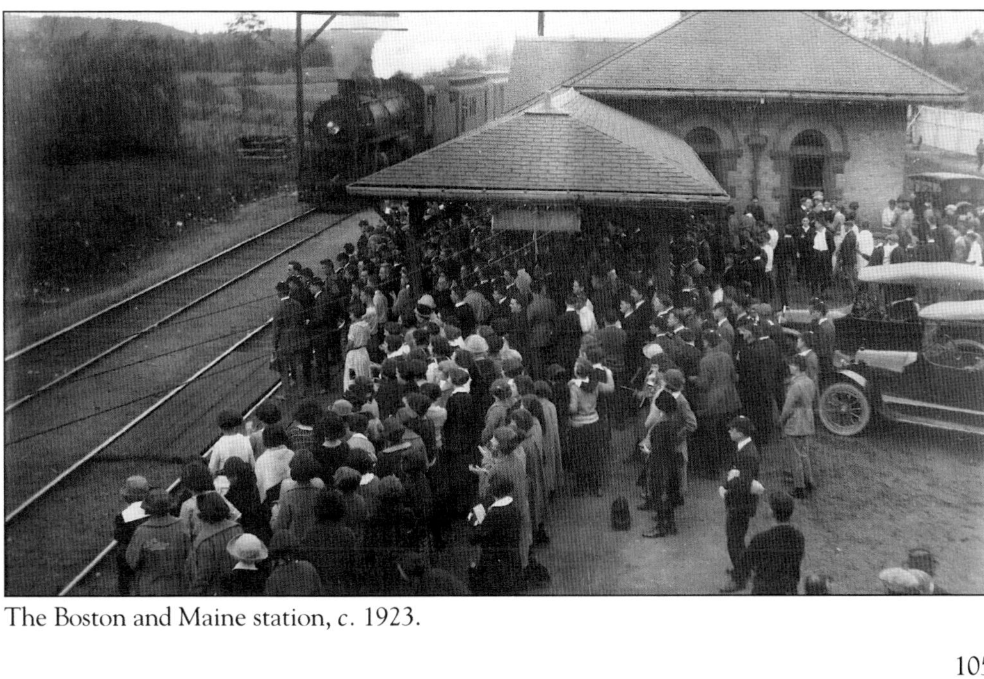

The Boston and Maine station, *c.* 1923.

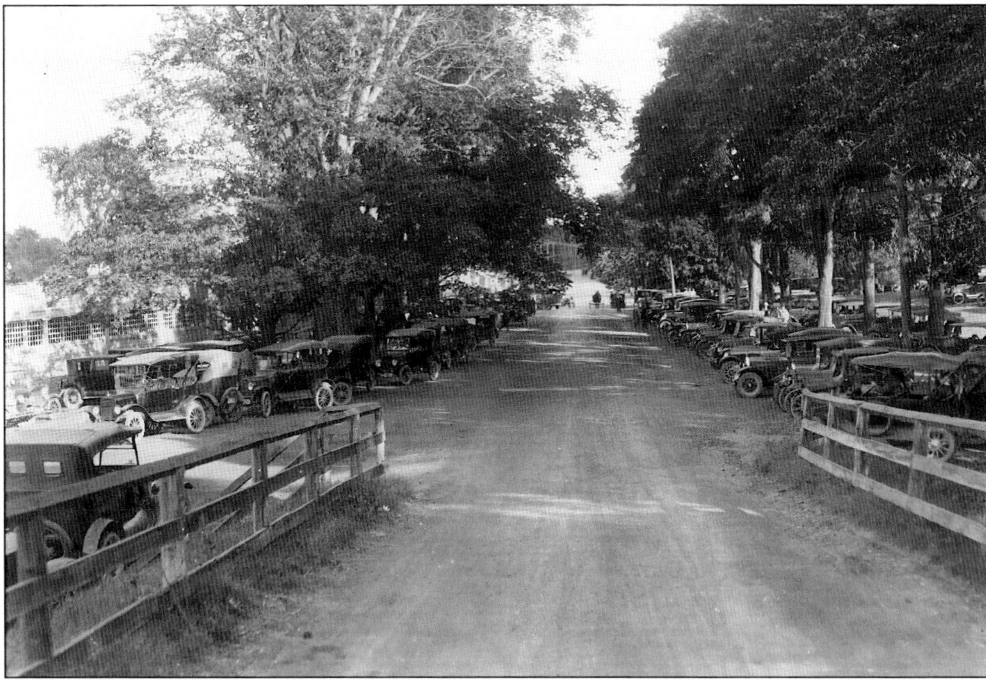

Cars parked along Main Street, near Memorial Field and the railroad overpass, during Farmers' and Home-Makers' Week, August 25–28, 1928.

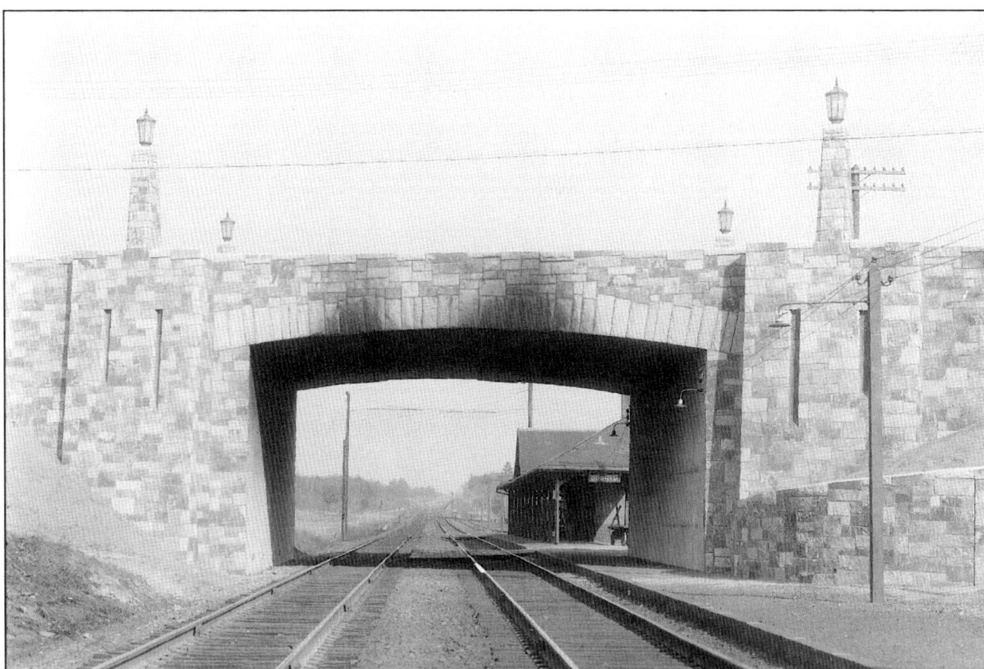

The new Boston & Maine Railroad overpass, shown here shortly after it was completed in 1936.

Five

Faces in the Crowd

Durham's history began a full two centuries prior to the development of modern photographic processes. Nevertheless, from the 1840s onward, there is an increasingly rich photographic record of Durham residents and the diverse lives they had. This concluding chapter contains a cross-section of such photographs, ranging from formal portraits and images of ceremonial occasions to glimpses of day-to-day life.

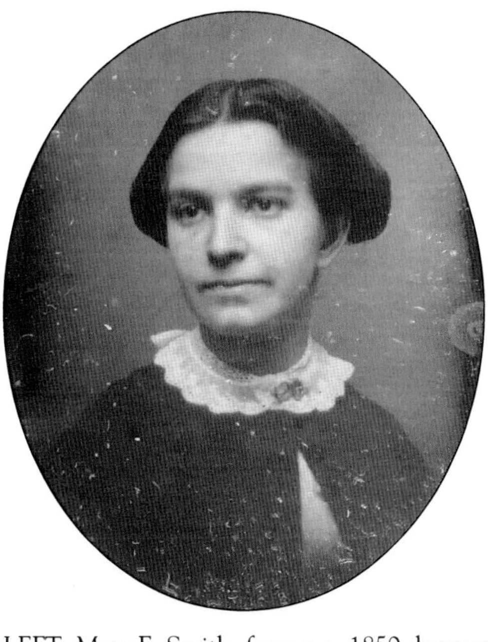

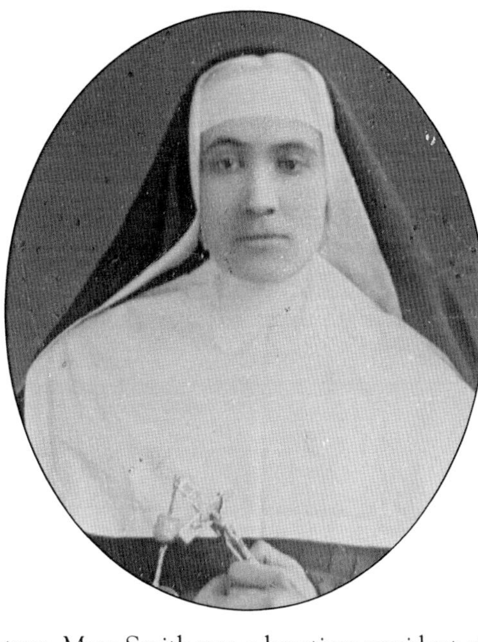

LEFT: Mary E. Smith, from a *c.* 1850 daguerreotype. Mary Smith was a longtime president of the Durham Library Association and organist at the Durham Congregational Church.
RIGHT: Mary Pickering Thompson, in an 1856 photograph taken in Toulouse, France. Mary Thompson was born in Durham in 1825 to Ebenezar and Jane Demeritt Thompson. Following her graduation from the Mt. Holyoke Female Seminary, she converted to Roman Catholicism and became an Ursuline nun. When she returned to Durham years later, she shifted her attention to local history and genealogy.

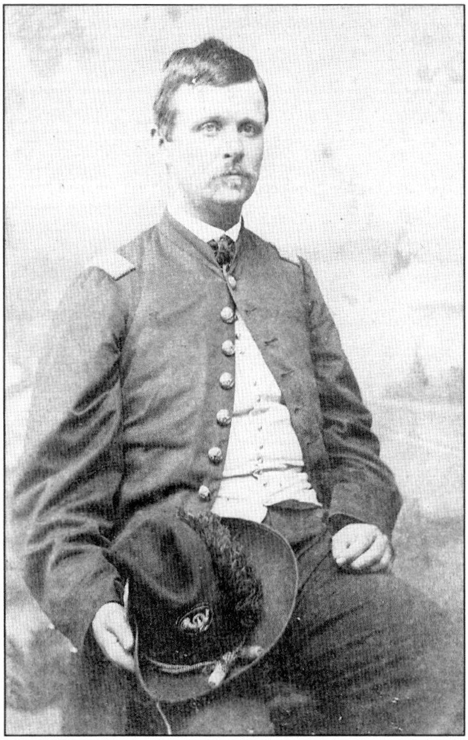

LEFT: Captain Enoch George Adams, son of John "Reformation John" Adams of Adams Point, 1865. Adams served as sergeant in Company D of the Second New Hampshire Regiment. He was wounded at both Williamsburg (1862) and Gettysburg (1863). Afterwards, he became a captain in the First U.S. Volunteers and fought against the Sioux in the Dakota Territory.

BOTTOM LEFT: Samuel Stevens, a native of Durham, from a tintype taken in 1863. Stevens served as a wagoner in Company H of the Sixth New Hampshire Regiment. (Durham Historic Association.)

BOTTOM RIGHT: Durham native George P. Doeg, *c.* 1910. At the age of twenty, Doeg enlisted in Company D of the Third New Hampshire Regiment. He was wounded in the ill-fated charge on Fort Wagner in July 1863 and discharged four months later. (Durham Historic Association.)

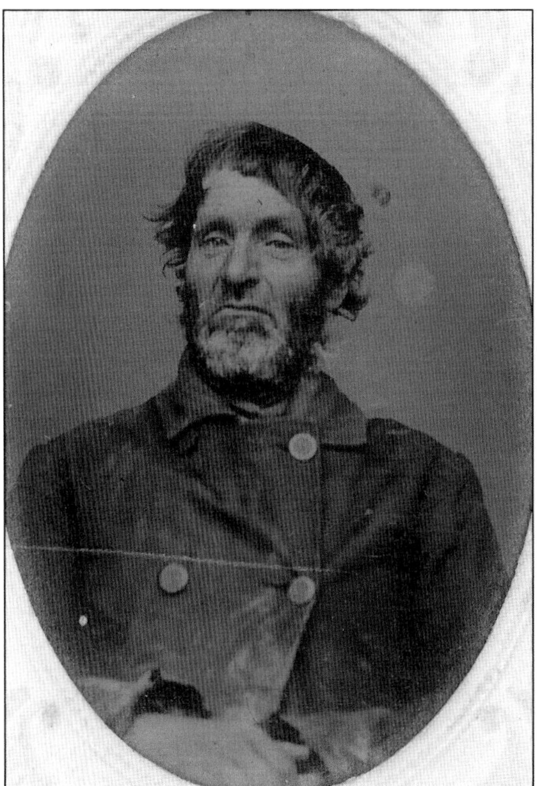

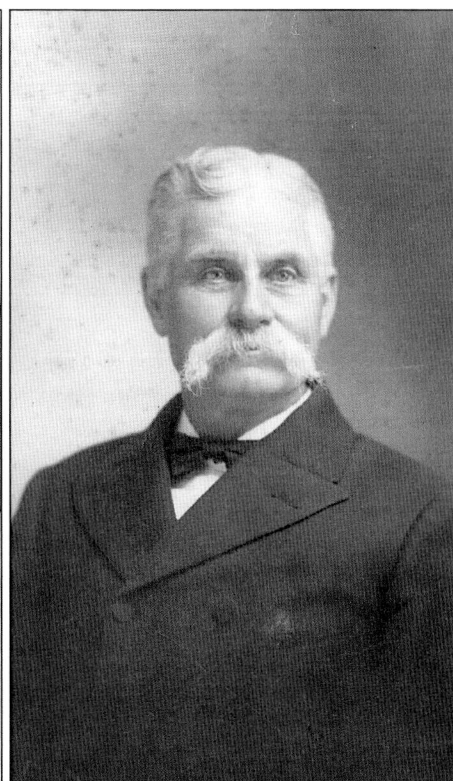

Reverend Alvan Tobey, c. 1870. Tobey served as minister of the Durham Congregational Church for thirty-nine years. In 1848–49, he oversaw the demolition of the old meetinghouse and the construction of the current church. For a number of years, Tobey also served as school commissioner for Durham. In 1871, he left Durham for a pastorate in Somersworth, where he died three years later.

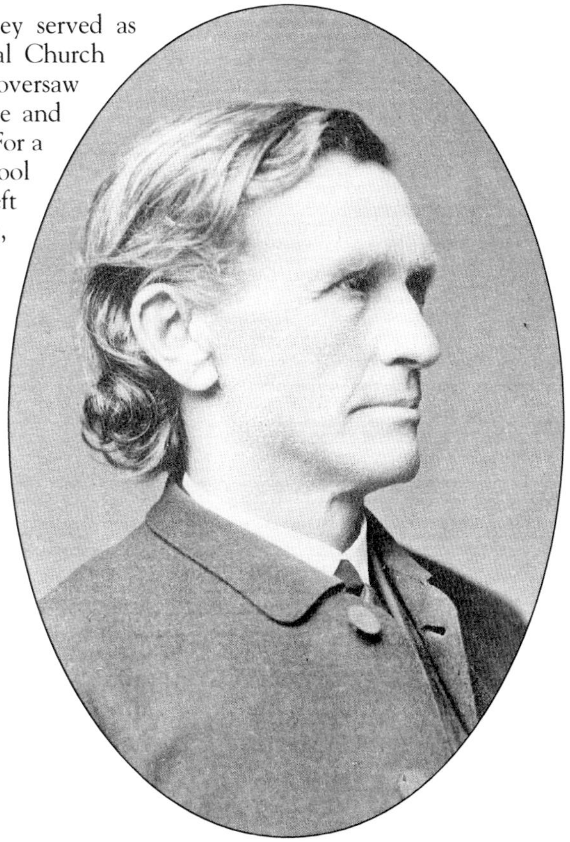

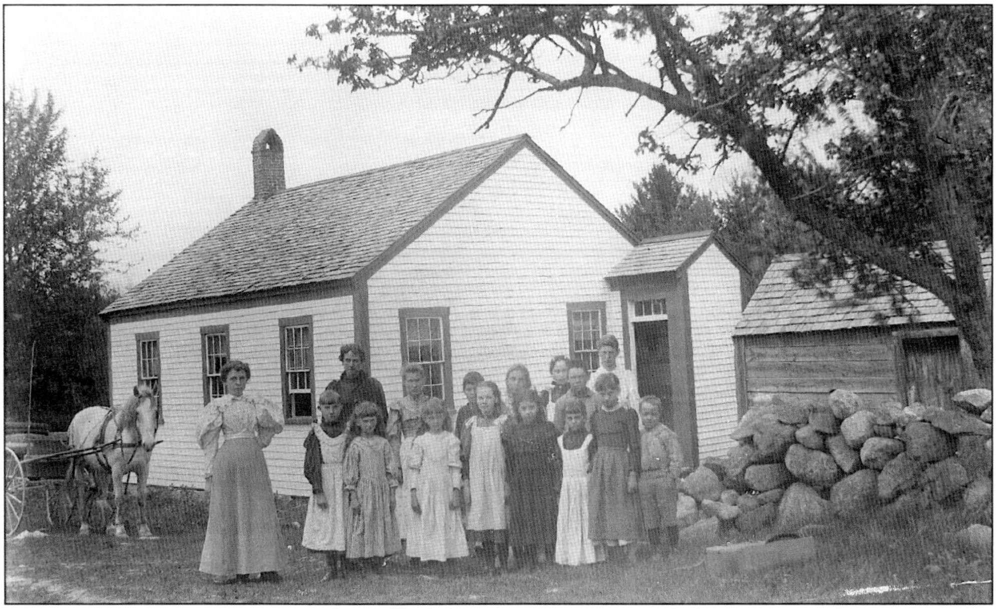

One of the ten district schools in Durham in the early 1890s. Prior to 1900, Durham consolidated its school system. In 1900, the Village School, the Packer's Falls School, and the Durham Point School remained.

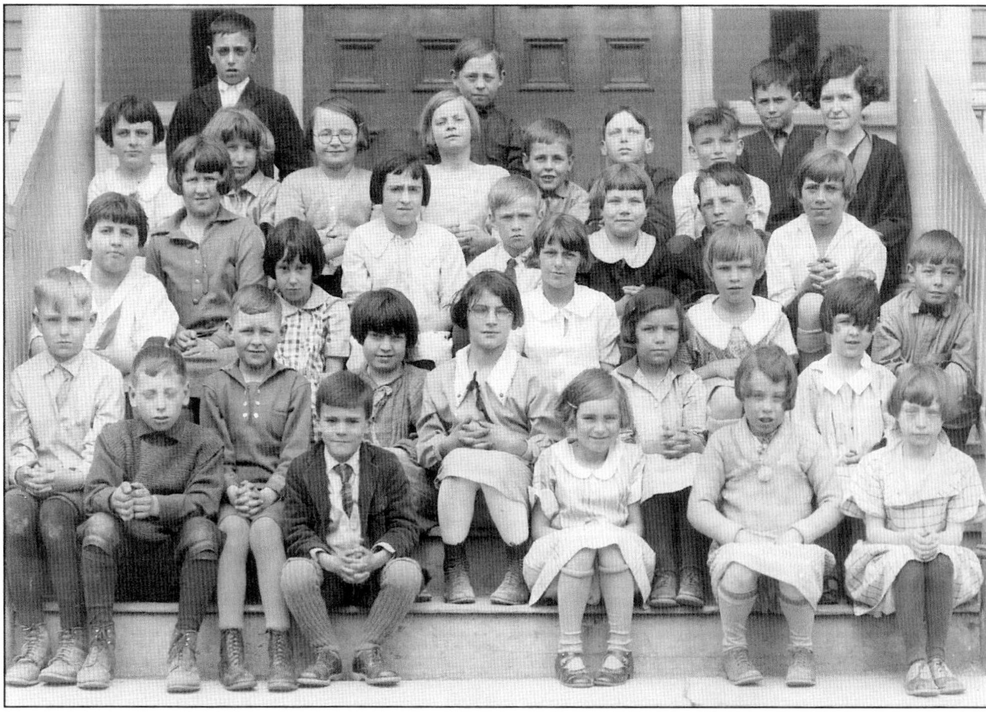

The third and fourth grades on the front steps of the Durham Village School, 1926. In 1936, a new school built on the site of the Woodman Garrison replaced the Village School.

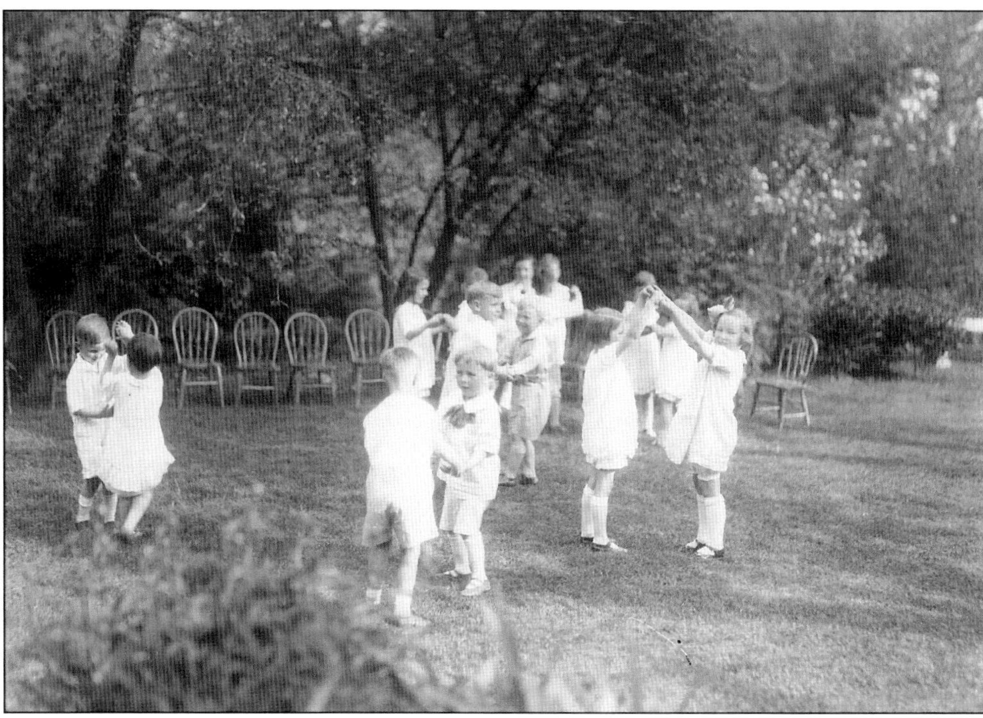

A Durham kindergarten class, 1929.

Hamilton Smith, c. 1895. Although he was a native of Louisville, Kentucky, Smith considered Durham his ancestral home. After making his fortune as a mining engineer, he purchased and developed an estate in Durham, which he called Red Tower. Smith died in 1900, while boating on Great Bay.

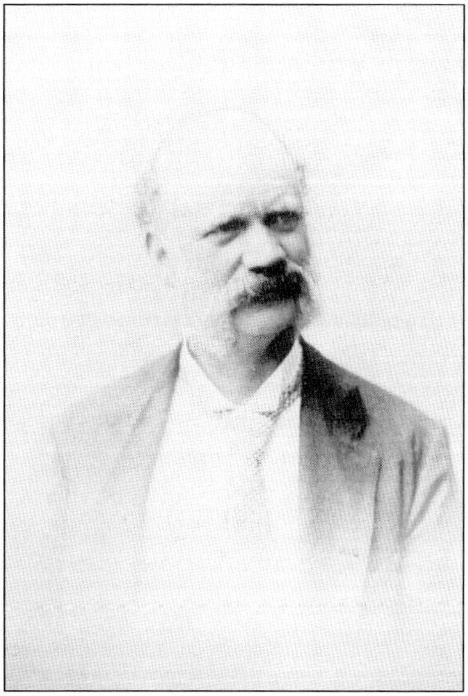

A wedding party at Red Tower, June 1901. This image shows the wedding of Edith Angela Congreve (Hamilton Smith's stepdaughter) to Shirley Onderdonk of New York. Mrs. Onderdonk later gave $16,000 toward the construction of Smith Hall, as a memorial to her mother. (Durham Historic Association.)

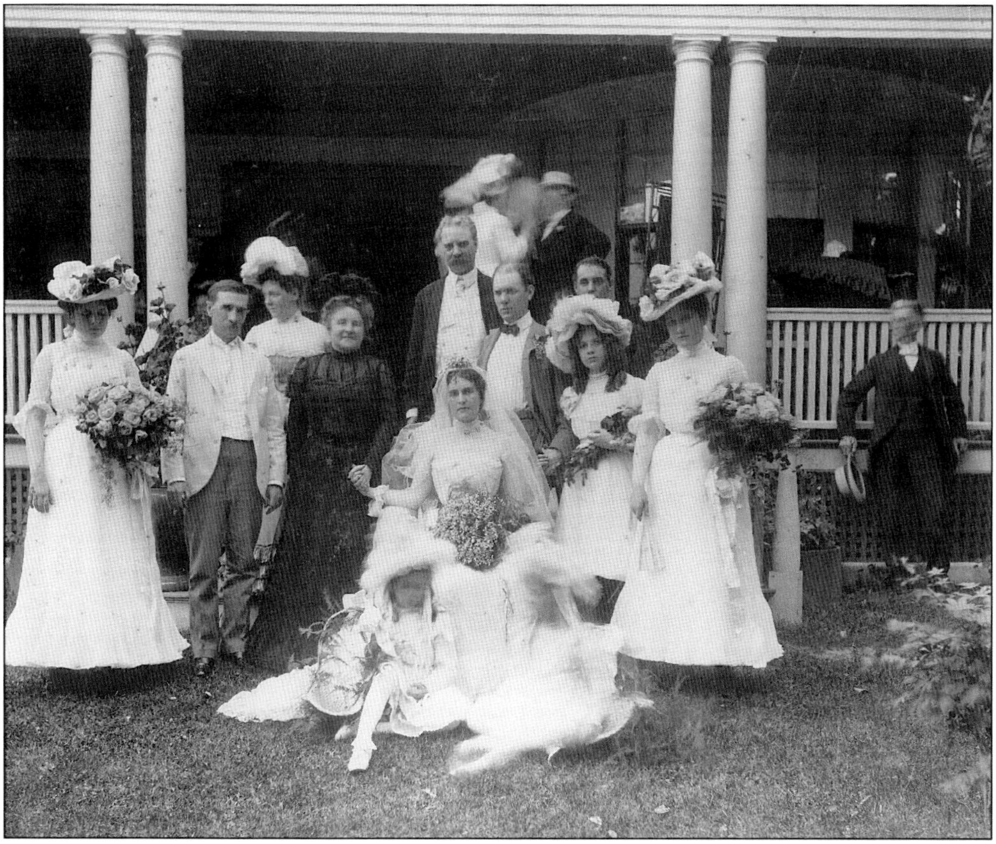

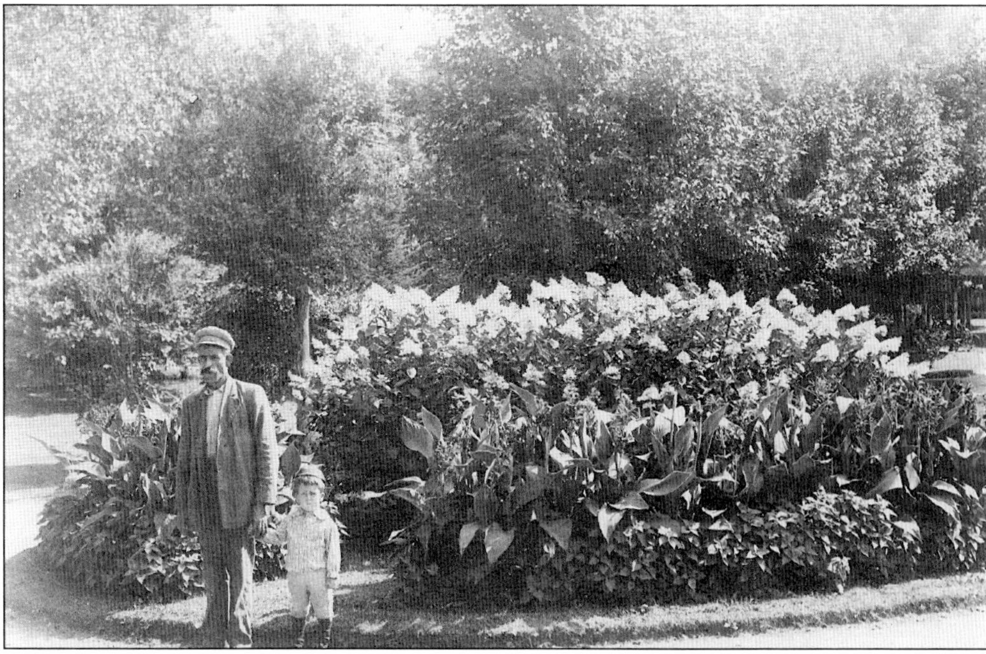

Joe Manley, the gardener at Red Tower, *c.* 1910. (Durham Historic Association.)

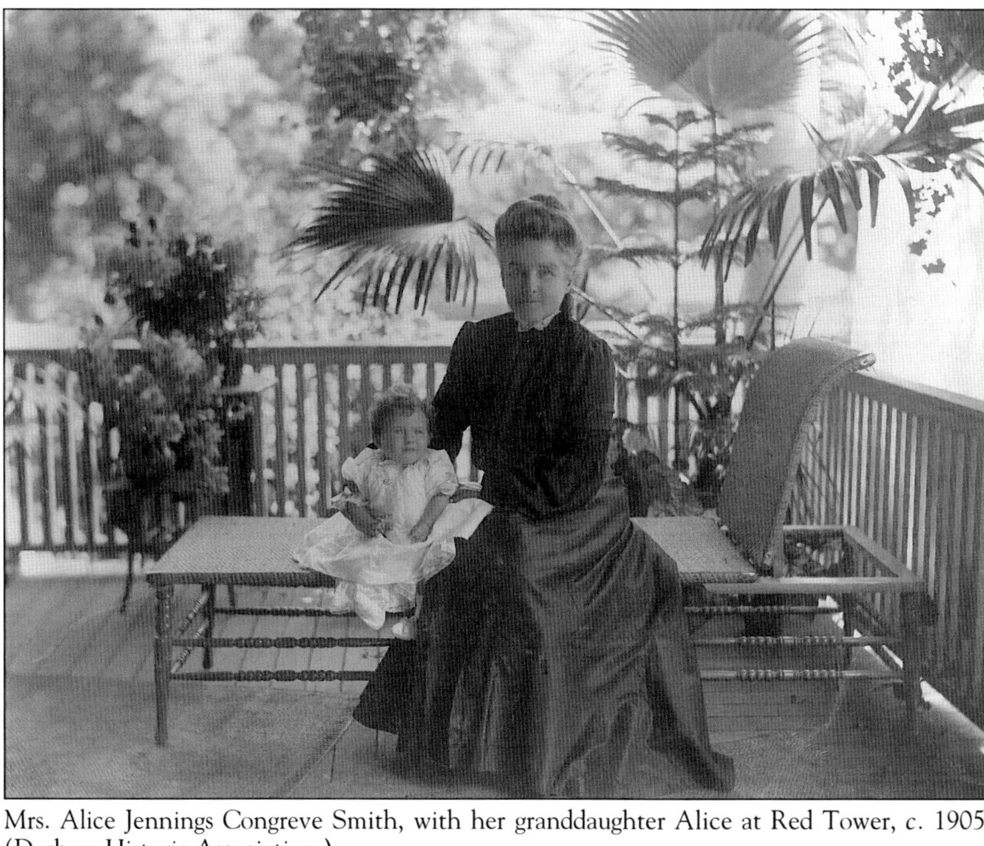

Mrs. Alice Jennings Congreve Smith, with her granddaughter Alice at Red Tower, *c.* 1905. (Durham Historic Association.)

Effie "Aunt Effie" Griffith, *c.* 1900. "Aunt Effie" served as one of the first presidents of the Woman's Club of Durham. She also served as Durham's unofficial poet laureate for over thirty years. She wrote poems for any occasion, commonly sacrificing meter and rhyme for sentiment. (Durham Historic Association.)

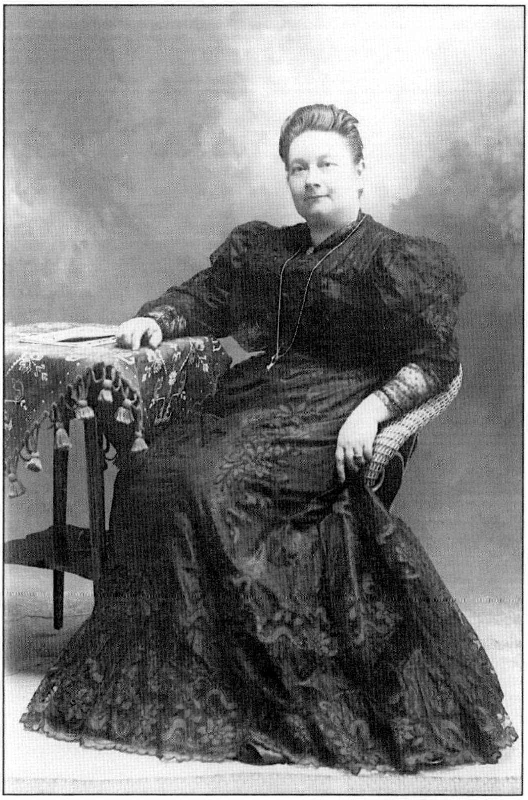

An unidentified wedding party, *c.* 1910. (Durham Historic Association, the Littlehale Farm Collection.)

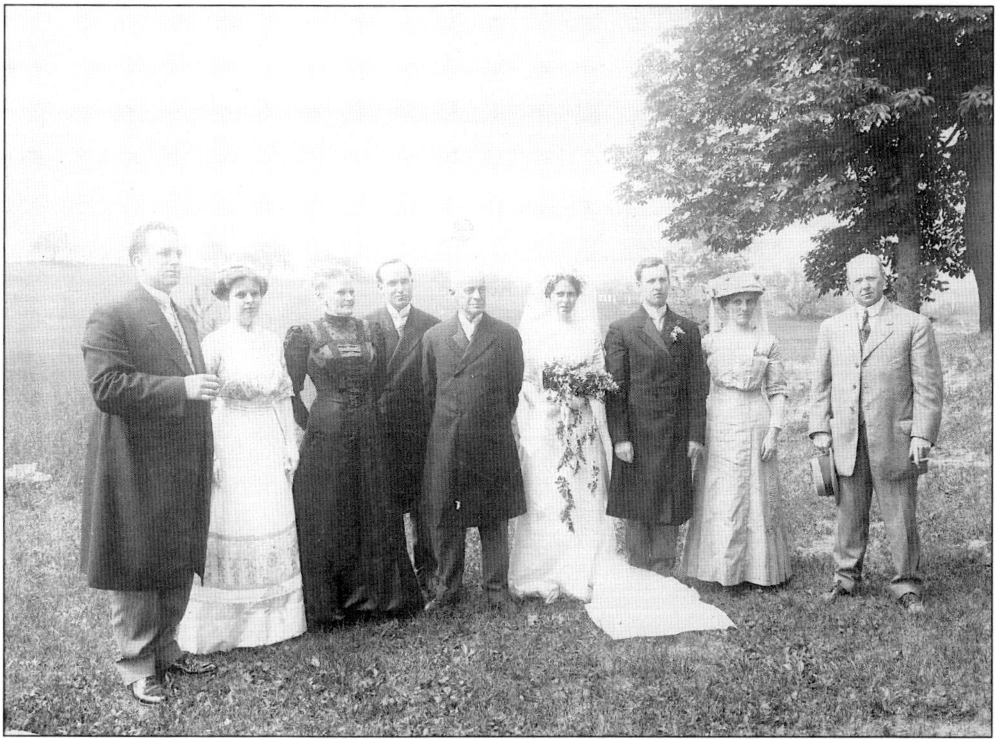

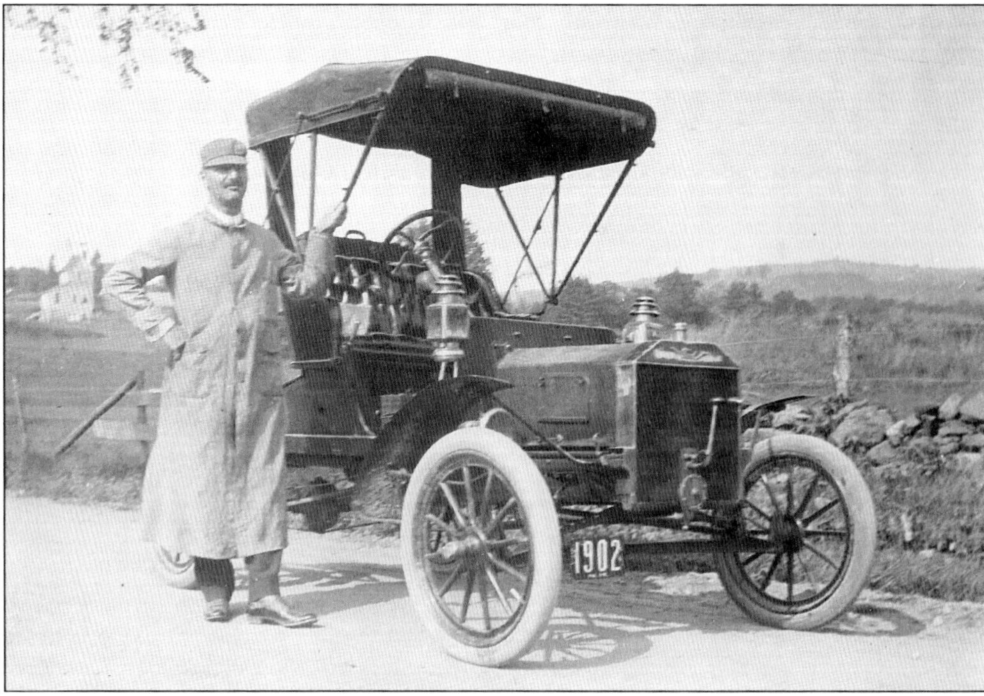

Professor Frederick W. "Pa" and Mrs. Taylor stand next to their automobile, one of the first in Durham, 1902.

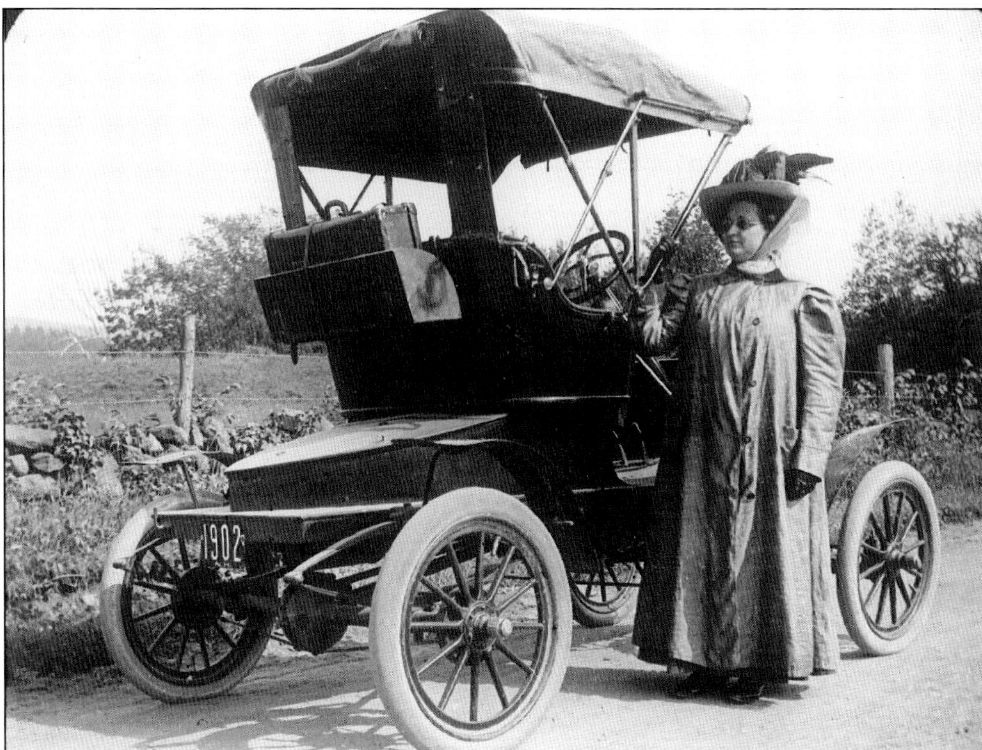

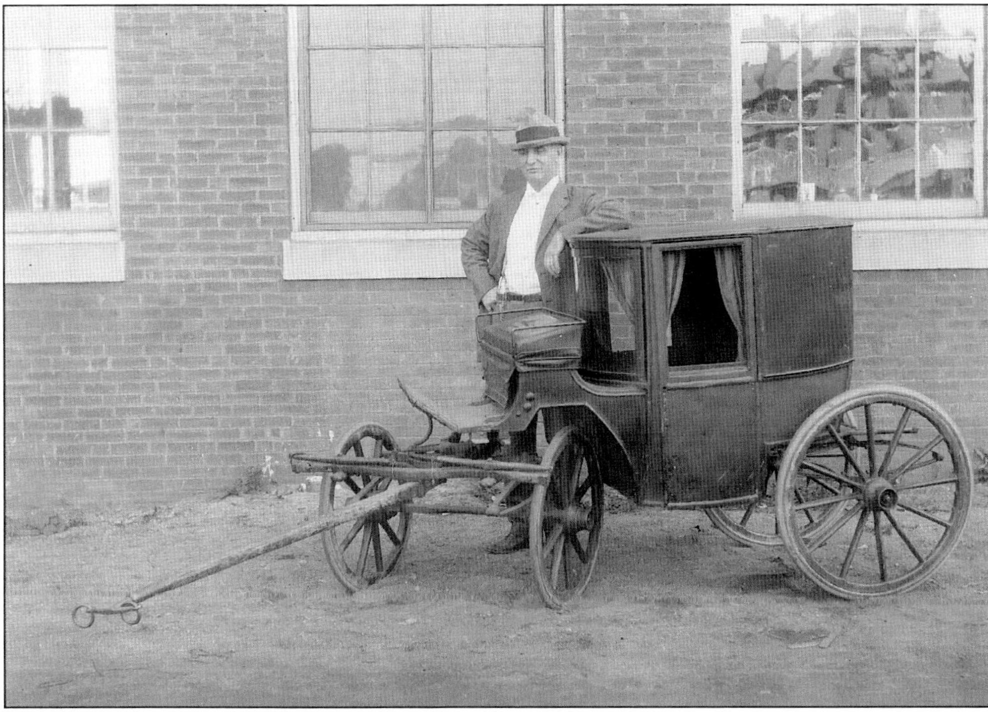

Professor Frederick W. Taylor and the "Tom Thumb" carriage, early 1920s. This English-made carriage was given to Mr. and Mrs. Tom Thumb, the famous circus couple, by Queen Victoria. It came to the college as a memorial to Maxwell Smalley of Walpole, New Hampshire. Taylor later gave it to the Henry Ford Museum in Dearborn, Michigan.

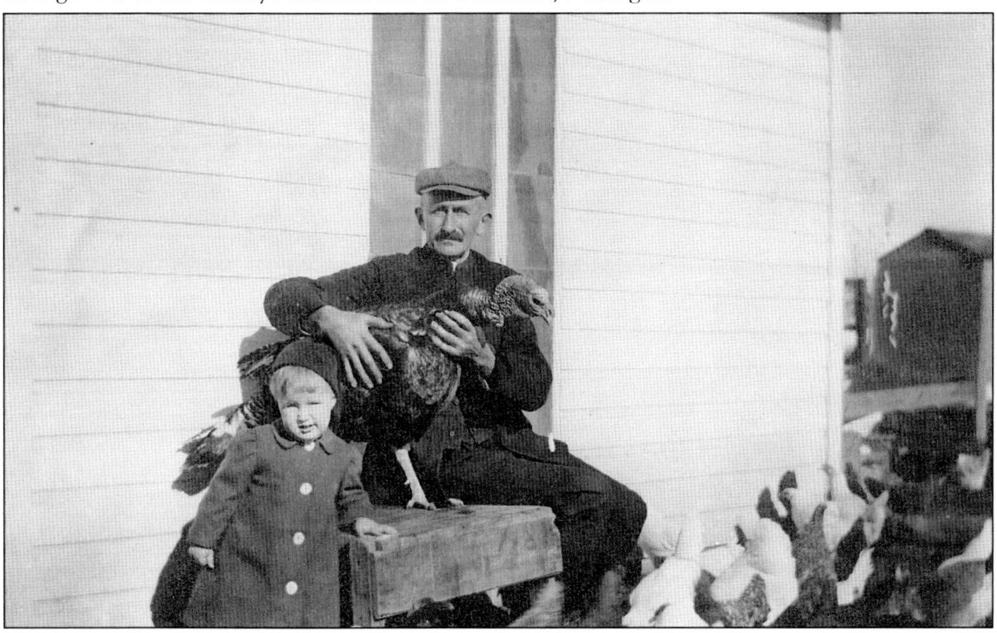

Lucien Thompson with a large turkey and a small child, c. 1912. Thompson was a member of the Durham Board of Supervisors, represented the town in the state legislature, served on the state board of agriculture, and was a trustee of New Hampshire College.

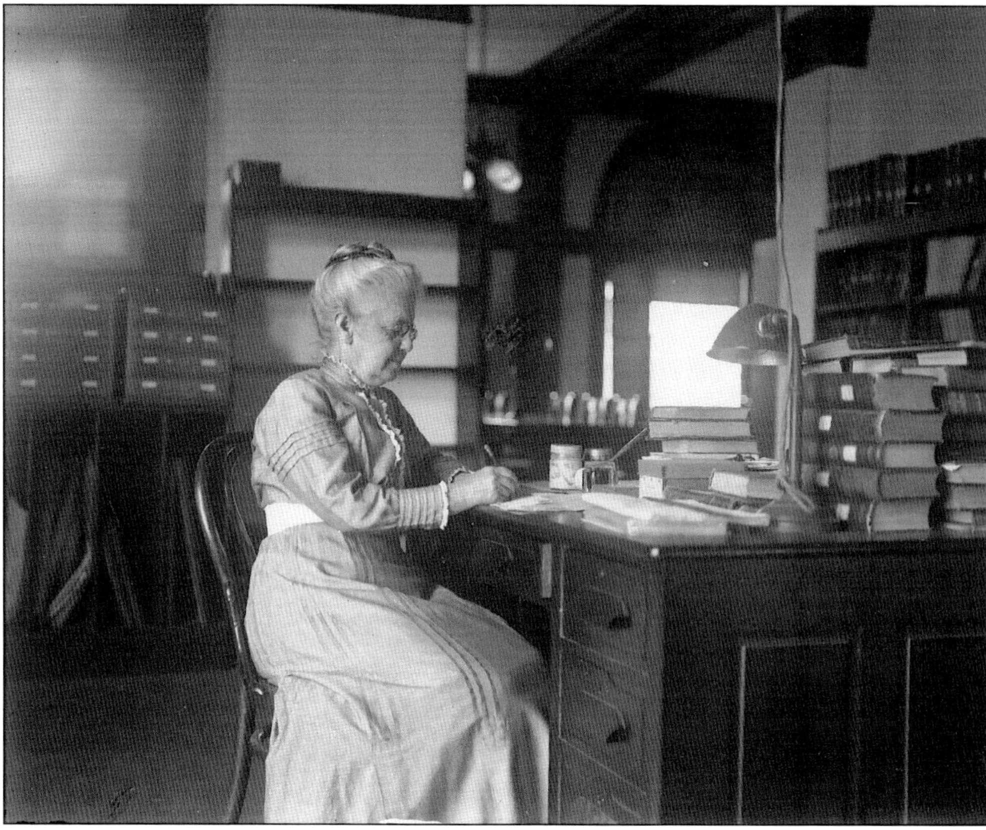

Charlotte "Aunt Lottie" Thompson, August 1915. "Aunt Lottie" served as the Children's Room librarian in Durham from 1903 until she retired in 1939. When she retired, the Children's Room in the University Library was renamed in her honor.

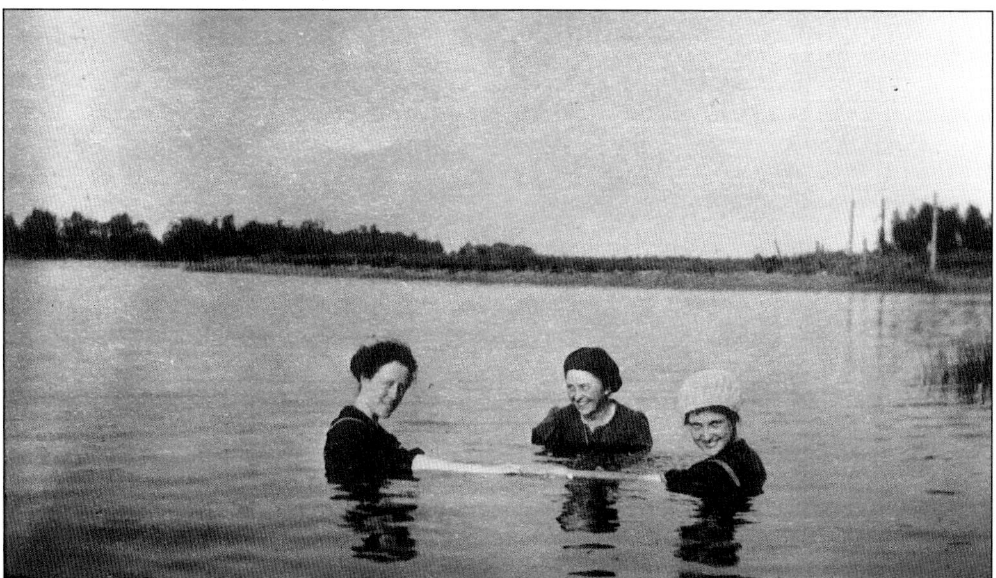

Swimmers at Camp Comfort on Durham Point, *c.* 1914. (Durham Historic Association.)

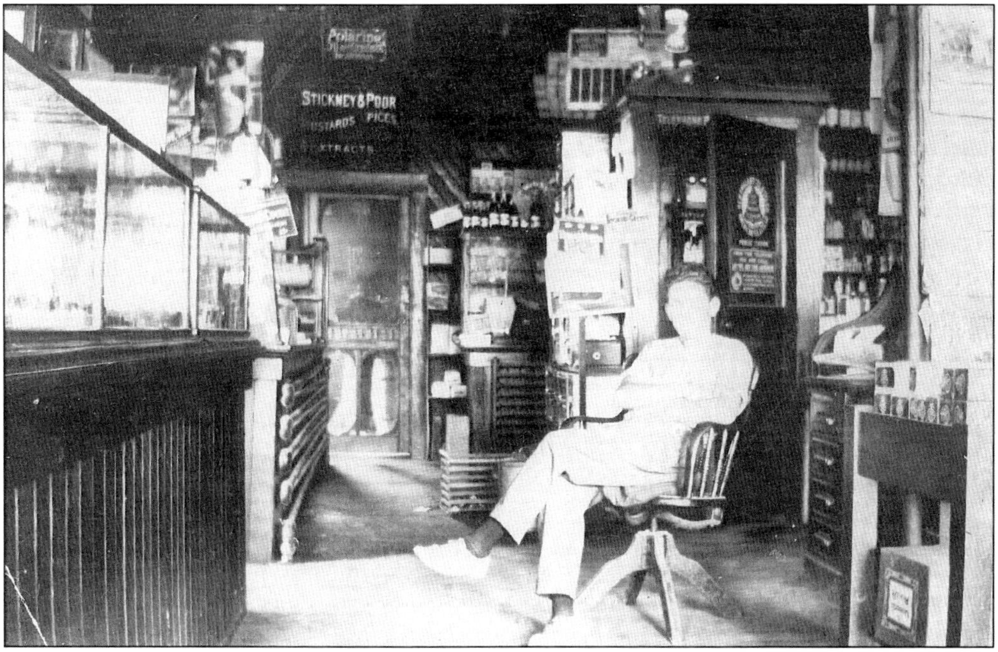

Store clerk Sherburne H. Fogg sits in the boss' chair, *c.* 1915. Walter S. Edgerly owned this dry goods store on the main floor of Pettee Block. (Durham Historic Association.)

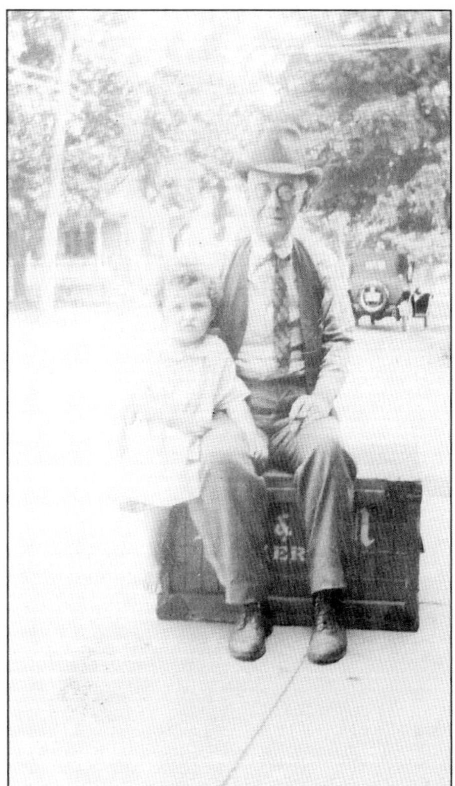

Samuel Runlett and an unidentified child, *c.* 1920. Runlett ran the general store near the old railroad tracks. When he added an ice cream parlor, he provided Edgerly with some stiff competition. (Durham Historic Association.)

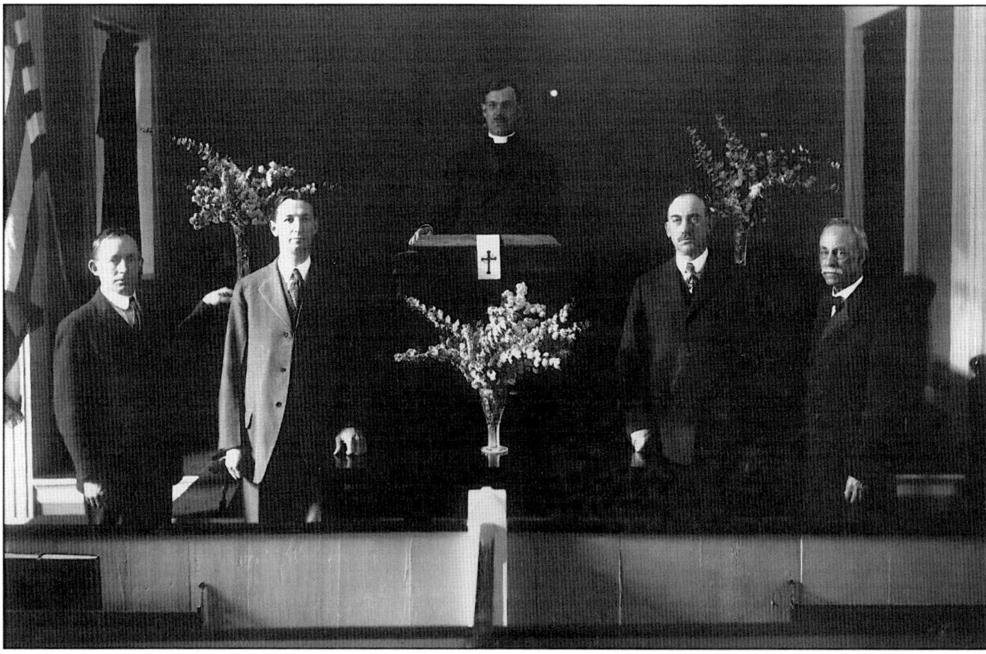

Reverend Vaughn Dabney and the deacons of the Durham Congregational Church celebrate the restoration of the old mahogany pulpit, 1919. From left to right are: Albert D. Littlehale, O. L. Eckman, Reverend Dabney, Dr. Albert E. Grant, and Dean Charles H. Pettee. Dabney served the town from 1917 to 1921, when he became dean of the Andover-Newton Theological Seminary. In 1918, during World War I, he took a leave of absence to serve in France with the Young Men's Christian Association.

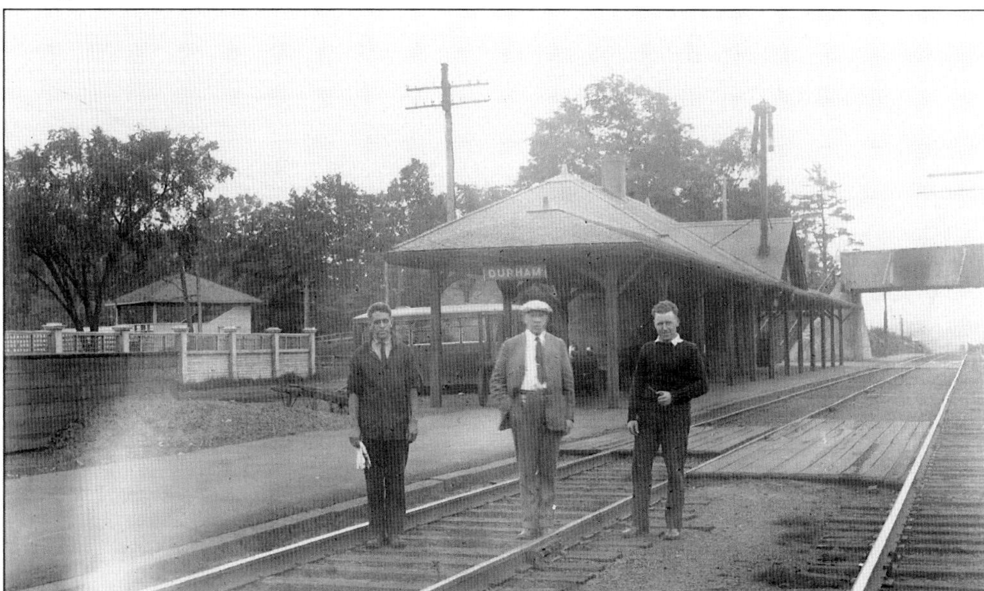

Charles Scott, station master, Charles Wentworth, and Joe Foley in front of the Durham train station, c. 1920. Wentworth served as the Durham town clerk from 1904 to 1913. (Durham Historic Association.)

Joshua B. Smith, former town moderator, town clerk, selectman, town treasurer, state representative, state senator, and executive councilor, at the Durham selectmen's observance of his 100th birthday, 1923. Clockwise from the upper left are: Oren V. Henderson, Samuel H. Craig, James S. Chamberlin, and Joshua B. Smith.

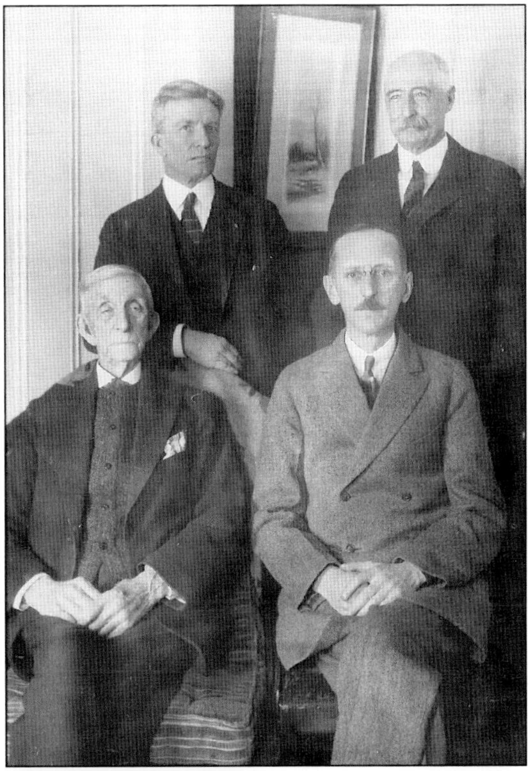

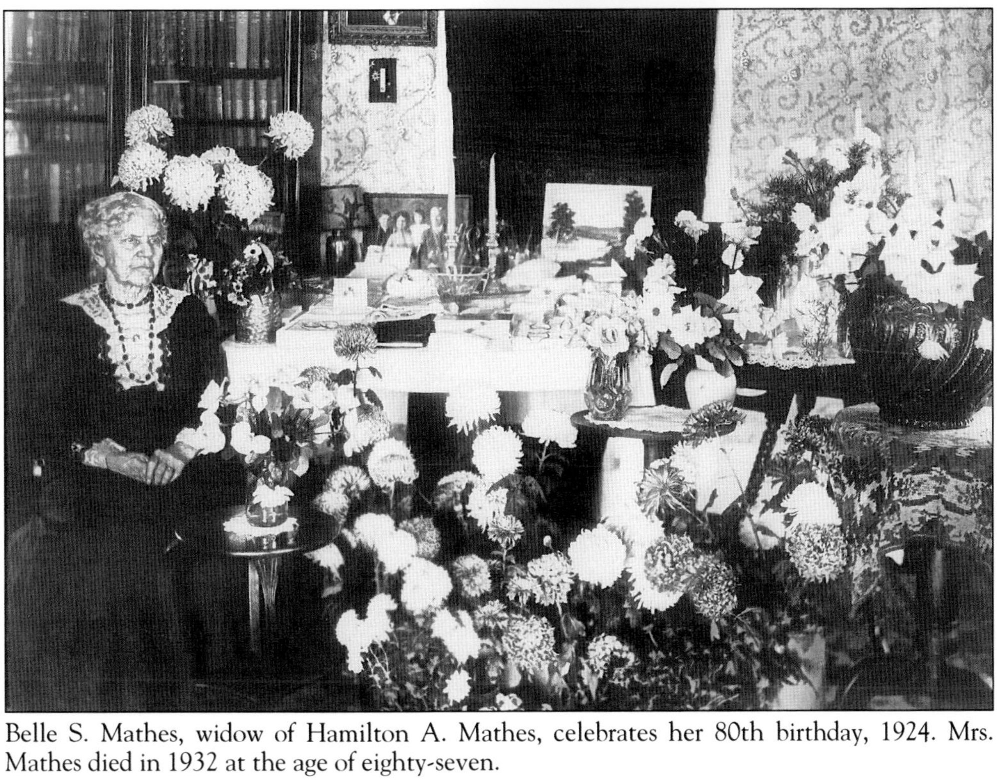

Belle S. Mathes, widow of Hamilton A. Mathes, celebrates her 80th birthday, 1924. Mrs. Mathes died in 1932 at the age of eighty-seven.

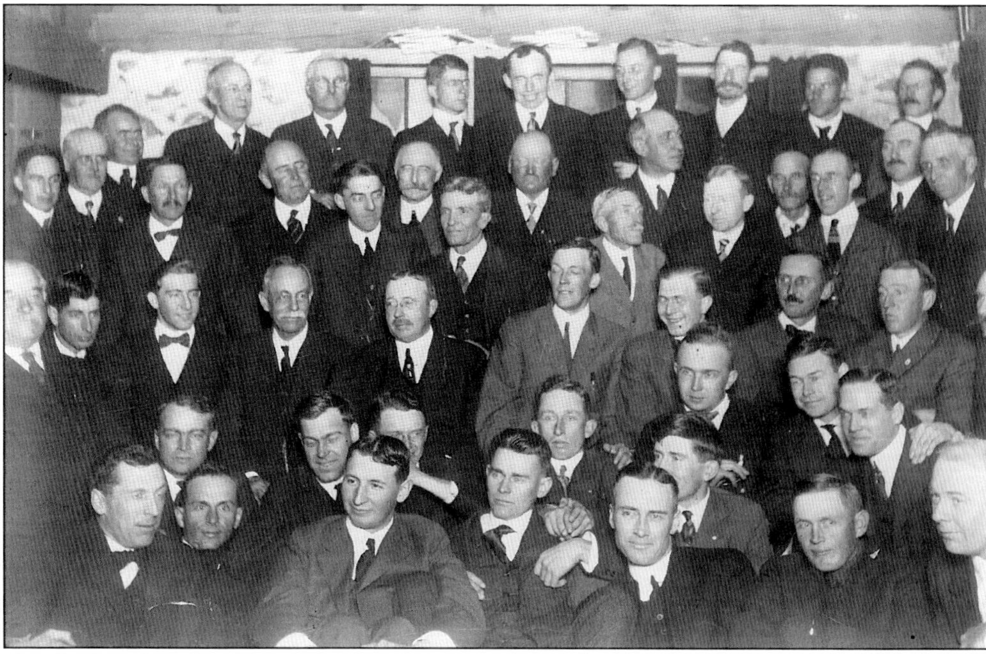

The Durham Men's Club, 1917. The club was organized in 1917 by Reverend Vaughn Dabney. It held its first meeting in the "Sawyer Cabin" near the Mill Pond. Among those attending the first meeting were Samuel Runlett, Albert Littlehale, Professor John Whoriskey, Ralph D. Paine, Dean Charles Pettee, Dr. Albert Grant, Walter Edgerly, and Reverend Dabney.

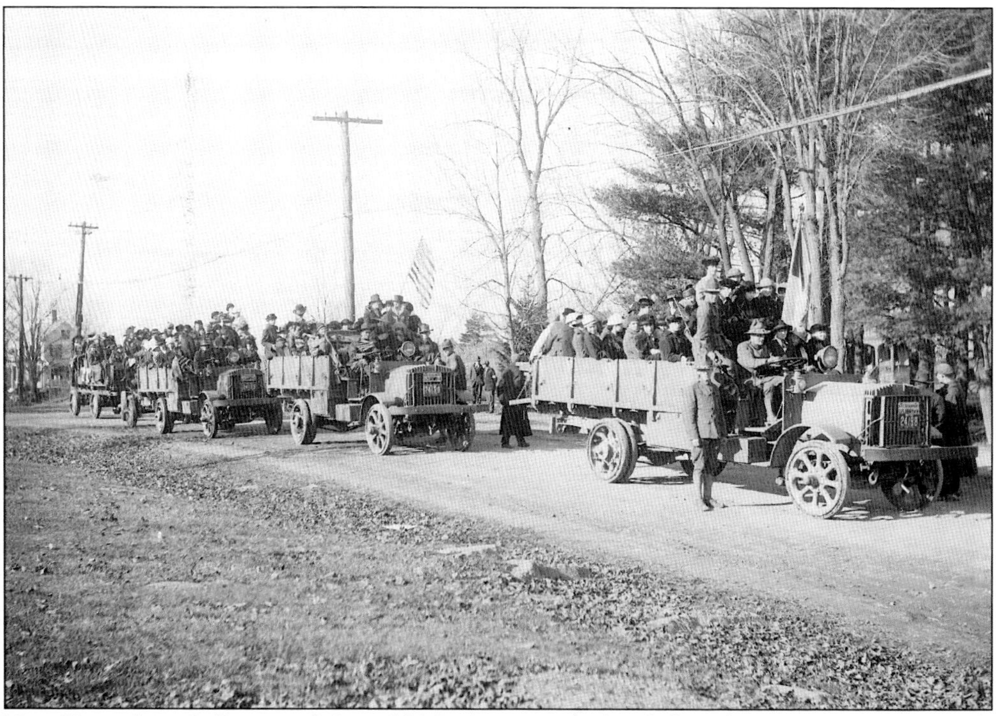

New Hampshire College coeds board U.S. Army trucks headed to the Armistice Day parade held in Dover, November 1918. The college men marched as part of the parade.

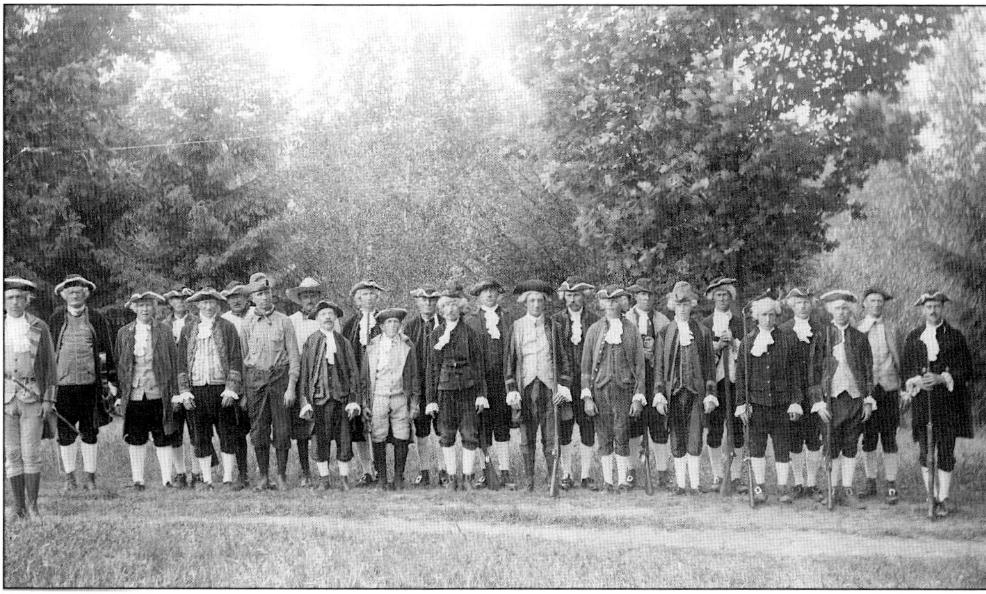

The bicentennial of the Durham Congregational Church. On May 30, 1919, residents gathered to celebrate the 200th anniversary of the founding of the Durham Congregational Church. In a town with a population of about 1,400, over 200 residents signed up to be cast members. Led by Lynde Sullivan, a great-grandnephew of General John Sullivan, these actors portrayed Durham's role in the American Revolution.

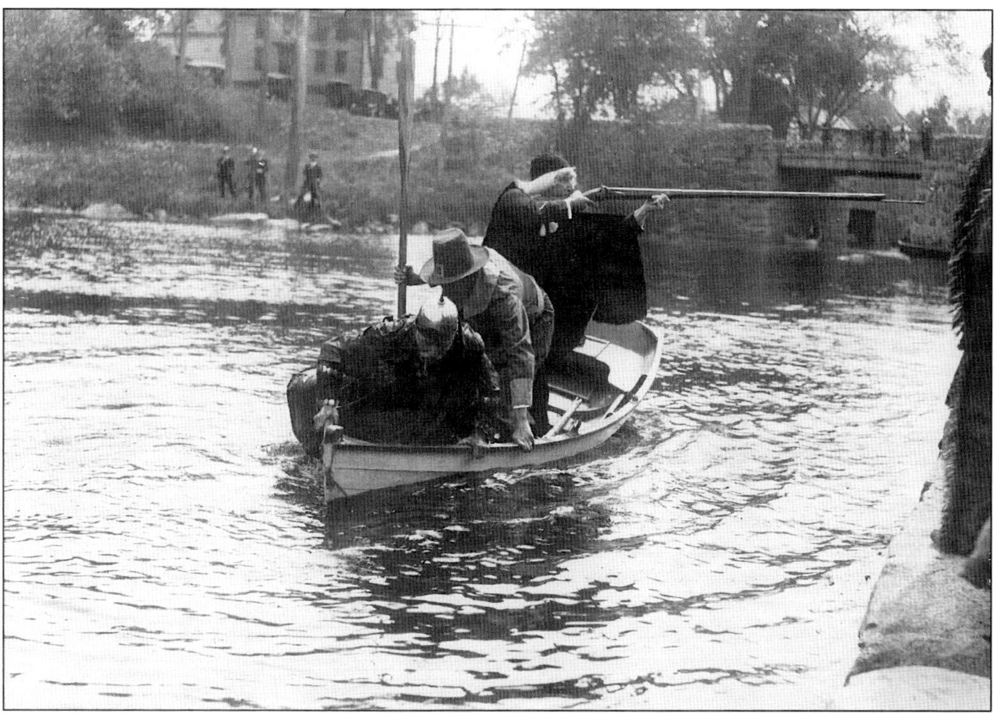

Not all the action in the pageant was scripted. While rehearsing the landing of the Oyster River pioneers, Professor Charles E. Hewitt fell out out of the boat into the deepest part of the Mill Pond on May 30, 1919. Author Ralph D. Paine wrote and directed the pageant.

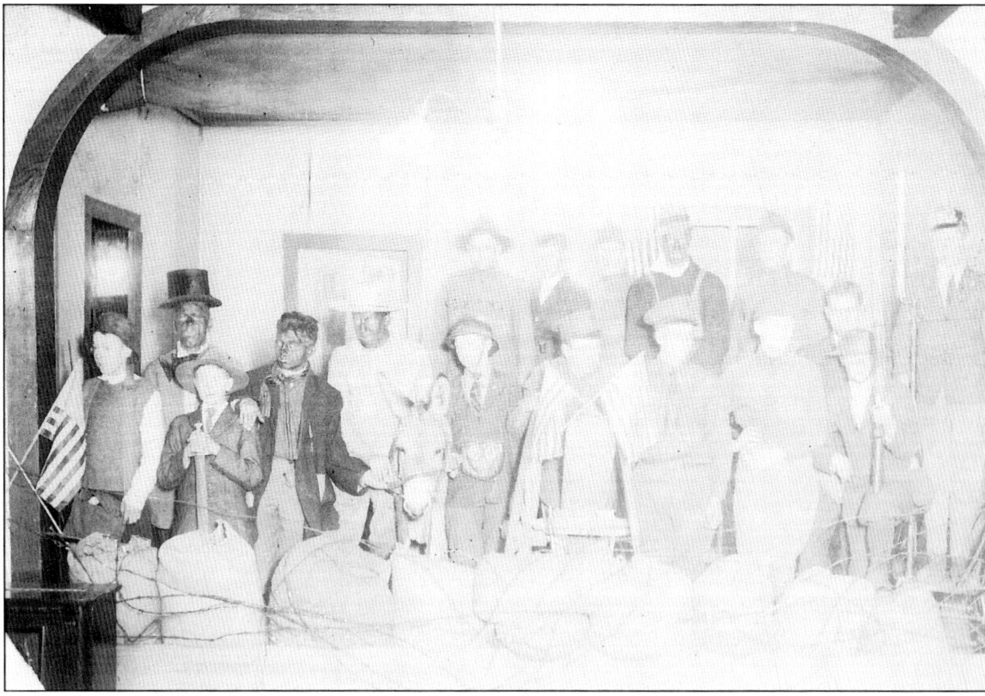

Members of the Durham Boys' Club perform in the Scammell Grange Hall, 1919.

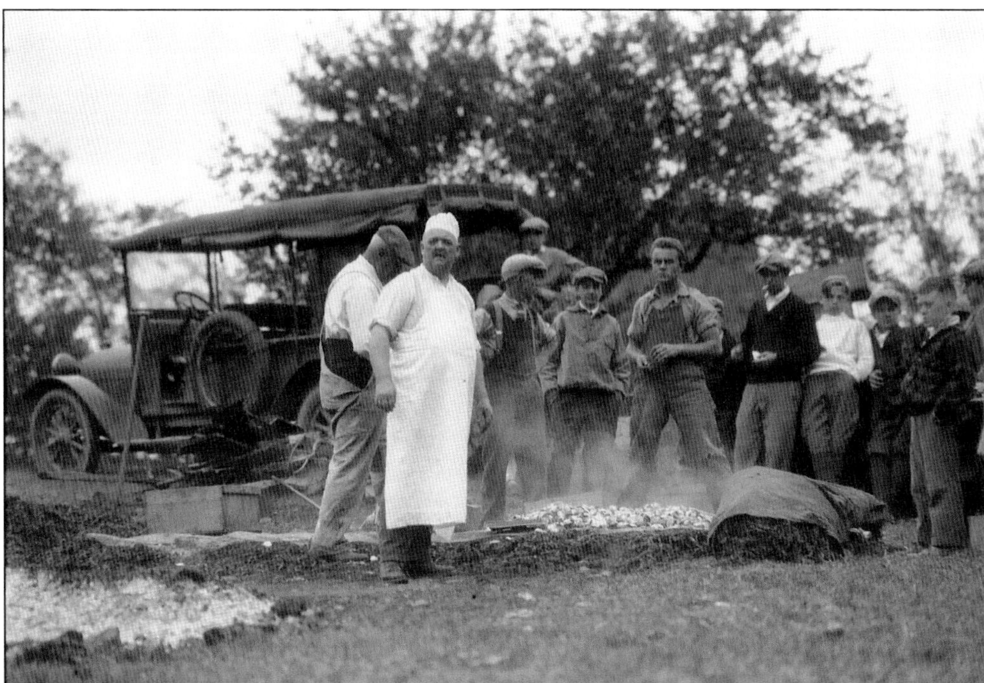

Preparations for a clambake at the Colony Cove House near Little Bay, 1927.

Mr. and Mrs. Willard P. Lewis and their children, Walter, Barbara, and Robert, 1925. Lewis was the university librarian during the 1920s.

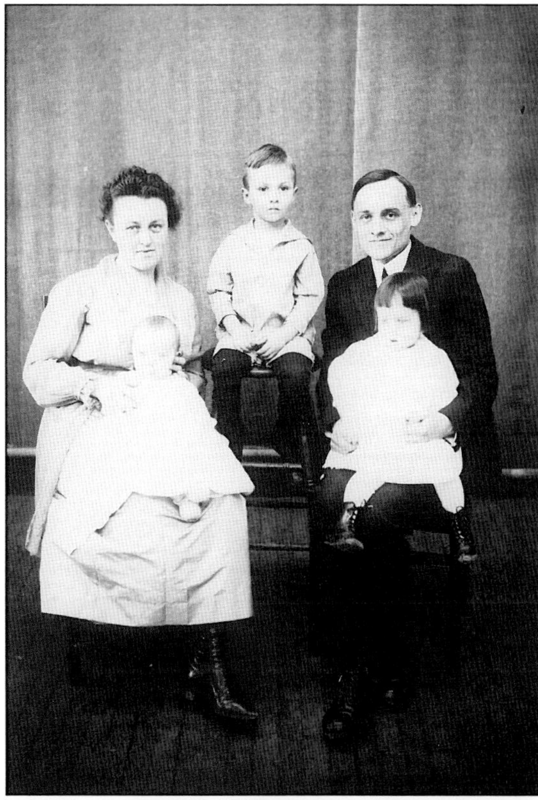

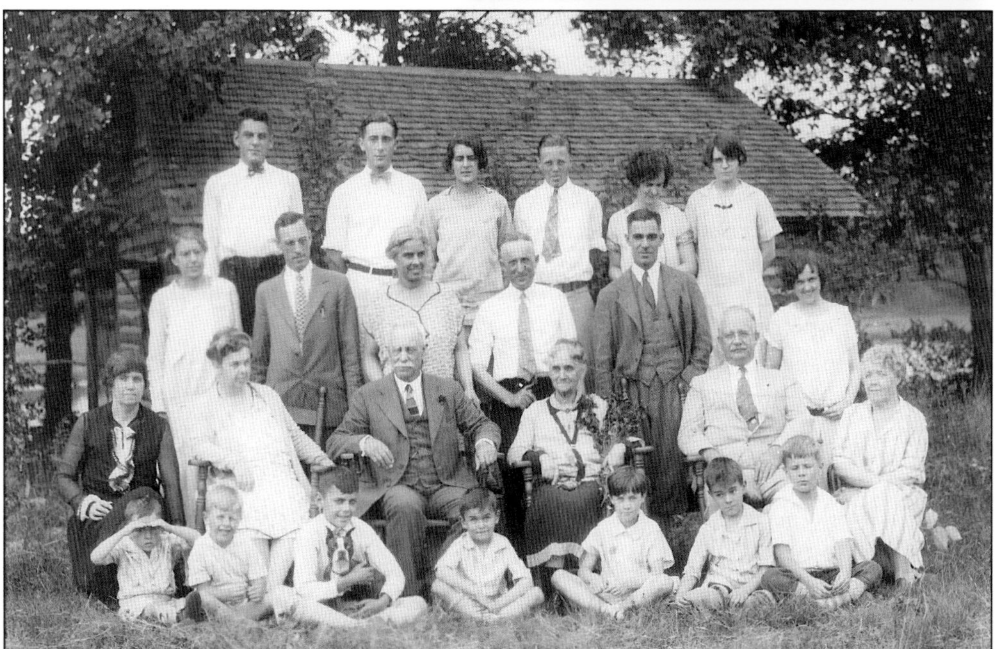

The Pettee family reunion, 1927. Dean and Mrs. Charles H. Pettee are surrounded by their children and grandchildren.

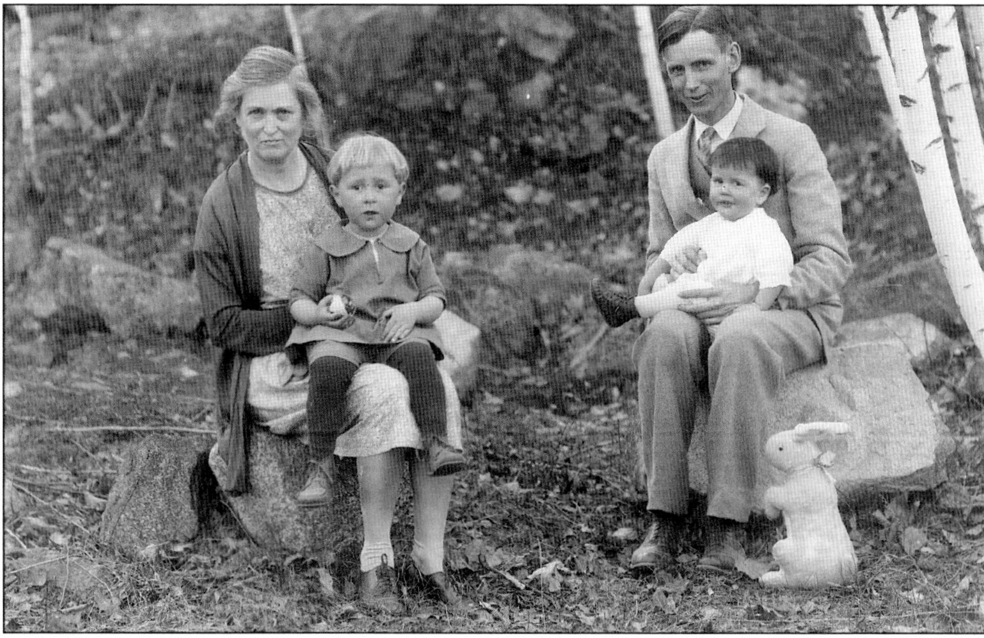

Agnes Ryan, Henry Bailey Stevens, and their children, Patricia and Peter, *c.* 1930. Stevens wrote several plays and was longtime director of Cooperative Extension at the University of New Hampshire. Ryan was a poet and prominent suffragist. Both were occasional "colonists" at the MacDowell Colony in Peterborough, New Hampshire.

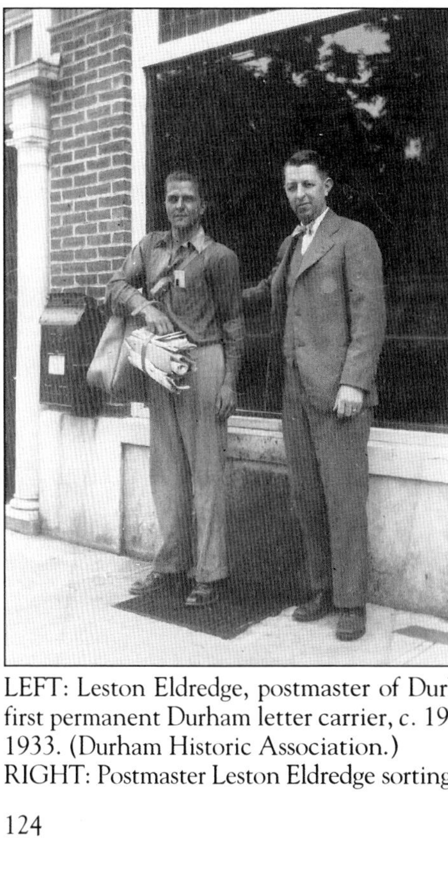

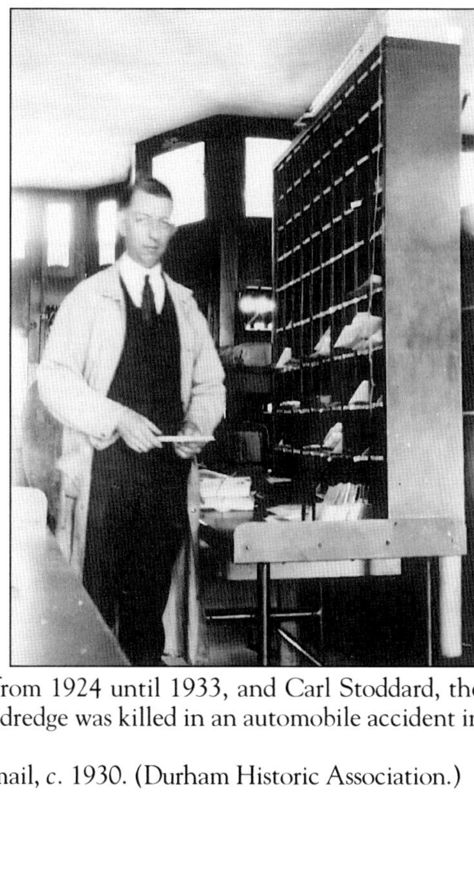

LEFT: Leston Eldredge, postmaster of Durham from 1924 until 1933, and Carl Stoddard, the first permanent Durham letter carrier, *c.* 1930. Eldredge was killed in an automobile accident in 1933. (Durham Historic Association.)
RIGHT: Postmaster Leston Eldredge sorting the mail, *c.* 1930. (Durham Historic Association.)

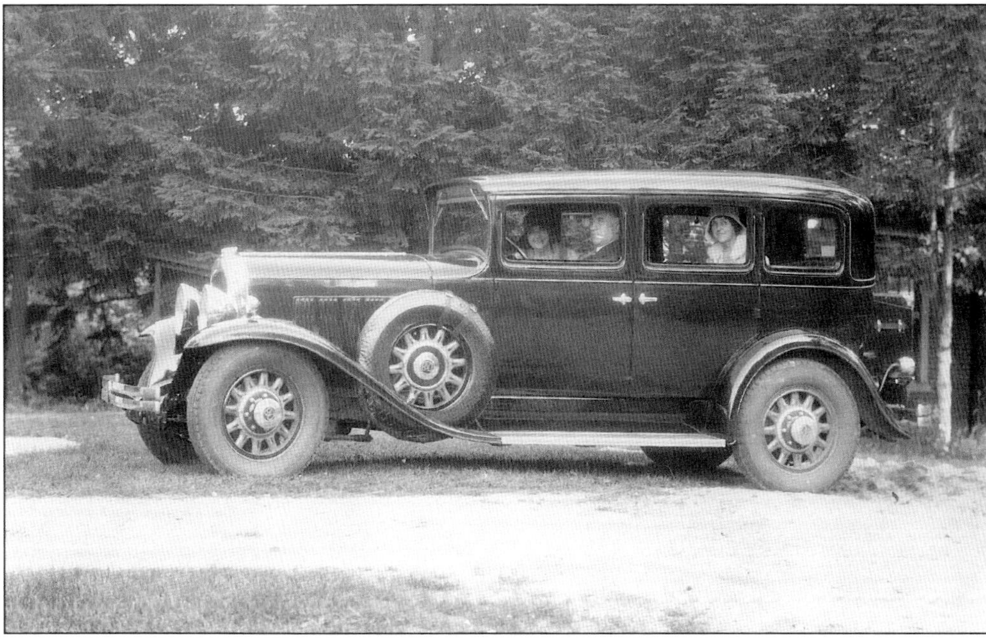

Dr. and Mrs. Albert E. Grant and Eva Brown, c. 1930. Dr. Grant, a graduate of Dartmouth Medical School, practiced in Durham from 1897 until his death in 1933. He helped see the town through a typhoid epidemic in 1911 and the influenza epidemic of 1918. (Durham Historic Association.)

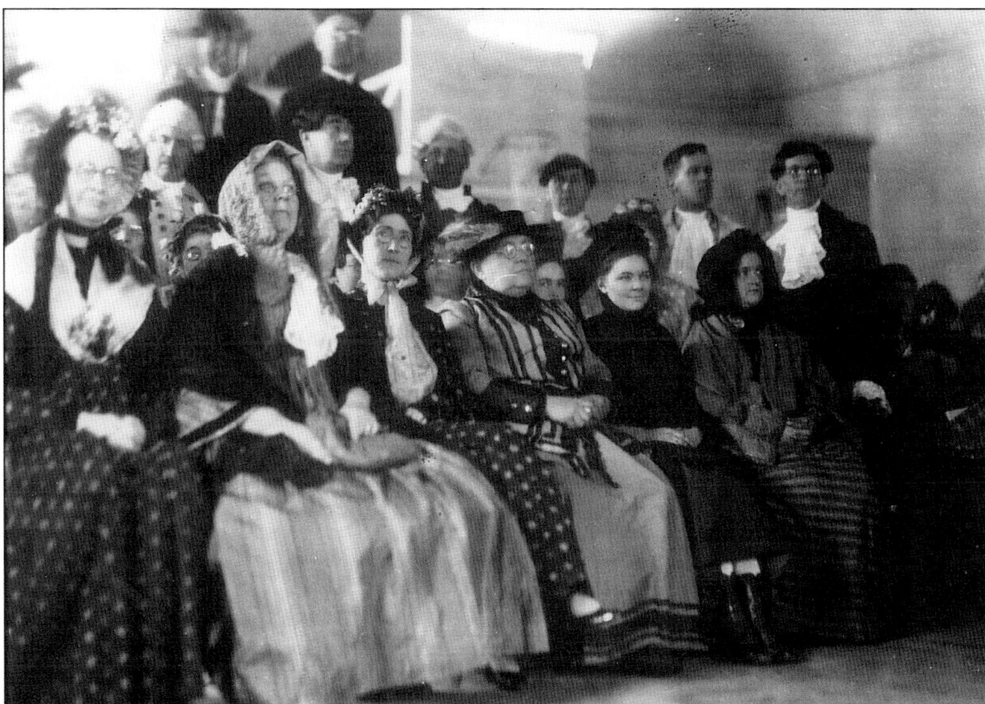

The 1932 Durham Bicentennial Celebration. Residents celebrated the anniversary by attending the town meeting in eighteenth-century costume.

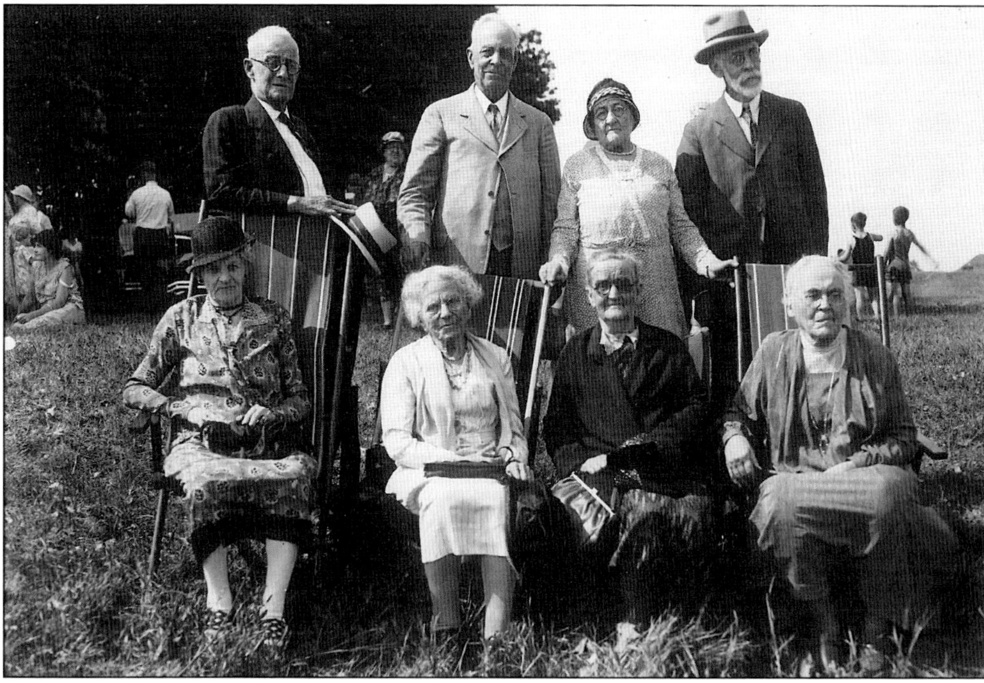

Participants at the bicentennial picnic in the Chesley Grove, August 6, 1932. The picnic featured a gathering of the descendants of the early Durham settlers. From left to right are: (seated) Mrs. Samuel Runlett, Mrs. Belle Mathes, Mrs. Hannah Shrives, and Mrs. L.A. Burnham; (standing) Samuel Runlett, Charles Pettee, Mrs. Zella Mathes, and Reverend Chapin.

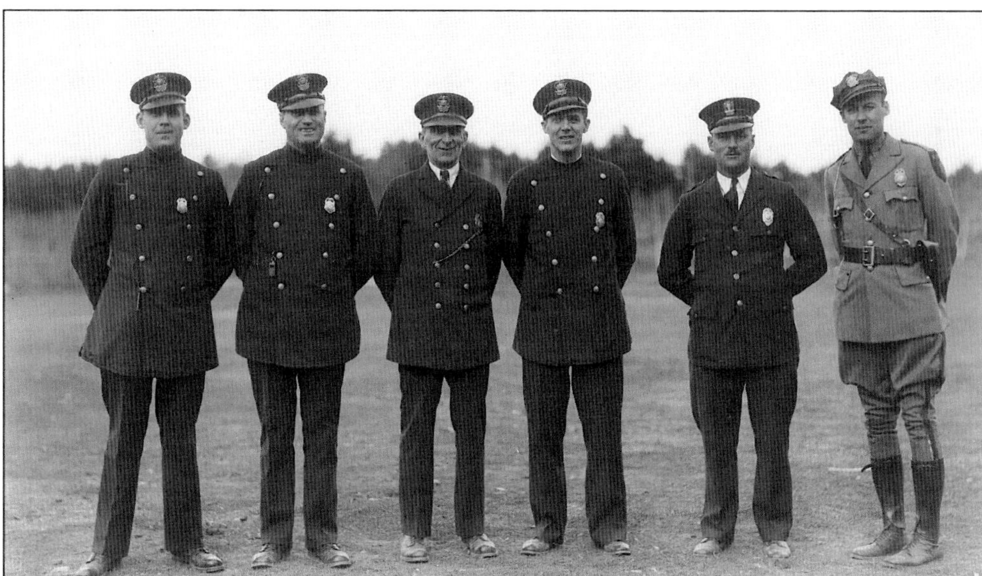

Police Chief Louis Bourgoin (third from left) and other police officers at a 1935 UNH track meet. Bourgoin began working at the college in 1918 as a janitor and part-time night policeman. In addition to serving as a full-time campus policeman, the town later hired him as police chief, a post he held from 1928 through 1955.

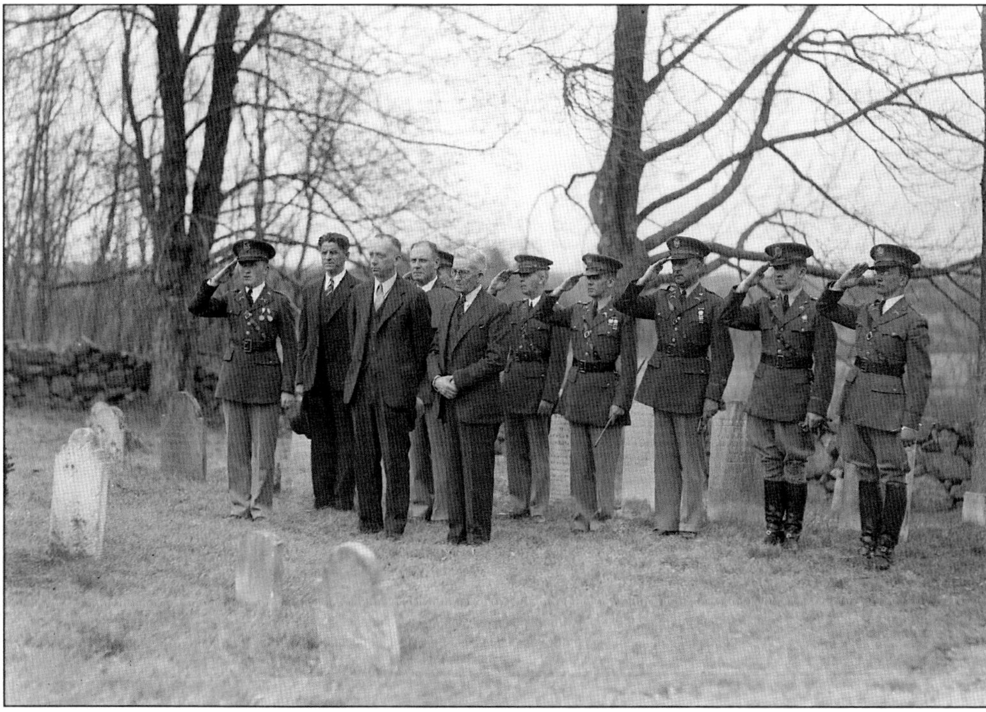

Memorial services held at the grave of American Revolutionary War hero General John Sullivan, 1937. Those in civilian dress, from left to right, are: UNH President Fred Englehardt, Professor Donald C. Babcock, Colonel Putney, and Oren V. Henderson.

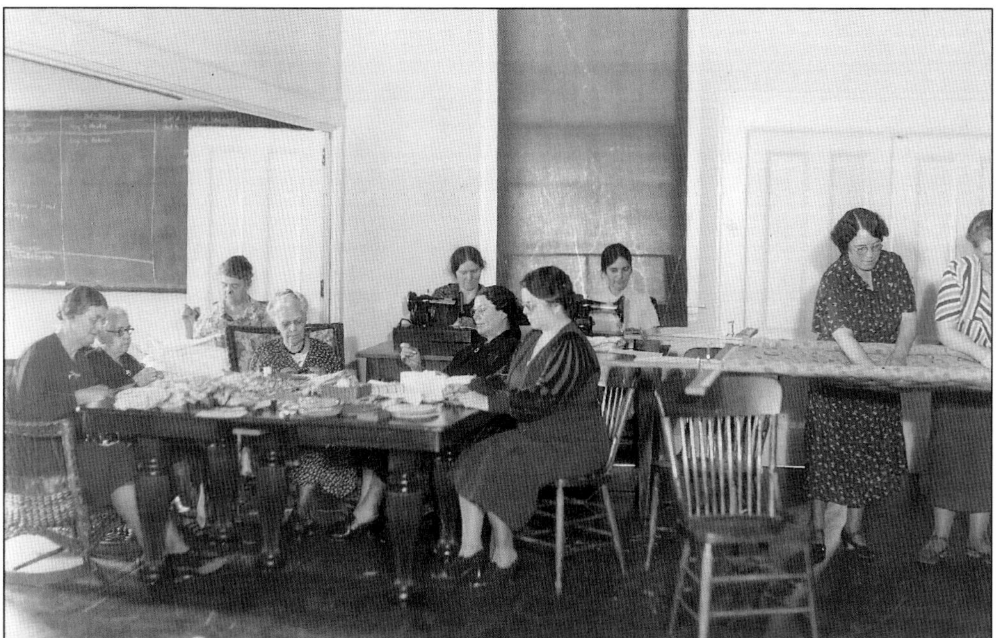

The sewing committee of the Durham Community Church Women's Guild, November 1937. From left to right are: Mrs. F.W. Taylor, Miss Thompson, Mrs. Brisbee, Mrs. Sterner, Mrs. Fred Daniels, Mrs. Edgerly, Mrs. Coulter, Mrs. A. Robinson, Mrs. L. Dodge, and Mrs. Chamberlin.

Additional Readings and Sources

Adams, John P., comp. *Drowned Valley: The Piscataqua River Basin.* Hanover: Published for the University of New Hampshire by University Press of New England, 1976.

Bardwell, John D. and Ronald P. Bergeron. *Images of a University: A Photographic History of the University of New Hampshire.* Durham, N.H.: University of New Hampshire, 1984.

Durham, New Hampshire, a History, 1900–1985. Researched and written by a Committee of Volunteers for the Durham Historic Association. Canaan, N.H.: Published for the Durham Historic Association by Phoenix Pub., 1985.

The Historic District of Durham, New Hampshire: A Walking Tour. Durham: Durham Historic Association and Kellogg Program Office, 1992.

Sackett, Everett Baxter. *New Hampshire's University: The Story of a New England Land Grant College.* Somersworth: New Hampshire Publishing Co., 1974.

Stackpole, Everett S. and Lucien Thompson. *History of the Town of Durham, New Hampshire (Oyster River Plantation).* N.p.: Published by the Town, 1913.

Thompson, Mary P. *Landmarks in Ancient Dover, New Hampshire.* Durham: n.p., 1892.

University of New Hampshire. *History of the University of New Hampshire, 1866–1941.* Rochester, N.H.: The Record Press, 1941.

Weed, Clarence Moores. "The Town of Durham." *The Granite Monthly* XXII (June 1897): 361–384.

Winslow, Richard E. *The Piscataqua Gundalow: Workhorse for a Tidal Basin Empire.* Portsmouth, N.H.: Portsmouth Marine Society, 1983.